BENEDICTION

LETTER MACHINE EDITIONS   TUCSON, AZ

BENEDICTION

Alice Notley

Poems from *Benediction* were previously published in *The Capilano Review, Raddle Moon*, and Oasia Broadside Series No. 87. A portion of "The French Word For For" was published as a broadside (with Ann Lauterbach) by DIA Center for the Arts/Readings in Contemporary Poetry. "City" and "Love" were published in *Grave of Light: New and Selected Poems 1970 – 2005* (Wesleyan University Press). I may have lost sight of some others who published work from this book, since it has been fifteen years since I wrote it: I apologize to you if I did, and thank you.

Published by Letter Machine Editions
Tucson, Arizona 85721
© 2015 by Alice Notley
Cover image: Burmese yantra of an unknown origin
All Rights Reserved
Book Design by HR Hegnauer
Printed in Canada
Cataloging-in-Publication Data is on file at the Library of Congress

ISBN: 978-0-9887137-3-4

lettermachine.org

Distributed to the trade by Small Press Distribution (spdbooks.org)

Part II

In Memory of Douglas Oliver

BENEDICTION

CITY OF TINGLING

city standing together high on that hill   voices souls

     We are the city

               in an act
               something like remembering
               will envision something like a city
               from before all curses
               I was, am, born here.

I'm coming to the front of things   though you may not perceive my outline
you'll perceive first   what you're used to seeing
framed, simply the clothes, the costumes of Ukrainians say

because most art is a portrait of national costumes.
my hair tangled and hangs down is it is hair real hair, understand? is hair real hair.
whatever i see, it isnt, at least in the city *down there* in the city *up here*
overlooking that one the voices click together glass leaves or melt together liquid glass.

i dreamed of my mother momma youre so beautiful. she was younger and i was im
older ive grown just to here. I'm two I's young and old. I'm going to grow
up again, differently Why
in order to change. No because there's no order and time isn't orderly

Sometimes it's so hard to be here in the right city   Can I see it?
I'm from each end of a spectrum   of I young and old, past and future
and it's so hard to get here With no form but thought or dreams   With no
forms but the already seen   Already seen down there, but where do forms come
from?   I want to be in this high bare place Allow it   Asking who
Ask me or you   How do you ask   Ask who?

Asking in the quick   broken phrases of thought. It's quick thought reaching out
and connecting   complexly needing only a few   A few wordlike things fan out
and curl   around other statements or expressions   How we talk here: We

think. telepathy, our true condition
Units of blue and red-yellow amorphous are seen against hills in a dream
units of two and three "things" combined into the amorphous tinted are seen
blue and red-yellow, along the hills   they could be anything or
us   they could be   us in
                                             ourselves each and same
Same-looking not same
                             Could be anything. Could there have been anything What's
anything?

Come with me amid this instability
permit me not to know what things mean yet.

                   He, just someone
                   gets up from the bed of Swing High, Sweet Chariot
                   high in a highrise down there in a city
                   in the world we know best
                   dizzying windows, in black and gray.
                   How unpleasant and how unpleasant he seems.
                   Get up at night to get high down there
                   One gets high down there, but

                   inside himself he's amorphous
                   somewhere inside he's here without knowing
                   So beautiful where the crystal wind rushes across the
                   bare highlands   Where we shapes are in our colors
                   He isn't the story.

You have always equated shapes, equated form with the good.
You have always equated stability with knowing.

I will have to be clear to make you down there come up towards me. But
clarity may be neither   visual nor aural nor verbal. it may not be stable.

This happens at many times at the same time. This house I believe is older than the first house I've been so far able to remember, the house furthest back in time I've been able to remember–past that. I'm to sleep in the high bed which may have a colored squares afghan or quilt my mother is younger than I've ever known her in memory. I'm a little girl and my brother isn't born though I know he's lived and has died; my sisters are there though they aren't born either. Young one with tangled hair, sleeps in another bed at the foot of mine, and another sister has a modern apartment in another part of the house, it's her real house, where she lives now, attached in a faceted time shape to a faceted time shape time is a diamond this house is. It isn't a cursed house, even though cursed events will happen have happened, it is a crystal faceted with different times. The diamond contains them lets them go

         Lets them go, to be a diamond   am I
                                  the diamond?

family isn't the story

your friend is dead he said, Life is for the living. That isn't true.
Was put among the ah ahs ashes
and told they were jewels

                              ashes the same   old ashes and told they
were jewels, but now we are here in this city. have been all along

i am the one born recently. i can choose what i want to be can choose whats good. prescient i can know prescient, green quality i can know quality, but do i want to there arent even any green or leaves, in the city except for crystal leaves, where is you your respect i dont yet we arent breaking the heart we might dissolve it instead to a dark void got started from can you remember i dont know. maybe i dont have to remember anymore.
maybe this is close to chaos or uncreated

But all our visions of chaos and nebulosity
come from previous art   What
could we know of dissolution   without total dissolution?
Would there be a we to know, if dissolved?

      i couldnt break that much, what is can't be that broken. our imagination's often
         full of lies.
      has never been that broken dissolve into the dark ring and find that you
         dont break

you dont even disappear. you are carried peacefully backwards to
the fact that you dont disappear.

They have broken our hearts with imaginings but we don't have hearts. What do we
have   My friend has a telephone cord
                a thorn cord a cord of thorns, black
                a thorny necklace wrapped around her neck
                it's said that she never takes it off
                that they are some sort of cursed house
Our hearts have been broken by imaginings but we don't have hearts What do we
have   We once had thorny necklaces telephone cords   wrapped around our
necks   but not here in this city, on the high hills

Life is for the living he said   I say, But there is no life so drop it.

Leave your body you have another body it is a pronoun in fact   stripped of
everything

there was a book in which silkworms became moths. i cant understand this change quite
they are worms then they are angels their gauze wings against the lightbulb, in a book in
the old early house. i am transfixed by the texture of their sudden wings the light through
their wings. outside, in the blue night are you. blue and yellow. oh mother you are so
beautiful, father asleep behind the door in this city families are facets of encrust the crystal
giants do we tell each other apart but we already have i cant tell the if theres so much we
already have done but ive forgotten forgotten much of it can forget. then a man comes
and presses his hands against my temples so i'll forget whats important, this city, and
come to be a citizen of the unpleasant lower city no not this time.

You look different inside   We see how you look different inside you are
different.   I've come here for that.

Down in the other city I've entered the world of another, the hall of her worth. She or I
feels vengeful or compliant, how we get along down here. Tonight I listen to her
performance, lying down before her worth on a long chaise longue. She reads from her
book—is she still defective? I want to judge—that can't be the point any more in this

dark intersecting hall facet of a black diamond with a gold light on her stage. Her stage. In our city there is no stage. In the unpleasant city I will allow her her worth and in our city is there worth? Not at all. She's still defective in that she's only for herself, what will we do about that in the city that intersects but transcends all worth

transcends my own worth probably? Wisdom the figure of wisdom   is also in this hall but   our city   transcends wisdom
even wisdom

        Goodness is in the hall but   our city
transcends goodness

          In our city there is no need
          What can it have then
          if there's no need.

I quote her words back to her I affirm her worth what difference does it make
if I affirm it   The gossip columnists are watching
                  So much for
worth, wisdom and goodness, subjects for gossip columnists   Go back to the heart
Of what things.

i walk through to, is it time, i walk through, is it to, i walk. i want to see you in order to be a. that can't be. i am already intermingled with you in. i am choosing a living shape of sorts. go on. did i choose. who chose us. who chose me, no one. what is a random beginning, there is no random beginning there was no. there is no system it doesnt conform to our words, start again with what then.

I have to take you to the doctor no you don't no you don't.
You have worms They live in my body they may need my body.
I can tell them when to go cant I
No you cant
   .

City of Tingling, to go there makes me tingle.
I i know where to find the city inside the tingling that i I knows
magical flux, memory potential and something realer and older but what is that?
suppressed sensation, City of Tingling

Take off your transparent black dress he says your black dress should be more opaque the night

           night he says should be as heavy as another's authority.

Where am I what am I doing? It's a beach it should be hills it's a vast bare beachland and someone is ill, dying and therefore doesnt really have to wear clothes my friend she's my friend a blond the air is magical tingling with death and also with size the empty landscape almost no color at all. I'm sisterlike she or I hug him her husband in identification but not theft of self there is death why not we're all dead, and she hugs him or I hug him on a bridge across no color. Child asks can we go home no we must stay with them another twenty minutes in the identification with them of their outlines. which is love

But I understand indeterminacy. The considerable concreteness of the unpleasant city in which I am made to conform to precise outlines suppresses its tingling.

i am allowed to choose it i am unformed enough to choose indeterminacy instability.

           If I look in the mirror I'll break it
           Break it like my broken friend Tony

complexly singing without brutal work. We can do that

                            In the city of Tingling
do that.

THE MET

in the earthly city we are interconnected Are interconnected even down here
by some invisible   grace which most often you   don't   acknowledge
...says his life's being paraded before him in a travesty of itself
as if it were a visible story: as in 'I'll pay you' god says   all the
immoral demanding   gods say god the immoral   demanding god the
goddess says too   such   impossible   dictators   Don't choose God

What is the grace that connects us the lost cause

                                                                The brunette
walks over to a car, in a shacklike garage   down on some farm or other
siphons sherry out of the gas tank so she can still drink secretly   always
preferred sherry in her small dark core to   glossy clarity, so she says   'in my
small dark core, only my exes understand me, I am the past which will never be
shaken   because I love obsession   its vengeance and rejection   the
paucity of dark small rings of feeling bursting petals of a black   autumnal flower
stunted dahlia.'

in her small dark core, only her exes understand her, so she turns people into exes she
is the present world churning them out old loves and wars
always presaging the new ones

but I want to change my past. I want to remove the bad from it

i opened it a book of clouds momma said its about the weather and how they come down
to earth in rain then go back up to heaven. the pictures arent very good do i choose more
than it seems do i choose the sound i hear choose the way i feel when i look at you.
choose that color that the sky is how it looks to me, choose how to hear the sound. when
it just comes up is met. we are sitting playing cards i see the hearts because i prefer them,
momma gets up to go have a baby. we must take care of these babies other peoples souls
whats a soul a baby no it is the site of the tingling sensation you have lost it take it back
choose a new body thats the soul its a new body. i choose it secretly for myself at night
now in my future life.

At school you'd sit at a satanic desk,   with a line of fire around its top
rectangular surface   a wire popping with fire small fires   and when you
made a mistake, you would get burnt   This happened to me   No one
expected to burn me though theyd constructed the instrument for it i   wasnt
supposed to get burned. they said
          now i speak to the
          flame   by admitting it into our crystal
          our telepathy chorus, all

In the backseat girl I wearing green corduroy
in the backseat I not girl wearing, in the backseat I thinking, not girl wearing
What you see isn't correct unless you see the whole thing   what you see
is usually a notation.

                    Twice someone came into the kitchen
                    to criticize what I was doing. Someone else
                    was doing it the Right Way in another
                    kitchen. If it's cooking a large dark whale
telepathy is different from that we will just talk to it. not   kill it and cook it

I don't know how to find the city yet how we talk or don't talk. I'm hung up on past
shoes, these shoes have thicker soles   but I haven't found mine yet.
Have entered the apartment of my enemy. or my semblance. She has a large apart
ment   I'm not as apart as she   is, from the crystal air. This message flies
She doesn't want me there. The figure of Life is there is grouchy and has a new
hairdo. Life's hair is a redder tint, it is short and curlier, the figure of Wisdom is there,
dull and quiet. My enemy wants me to leave, because she's upset about something
I'm not going to be   upset about something. looking for my shoes, under the bed
can't find them and leave leave for the last time, no apartment
for me large or smaller The high city has no   apartments What does it have

Does it have the Met. whatever is met   that is, already chosen   by what?

                                        I entered the Metropolitan
                                        Museum of Art and turned left

where the Greek and Roman statues   should have been but it was dark
walked across darkness and then down some stairs   later walked back up and
across the same darkness   which was tingling   I thought, I'll say,
The met   is so   beautiful!   I suspect I've been taught to think that

What is your sexuality I don't have that though you say its met
there is no sexuality.   And in the city of   there is no hope,
the fact of no hope tingles
                        I entered the met and turned left   across the white and
black tiles   walked down some stairs   but didnt see   what's in the
basement of the met
                        what's in the basement of the met?

only the buried   is or are breathing,   really.   where does the met
come from, the basement of the met?

                                how does it get met

                pretend I descend to the basement of the met
                walk through dark statues dont pertain. no statutes
i see you star flaring there   does there have to be more i dont know
only if there is time the meanings are all double   but not i not i at this
        point   finger   back at small star flare and bigger
it isnt any way youve ever thought

the star is getting bigger it lights it up.

i see a face with a smile the met i or you demented that is without their mind You'd
think it was a vampire   a demon   So beautiful

                                        i am a demon

Identification with others floats   a floating soul like thing   I identify
with the other since I was born   in and out am not them   identify them
by being so   separate.   I take her on as my double, since I   identify   with
her, how she'd hurt me,   even if I would not do the   same to her.   I'd
like to cease   to identify   with your outlines as someone who'd hurt me

I'd like to identify with anyone in the crystal city

nothing lush here all the luxuriance is in the tingling not in the messages the
luxuriance the tingling is in me

       We're destroying the other species
       though not in the tingling.
       How then can you discover
       this city?   It's the only thing to do
       The only thing that will not hurt them.

       evolution is a tangled line no one knows how
       long it took one second before she identified herself as similar to
       another there is no time line of that right away it was a right
       away. the met   isnt evolution

save these beings who are you married to america or what
                           not i   i'm
just born and have never been married
                    to america the map of the world the
unpleasant city
       We were married to the
animals and plants   Now only our spirits   can be married to   only
their spirits   as they die.
       In the crystal city?
             I don't know   It is much mind, this dying
as i'm being born born   what's the point of being born   to witness such
loss   which i don't choose.   In the basement of the met the animals are sick
the plants Why did i think i could ever be born

the map of america fills the window

The crystal city the real city is not a nation it is everyone everything a lot of it is dead.

have i no right to beauty
there is no such thing as a right, not in the beautiful tingling. where does the met
come from.
                        This has been so wrongly
done these thousands of years then this couple of hundred   In the lovely city are
the souls of the discarded   What time is this? our minds are reaching out to
touch it has its teeth and wild wild eyes why would
anyone   want to be alive in   the nonimaginary now   Do you
understand me

born above   can i identify and be   above   anything both there is no
both   there are several worms in

me and i must repel them now they are my doubles they are not worms they want my
sympathy in a vicious   way. what is vicious   when i was four i thought
there was no vicious but now that im five. a sickness that city is sick   The
worms will rob me of tingling   expel them now
They always come back This time dont come back. they arent the moth kind

whats in the basement of the met why is the room on the way down dark and what was
there woman with ragged hair i am coming to the fore there have been two versions of
this so far one for I and one for i but soon it will be this I the only. I am telling you the
rats were splendid a pond with something on it like saliva might be clich could i ever get
past when not asleep and dream in the dark for if time is knotted whatever happens then
is happening in this now with worms inside i i though the one I is coming to the fore. raw
raw splendid what did the first pondscum eat then, raw color and water? down in the
dark cry before you step to hear of echo. its more like and like the first thing ever was
telepathy not a one thought but a tangled thought that was rooted in an individuality or
more more than one. why not that instead of milksop see if i care what should i care

about except who cares what word wha shou i and how many letrs do you nee to get mesage? just so my frends. down theres plenty of tingling and you have the sense of sparks inside it go in down the just there more stairs hard.

I have to keep trying

if i can reveal the city   and tell you   youll stop killing species–

the faces in our city, are nonfunctional and imperceptible. anyway i realize ive never seen a face and theres no such thing. i see you what you tell me how. we're married arent we every one. if the only relation is between everything points of I. am tingling again.

AM A CAVE

he doesn't want to say it
                "and bring people down"
a john's wearing his leather jacket
                and doesn't want to say it–how
endearing–I, myself
                "bring people down,"
                            Trying to take them up

This is no story
this flits by   are there no longer   enough birds to flit by   The purpose
of the mind...but   what is the mind asks the chorus I   other than everything
what it   has   isn't a purpose.

See a car turn into a large baby shoe.
                Rooms full of people working
                keeping the trash world going

Let this world collapse

                See the car turn into a large baby shoe
                dunked in bronze
                on a revolving platform at the
                annual automobile show

                the night is splendid, full of people worms
                in fine clothes–I speak with dispassion
                not angrily. I'm looking, I see

Let this world collapse–the chorus sings dispassionately

Reborn in loss? I sense the look in the look of the   chorus or city

the bones of the bigeyed its skull the eyes are not for seeing but for being but thats not
good enough the proportion of earth matter involved in the debacle and continuing

anthill anyway like good little soldiers. please leave it please stop. white mist armlike minds of the crystal my other choux i'd just as soon. i enter a beautiful grave of hair and soil again no story the one bright fingers connect like smoky mind to and saying the crystal saying come here in order to love is it the place of death must pass through to attain must enter the hill first to climb it well i did didnt i said the reborn i say i myself a good little soldier too but let it all collapse into this fertilizing grave and then i might stand with dispassionately loving and lovable eyes on top of the hill of the crystal city. ive ceased to believe in our world one single aspect id passed through the ceremony previously of dispensing with belief in our group or groups i only believe in the telepathic field that is the universe in this moist grave which i must have come from i have left as much as i can of the previous life many of my feelings words and memories left a tone or two a certain useless breadth of knowledge as if that were a thing, left heart left. this is under the met or under the hill if i choose which it will be a story so i wont choose. ive left a lot of what you might see any day. there isnt anything to see, and relational struggles are, or arent even, childish. reborn in the skull of the bigeyed. listen to trees with rustling glassine leaves. as a lot of beings know it is better to be dead it is a kind of living life rather than a phantasmagoric one and we are better at loving each other i would suggest being born dead or reborn dead. tingling tingling is only for us dead reborn but dead.

i will be married to another soldier like me   we will fight for the hill
     not fighting really but being, being a certain way
     i was poisoned by heaven, so i can't live on earth
     where it rains but the rain isn't natural now

     must stay the night in a house that contains large bugs lightly striped
     which eat one's body and replace it inside what can i
          girl of deathly face
do. the doctor was blue and you too
          there is no doctor.
and leave the métro car carrying a briefcase So?
ground that smells like dirt and shit is home. a simple
sentence
          the bugs have eaten most of your insides.

          i forgot to make them be worms

i will be married to a soldier and will be a soldier of sorts   the bugs have not
eaten my insides

        won't let me talk on the phone to heaven the crystal city   say it's too
dangerous for me i might be crazy go crazy   but I'm an agent from that very
city I'm in the ancient bedroom of the house I can't even remember i know i cant
remember this house im dreaming was real   it has blue walls blue for reason the
thought in the sky

then there is a beautiful intricately rocky cave with a black black entrance
a beautiful cave with almost curly rocks at its entrance   and she stands there
or I stand there no   I am the cave   I am the cave   her body enters me
the darkness gradually becomes   lighter   grayer   paved.

I am a cave   and the she I am split from walks into and throughout me. I choose this.

later there is all of this beautiful water in the basement   in which to purify oneself—
is it real water No, real water is polluted

                    I am trying to call you
                    near a medieval wall
            I want to hear your voices melt into heart of me:

                                        we are not
factory. the wind positively carries us together real or unreal however youre using
that word today up here are glassy eyesockets full of thought sent out and received as
we continue to be   your better you we are your yous all of you down there we are
you unconscious   we grieve for your wrongdoings as well as for your
losses—you   hardly know what those are   you think they have to do with
eros   status   or personal death   but you have lost us
and you are losing others.

question her on her moiety or theirs their other halves who is whose soul en effet i am so
no it is older i who is strangely split. we are in a cafe of the lower city or is of the
underground under the met it is fall in the world cold the costs of the tea rack up we are

begged by a site-specific man not to drink any alcohol but which site is that and which i am i here? all of this is happening in a supposed life somewhere I live in Paris in October of 1998. running downstairs so fast that my feet dont touch down and down. I am a poet I live in paris where I'm what's called real but telling now in these pages what of me is real how and really where I am real. the waiter who works in a city described me as an other half that is une autre moitié i say to the girl, of the figure of love he is there but I am only a whole at any instant and he and I may be each others other halves but I am also my own other half. young half and old half soul half and struggling. half in the city below and half somewhere with all others other halves there is no where though I have been enslaved to these gruesome dimensions that ages of others have insured, we must undo them. We are committing too many crimes within them.

mary is screaming at me from another toilet stall to stay here but   these toilets are unusable   small pieces of shit everywhere

in all there is, in the universe, is there such a thing as too late–cannot get rid of our shame of it this this planetary disaster and this insectoid culture of enforcement

mary is screaming at me to stay here and talk in the shitty stalls i am gliding downstairs i am the cave and therefore i dont have to find my secret elsewhere

there was hardly anything to feed you before. corn and milk said the lion, that's a good meal. but now I've discovered there's hardly any corn just milk. what will you do without your corny corn?   just   milk   served by one rejecting corny lionhood.

discarded on the pile of used
urgencies in the big dump.

I am running eluding everyone again   in order to get out of the house rushing down successive staircases   again   in order to   get away from you   so I can be with you in the crystal city.

havent you seen it forever. being the cave of myself larger than house drama and somewhat recessive from wars. this is all a landscape of hills shapes that coalesce and emerge young being i am the young being standing on short legs selecting airy pieces your sayings your notions your feelings you have your rights though i will always be my cave in which you i get lost could get lost. closed to the world of the dimensions. im maintaining a somewhat consistent shape, as you perceive, though you dont know what or where it is. *you shouldnt be impatient for a world you can recognize, you dont do well with those* the crystal others have joined me in speaking these last words because being still growing i cant quite say them. im a few years old. im thinking about snake and scorpion, tarantula. im thinking about desert willow and prickly pear, i know i talk to them in this city they are citizens come out of the hills from time to time to tell us about crystal or whatever the ground of smoke here see it smoky highlands.

> am met by a tall woman
> there are a lot of snakes here.
>   she
> says ive already been bitten many times
>
> jokes that i will die but everyone here
> has been bitten numerous times
> my fingertips are tingling from the bites
> tingling

is this corn or milk?

this is a role of the snakes. if you are bitten here if you leave you die if you stay you dont. These are the snakes of heaven. But you are poison to unheavenly people. Because you stay here in your mind. Because youre always walking around in the other world anyway. im poison youre poison robert johnson is poison, all in the heaven home. there are no houses higher than one story here. in the tingling i can trust you only in the tingling can i trust more than four or five people. trust not to hurt the world but if you come here you want to stay is it partly that the snakes bite you and make you stay they are corn snakes and they have poison and we all eat poison. snake milk because they milk snakes.

half the landscape black burnt swamp demilight. now i remember, that was where i am depressed even so young. you know you arent really like that you arent really mean and narrowminded you arent really a judge. demilit burnt black half where the school desks are designed to burn you if you get the wrong answer. in our city we are not superstitious, there are no presagings or omens, because we havent decided when past present and future are. one bumps into them the met a different kind of met. not the museum that the present is, is is and is.

you can see through jackrabbit's ears

you can smell skunk in the pines. it is a foreign landscape the trees are foreigners. why, that ways canyon after canyon something smells like vanilla too its in the bark of one tree they will catch you and tattoo your chin their ways are as unfriendly as ours, but they will join us in the city which isnt christian but is instead leveling the way all air is equal because we cant see everything everyone knows this. we have to put up with everyone here, unconscious everyone is here. some of us are consciously here. living in crystal you can walk through the walls of talk through the walls of.

CHOICES

choices, or is there only
the met? (chosen from, so long ago)
        At a workingclass seaside resort   beach of nakeds theres marilyn monroe
breasty-nude in a bridal veil   posing for porn. i wouldnt choose that
another blond on sedatives   to study,
                to stare at
the white earrings of playfulness are possessives   hers.   individuality
without possession   is what i am choosing   because nothing was mine once
in   the world before world   i have no choice. i must unchoose

             More choice of story is offered, I

go into the duplex of a woman. her house a solarium   is divided from the cafe
of the met   by a bank of green plants   there is a long wooden plank bench
on which some of us lie i   am zapped by streams of red sparks emitted
from a nozzle on high.   this is the woman's job i am told.   shes some sort of
evolutionary technician   for we are now   lying nude   on the
bench on our stomachs   we have short flippers for arms   and prominent

spinal indentations   i as a consciousness am outside these proceedings as ever
ever i   no matter my shape or origin whether   the nude bride of the great
pale beach (oh wouldnt that be mythic)   or the first little blunt headed
salamander   Oh how could i choose   a version of origin   The woman is
zapping me   with red rays as if   i as i came from outside myself
but all i know is that im myself, right here,   with nothing.

in our building we are hardly aware of each other today inside the crystal where no one
has to matter. i am no mystery to myself but i cant find the sense of things, so maybe
theres no such thing sense of things such thing ess salamander i on bench is still same
inside cave or crystal city star i wont stop there is no stopping even if you jump in front of
the train in the métro. i enter the cave as if to try to find figuration, which may be the
beginning of mischief, can there be life without figuration but i am no mystery to myself
and somewhat unfamiliar with how i look to you. being born being born being zapped

with soul or consciousness sparks im still myself before im born ever born im still myself whether i have flippers or not id be a salamander they are probably endangered i am endangered though not as a species am i a species you made that up though certain creatures have said goodbye and left many creatures are ghosts now swelling the unstable walls of our crystal buildings. a wholehearted spirit of i telepathing through the daynight noonmidnight of this city calling crying out *not over it.*

way back in the dorsal fin in the flippers era...these family attachments are beautiful

demonic we are demons together that is magic figures short and tall who try to do good we are demons because there are rays of connection between us of attraction communication comfort preference. we have emphases, which is a demonics.

i dont know if thats negative

i didnt choose my father   yet something about him tears me up. i keep trying to choose my family because we're already demons together. ive waited a whole lifetime for what i would choose the met or really to choose which principle we seem, that the city of crystal is founded on. is there nothing to choose from down here except for whats met. or has been met. there must be more

i love to push my forehead against the water and move along the bottom hushpuppies are creepy swimming turds. anything you might be down at the swamp

the point is we have nothing because we're dead how can there be evil no one has anything not even shoes.

there she is the lovely blond hooker
in black chiffon goldtrimmed   standing on dark
corner two of my men friends have just been with her and now I
know who she is I remember a nurse for important doctors to date
now she's in my old apartment   so I can teach her how to say
mnemosyne it's time to leave   I give what man a plastic soap dish containing a bar
of soap, used, and a coin   I'm paying him   to clean my memory   of her perhaps
or being like her   do I need this myth or story do I choose it. I unchoose her

22

A man

wants me to watch a story   at his house tonight on tv   I decline and he's
angry   another man here   has asked me to be in a film   in which I
would play   an antiquated bandit elegant   you who are story go away

with much anger I can't forget   the brunette who requires my constant
memory of her   memory story myth do I choose it night is leaden with it   like
another blonds tumor on the brain of her skull in the eyesocket I   dont have to bother
        bother to remember   if we are all here and
dont have to go with   going to the house there is no house you were mistaken
you have   no house   in which to watch stories in the crystal city.

I choose to wash away   those memories   of blond or brunette
I choose not to have a story double.
I unchoose story identities.

in order to dissolve these dimensions.
                        and so im changing back back try to go beyond
the pre-fetal fins or flippers

layers and layers swimmingly rushes water or air or hot rock so they said but what have
they ever do they know a thing. i have the demon shine again in the tingling as if to be
any thing is demonic or eerie a light in a swamp where catfish have small lamps on their
bumping heads. knowing each other. knew each other from always. do you know any
thing not yet really. i dont have to no ones made me. someones beating something. if i
could wrench off what i will be like a lot of weird clothes chosen for me. do you
remember learning names for colors those are smashed green sticky locks   but
they arent locks they are emerald grasses   im messing up the categories twigs
failures i have called thing a wrong thing in the burning leaf or rock   there used to
be so much burning here they say.

you say i have to choose the history of the planet as you tell it
you say i have to choose an inherent fish
you say i have to choose some symbols you already know
you say you say.

                    that in case the brunette has AIDS
shes swallowing Geology, a drug. the fixing
of layers of being as if we were
personally rock to be read
I am the only poet, says she

in a room where people lie on the floor
as if at her feet, worrying
about her but
anyone we know might have AIDS and
anyone else might have AIDS, I say
must you choose
someone in particular?

o dissolve the given dimensions well thats what im doing in unchoosing. choosing as hard as possible not to be there down there this is the matter. leave the tainted leave the thing leave hurting by floating away all. telepathing sweetly to me these new kinds of drifts. so the hunting didnt ultimately hurt anything you south seas islander? he says, yes im still crying out but oh its because i cant be an ancestor if there is no tribe or linger near helping but i can be i can be here in this strange intermingling city. i say, is something selfish here the sort of g regression i need to find you earlier you and i as if one before you were hurt though we separate but have this capacity of same mother mind the web of a dea ear earlier dew. before that mud and before you made your women be different whether youre a human or an animal or if youre a plant a yellow i thought of a yellow last night what then was the pleasure of forget it into the mistaken attachment to words. screw the evidence and then the moths and the worms and then the forehead before that the dorsals and before that this exui exquisite almost slimey mind thats i do you know it can i meet you there, he says No im frightened Past the establishment of your dimensions which were different from mine this is not dreaming this is another kind of world. touch you with the potential for fingers in the slime. and i say, and when you learned how to build your big churchy halls to invoke spirits and to keep women out you were so proud of it those were dimensions and the island and the namings so different from ours what was science later to your world but lies and a sure winner Up here we will do better than that its all floating we dont have a thing its still floating

                    red/black heaven
dorsals and before that it can i meet you there. before the choices. if in our strangeness
you once knew me and we knew each other. im just talking talking to you in our way
here tell me night golden fact how the boundaries are slipping

small well-dressed dolls i wanted the first time i was a girl   but were too
expensive why does the famous dead poet have some which im dusting because i
miss him   and think i might feel near   him again, if i dust his dolls   but i
dont choose dolls   and since there are no dolls in our city   i will talk to

him there, without his fame   His reputation is dolls   your ideas of yourself
are dolls   but you are in no wise a doll   dont   be a doll   in a silk dress
with trim around the hem and   platinum blond hair.   how much will i
like him   without his fame   A lot

                                        pass the sherry
                                        the gin & tonic
                                        in the hotel lobby
                                        this cant be our city
i sing and dance, little douce coupe
we have our own   cupless cup The brides impassive
In this hotel lobby marriage   not in our   city, we have our own coupe not for two
but sweet full of tingling bubbles, dont we sister dont we brother There is no famous
bride

        A well-dressed well-made-up girl, approaches me as I'm sitting on the hotel
lobby couch, introduced, by a voice, as some man's wife. She says she's only ten years
old. She thinks she may be pregnant. She says she isn't too young for that. She has
brown hair, and brownish skin, shows brownish at the edge of her makeup.

This
huge crystal
contains disturbed dimensions   says a crystal member, Look at them if thats
what you do   (obviously a plant   doesnt do that)   They are jostled and
trembling snaky lines accustomed to be chosen. if you dont choose them soon

time space & so on   they will collapse and die
                            they are collapsing now
                            they are limp and can be used for ribbons decoration of a
doll   There are no dolls   here   but there is talk   its not talk
There is this

the city of all unconsciousnesses can come conscious
I dont remember where we bright shadows were, clearer than the sun
kinder than light last night how had we previously been so attached to our
actions down there
I only wanted to find you near the river of happiness and hand you a glass of it
I cant remember who you were,

a previous alphabet being poured out of a cylindrical container i thought it was a scroll but
it was a bottle wasnt it   the previous alphabet   was as a liquid
which id choose   as now

FOOD

they say it in a different way they singularly sweet
are singular too, each.
I've been in lots of places and times with you all you
we've been here together and dont have to try when you met someone down there
he or she was familiar.
it took such a hardening to conceive of enemies

covers my face with a cloth   happens all the time down there   Down there
I'm sleeping high up   next to a famous and polluted   river   and over
highways of cars   covers my face with a thin but suffocating cloth a veil of
pollution?   a veil a thin veil for a woman?   a veil thats thin   because I'm

high up but still near can't breathe fair   isnt fair that I breathe if there's
another woman with a covered self another person with a covered woman   though
those who are starving elsewhere   more of them women and children   are
utterly naked in the bone   flies near mouth   some men there also starving

who aren't at the war.

        'i too am in your crystal city   which isnt yours

        between the i who's become only hungry   and the one i
        was born   is a   burning tunnel burrowing path   connecting
        ends of a cylinder   i am walking inescapable breath still
        marking dry fields parched   gums   this

        is not a time   this infinite   hunger   night colder dryness
        and we're bodies   i forget   to be anything else   but my real
        self's elsewhere   where its always   been   i cant know it like
        this   famished   i'm in your city   but i'm   here   famished'

if i stay small and stay back here i wont hurt her or if i dont eat   i have to go on
      i think.

I'm supposed to go out and teach a famous poetry   that that's vanity   I am
being a poem   and I can't teach   that.

this hill is so high these hills are so high and beautiful (my love)

there's a cubicle in a hospital, like an office cubicle, in which a man hysterical exclaims that all of his skin has been cut off, that he has no skin now. But I see that his skin is there he's blind and insists that he has no skin I stare at his body again his skin is smooth and almost luminous, youthful. Afraid to be a soul, is blind. If you peel off a man's skin, if you starve a woman   are you destroying yourself   forever torturer is there a torturing
spirit here in the city unconscious   where on these hautes alpes on these fair hills.
I don't know where he is   a small scurrier a blunt shock inarticulate in our ways
will he learn to speak like us   after cloudbanks of what isn't time. is there a ghoulish
murderer   a brutal leader?

have always been communicating without signs

towards a further alley and then more of the alleys which i can walk in because there are no cars there no extras that dont belong. they keep making things that dont belong. i saw a snake. i dont know what it knows except itself you dont have to be better than a snake. there's nothing better than a snake. down with the gods. i am a god. you are a god a snake is a god. youre not a body with all its things on and all its insides like things on. especially not when youre in the air with everyone

In a world in which a snake and a tree and oneself and you   are equals.
you talk to them and they talk to you. songs   a song talks
Its very dark and so the snake might be   up in the tree, there
a snake or an owl a snake with round eyes streaming water.
                                        The snakes guard the
spring in the canyon you cant see them they're all enwrithed in the grapevines that
conceal the source of the spring.

there isnt a special god there

          one   tree in the yard. there was one tree but I got it
          one   I saw one snake and I got it.
          I know what they are Im about four

There are fifty of something   what   we have to teach fifty we have to eat fifty
fifty states   and fifty plates of couscous   fifty years and the fifty children
of hecuba   The greeks more or less ate   her fifty children   didnt they if they
killed them   so She ate someone back   she literally ate a Greek back
          Fifty plates of couscous at home then I
should at least eat one, Take it someone says, a knowing caped man   Now I have
two of couscous but one of sauce two of couscous it is
                                        writhing   broken
orange carrots.   Fifty years, fifty plates eat   what you have earned   I am
young I am young   I dont want to eat carrots   I dont want to eat.   In the
city do we eat

          we are done with eating and those we ate are here.

          'and those who ate us

          the countries the peoples   who ate us.'

we are an eating mechanism they say they think they even understand the first time
something ate do they   what did it eat   it ate air   it ate god it ate itself?

im now about six and i still dont care about food. like it later   but when i am
young its so un   important.   the egg slimed in the milky drink   because i dont
have an appetite.   i dont have to have something   appetite or
something   if im i like this   i dont have to have something
shes making me drink the egg slimed milk because im too thin   too   thin
          there is no too is there?   making me
eat when there is all this other   for the mind and the skin and the eyes all
together   mixed in with feelings from others   day's all their feelings
coming at me hard.   though not much is new   i seen it before dont say
that.   like it later   its a gross pleasure. to eat you up   you dont eat youre
all eyes and asshole.

          Whatever you say   oh whatever you say   But

          Whatever you say in the crystal city   is taken lightly.

hes coming to save me but i wont be saved this time i dont have to be saved. I told
you later I dont have to be saved, I'm always saved. I dont have to have, you dont
have to approach me with something because   I dont have a quality   there
arent   any. He walks across to pick me up its flattering but not necessary.
These are some thoughts I'm saying to you of the chorus or of whatever are you

getting them? Pull   the onion ring   instead of a wishbone it wont break it
has union it doesnt wish it dont wish it aint it caint dont say caint, like grandma.
she put sugar on my toast, with butter and i ate it   she was eating it too   grinning
sipping her tea from a saucer   i caint find my.   you never lost it
I always like to hear her funny voice up here in the crystal trees their painstaking

casual   ness like being itself like basal being, casually   theres
only one basis   and there are no other options   being, being me is exactly
what it is without   havings   havings or qualifications.   grandma's
sense of her being   was casual enough   not to hurt any frail mirror
she ate air   no she didnt   she ate toast   and small hamburger

sliding across from this to this   from me towards you for example
slide the icon a mind one   slide image thought from me towards you and back
without bothering to notice the towards and back   whos   thinking
who   cares?

                    the lyric baskets are my eyes
                    the lyric baskets (voices) are my eyes
                    and my skin   and my nourishment.

knocking down dimensions, just what do you put back up when something collapses

                              small white flowers not showy but real
hidden in the grass   of that empty lot   are of no importance
                                                      You might
choose everything that has no importance   everything dead to the senseless
senses of the world.
things wont be eaten or changed into food

i ate her biscuits there   he said a diamond could break a fork   see this fork a diamond   is hard enough to break a fork   this   is   the notion of industrial diamonds   i live in a diamond   we live in one its so hard that nothing can break it.   We eat meat made of diamond   We   eat air   we dont take too much of it there is no much.   You can have the most there is no most.

Someone I trust is saying our world down here can sustain us for only a few hundred years more. We are
all dying of little to eat in the future

...hands me a small a package of something like Neccos Necco wafers–one of the foods i like young, wafer-thin candies wafers   religious?   oh who cares if its that category or another   And says that one wafer   contains all i need for a meal. They are brown they resemble   chocolate Neccos.   tarzans upset while i eat a necco   he must handle the panther men   there can be no special faction in the jungle: both the people and the animals   are too scary for that
         you are kind and brave and beautiful   these words   are factional describing portional qualities   but one must be those pieces of thing as wildness vanishes and wildness arises, a   wildness to come unlike one   we've ever known.

a redwood like forest of crystal trees a crystal forest a forest of soul a gathering of tree souls or soul trees a beautiful forest is here   near our city.   The place of sorrow in such a huge event as the destruction of down there   which the planet has suffered before   and if our speci but i cant say that word which is not a proper category not a proper piece of thing.   i have no right to this sorrow

the consciousness we are all of and which this is and which is also an unconsciousness

i know this as young as i am   do i really have to learn what they know   no thats why im reborn   in order to choose   choose again

the streets are as wide and bizarre as stars are. the actual is very bizarre is not natural the dimensions are further destroyed, by a rampant fire in the jungle a grisly destruction a terrifying happenstance from nowhere. because there never had to be anything on this ground? it could be dead as mars. would i still be alive somehow i think mars is conscious. or do you think a different and as you think and as you think are you like animals or are you like mars. i am like mars. no one will read this poem in several hundred years. it is cast into the air which is the one thing i have confidence in not the breath air but the crystal air

a cup of coffee in a cafe a wafer in a cafe down there with the fisher king. they're after him and he's scared. you can't see the cracked barren ground
just the tall buildings behind behind the coffee shop. later
a young man won't let me go home until i've had more to drink more wine but i want to go home

i dont want to eat eat or drink a starving woman

TIME

the clothes are a liar
in the future we are sad but
sadness is not a fact
it isn't big enough (she
and she is in the future

writes at the table wind)
dark curl out   curl of storm   the
window.
                a universal beloved beyond the
planet   a universal echo ch system

reprisals friends   reprisals from
nature   are   friends.   soon my turn
to be reprised upon

a universal beloved is like i.

She is in a small   clean   kitchen

(has taken the laundry out of a washing machine
in which city has grayer hair in the future and
is I.)

to see this I have   floated   over the time line into the future

I was in a small clean kitchen i will not be in which city so where was i really or am i am i
here. suffering loss of self on a soft beat connection wind freely this is nothing nothing to
speak of not the hurrican mud the hurricane mu true future we have engineered because
we have suppressed our other city soul and so have engendered reprisals friends from
nature. who will destroy us down there. view this on a dream screen against a backdrop
of the constellations. i am what age now i am ageless without any counting when i am six
seven being a bottomless forever into the future of no earth as we. you must already
know what i am talking about. hovering over the time line in which we destroy so much
the rain forest for examp in the next fifty years (i speak from in the timeline nie nineteen

ninety eight) so we yes must proceed to hover over the timeline rather than be in it
destroying the forest or natural troy instead we must hover timelessly in the crystal city
and not break heart mud of heart in hurricane and volcano you have already done when
the weather is exactly our fault. it is my fault.

the weather is my fault
ravaging of an isthmus

the clothes are a liar all this poetry   talk is clothes is clothes.
Chorus repeats echoing the clothes are a are a liar your talk is clothes and are a liar liar
liar. Everything you have is a liar

something under construction
a basement to protect him from sand
m he must be protected from sand   here   the unleashing of future sand
        because he is special, a beloved poet
wooden beams   and concrete   for this basement but   no one
        —what are the beams for? special—
will be protected from the sand of the future   and when   all basements are done
when time now is done   and folksong too will i remember what a concrete
basement   is?
        special he   what are the beams for special   there will be no beams of
        that   nature   our   nature will be no.   so go on

two of me have landed
in an airplane wearing an aviator's leather tightcloche hat with a strap.

        Try to explain, again, about the construction, which is not special
        of the other body. It is being constructed at night while I sleep
        I dreamed this, but I didn't I awoke dreaming and was the second
        the second body the first lay beside me and I was really the second one
        painted with white washed with white beams flat like light.

        it is the white one that has been reborn   as a growing child again
        that knows the crystal city   and hovers over the timeline

34

I am trying to describe the city as I hear it
the poetry of not words but   not words but not style   just a quickly
continuous communication

                                              of eyes i have the biggest eyes around and can.
can see. but you dont you see auto automatically i cant control what i see when im four
seven or fiftythree see as in dream i mean see as in think image think cant control those
images why are they really others messages from other or other i wha how its realer how
old am i now? im having no age isnt that what we wanted. as young but having no age
one might see it on the hill a girl in underpants practically baby or that old what what
difference do you believe in the meaty body not particularly. the meaty body full of its
pains its literalness but what is that in time which refuses to stay in a meat present there is
no pres memory ensures hag nightingale night in gown i am so young i die i grow so
young i die a girl in you have no nature as a hoax another hoax of naming. dont want
any more hoaxes of naming. control your dreams you cant because time wont let you no
time but time wont let you it isnt the hoax of naming that we have accepted you will
never control your dreams. yes i will. dreams are the key to time outside the line

   I've never done this before crammed for a course. They have weird food here
   a cheese containing another cheese. I don't know what happens when you eat
   it. It has something to do with learning from a disciple goo within goo the bible
   the goo book costs forty dollars and the town named after a saint has a zip code
   after all so you can learn fast but do I want to be here in somewhat a hoax of
   naming is everywhere but the elusive city a hoax of naming? In this saint town
   is the last stand we will defend our north american values against all of weather
   and others of our crystal friends, here. We will defend gooey cheese within
   cheese, in san antonio, at the alamo.

On an airplane having gone backwards in time in October 1998
I dreamed awake   in a rush of short episodes   or was I
only remembering dreams I   had had a moment before
I was frightened barriers down was awake and dreaming beyond control   Then
I went into   a prolonged state of deja-vu   whatever she, real person, said she had
already said, for example You two have the same nose

Please consider time differently   it isnt in place as you think it
in words we have inherited   to make us go to work at the   right time
to ensure that   we not see into the future see the consequences of

a dream being dragged like a hurricane across the room. white it whirls round a
center   we have dreamed a real   hurricane   into existence by
countenancing time embracing and countenancing such a god as the time created by
us the needs of such a time of such pressing consecutive hours   which close off the
future a burning eyes man men standing in columns the eye my point of
eye follows from genitals to genitals why in this dream among trees near an inn a lake
that was septembers old earth   the engendering of time   could have been

beautiful if dreams had been known as their own   time.   armies of time
permeate our civic house   a chamber in the shape of a rat   rounded building a
snoutlike entrance   and elsewhere you in your large   or even larger
apartment pretending   youve got trouble, some kind of landlord trouble
but youre always in some apartment   as we are being kept quite well   in the
dream we've created of famine and hurricane   which is real   real dream
we've made   really hurting others.

Have gone back in time to the youth of the brunette a clear young woman
nonsmoker's skin and has escaped from a great fire in lower new york
explains the escape against a backdrop of sheet of fire at night on the lower east side
it happens again she explains it again

Will she escape from every fire
Will we escape   from every fire what   does the world   look like
why not a folksong   a man has escaped with her   they escape and escape
        again   but will not always.   This is a folksong   not science

this is differently true and they   song knows will not escape   they havent
the right to escape each time   they cause a fire   did they cause it   not the first
one but they have caused it now, are causing it too   because they've learned how
to escape.   So they can cause it.

i was born to be part of a great destruction. i try to escape from the house on fire at four five six and later i try to tell them to leave it because the flames arent so bad at the moment i cant get my mother my father, my sister and brother, to leave. i must be in all time together or i will be wrecked wrack weed human weed it says written in objective fire the smell is leaking out of the ground and in among the trees there where i round the bend running, fortyseven years later. this is a stagnant shallow pond that no one cleans. i only have to wear underpants. the sky will appear to run with blood being hot fake blood, you can make weak   blood with a chemistry set.

this doesnt look like blood
your tonsils are rotten. oh mountains to walk out and see you morning again what was ever so beautifu didnt know do know now know in backwards motion how beautiful   time in   some shape a martian would know
a martian bacteria a piece of rock a fake blood any old thing
this doesnt look like blood
then it has some other name any old name. im not blood im not full of blood i dont have genes or what you who are you say im not what you say am not a say am not even here.

Time won't let us find the met's source
won't let us enter the basement
of the met because what's made there
is already being met
by us on the way to So we couldn't
stop a met thing at its source So
we couldn't create a at the source maybe if
I can sneak in quick but
how do you create a what thing?

that's why I can't concentrate

apartment several stories up linoleum floors one roomish dominant sense of kitchen faint blueness reason is quiet I am being presented though there's no presenter in a prostitution situation how do I know how am I so there so right in it that time and situation in a white slip? someone's arranged this and he the man the john is tall and familiar with a gray high topknot of hair he's a rooster he has a son and asks him who is perhaps ten if he wants to watch but doesn't and I guess the scene disappears then though in another dream I wonder and eventually ask him if he used a condom he says he didn't think he had to one can judge these situations and he and I are already connected in friendship through a friend named John. I'm weary of such scenarios

courtyard lights night where library once was

think he was supposed to pay me.

i will not grow up to mime this sexual drea i am dressed in future rags and am glad in any time i want, not just the time of the topknot. morn light sweeps across lot

i will not grow up to mime your worl. up on the bluff in the city.
i am acquiring rag by rag crystal rag to wear time itself seems tattered now
i want a rag i invent a rag a rag.

remember the machine that takes dreams into the future dreams wound up in cells it lets them out its in a cave its in an under i am older and assume that something is using me. not a sex or animal thing something else is using me i wait for it to set me in stories because i can only anyway choose already stories the already existent so i wait till it does it i dont pretend i do i know they are only some stories. get out getting out

in our city all our stories are blowing away rags in a hurricane

NOT AN IMAGE

magical lights beside doors of
twostory small
motel-like apartment complex
near the big street–

here in mild night
these lights outside the
adobe-colored earthenish rooms
are alluring and I

I'm just looking at them is there another thing to do?

at night among magic lights
demarcating doors of individuals

to remember a thing all night
      never
      try to
if you have to you'll change it   there are three squares flat on the ground   what
are they   past present and future   white and blank so the same   in-
distinguishable?   when I walk near them a strong smell of Witch Hazel.

      Are the basement of the Met
      the source of images
      and myself
      different places
      or not?

take something out. you cant take it out if you do it just goes somewhere else you. i
didnt like it what difference does that, liking it, make mac is our leader well fuck him what
word is that. take some out, you are not being, consistent in character, just goes
somewhere else you. do you want to be the leader or leading what what thing i am the
leading thing today in my underpants which ive put on insideout again. so lead on down

and pretend through down below the house under the where the spiders are and under far and through and through. or out on the hill above the clinic where doctors are doc. theyve renamed a french street and a métro stop bugs bunny street. the old clinic though not the first clinic. im not being true to my age of four or five i thought youd gotten to seven or eight or fiftyfive no im only and always a light by the door age. there is a cave of light around here that is the source of the met but whenever i go in i cant see anything but light so how is it a rou source of the met i walk in and in and its only light try it again as if it were a weird folksong you already sort of know. go in/i go in/go further in/the blonds dead all dressed in her long brocades/further/the young brunettes necks snapped so her head lies limp to side there shes dressed all in her long hair/go on again/there they are the moths i mean images and you cant catch them/we will try to catch them/who/the city it isnt   just   you.

the next time i see the cave there's only light in it

if you go there you have to see it yourself and see how you are it the source of the things. we'll go with you and let as voices cool and warm both in the small child underpants folksong you be the i am i walking into the center of i am the machine thats not a machine that takes dreams into the future swirling its turning all around me making things out of hats peoples scalps no thats a but there is no first oh all of you voices so gold glints spiral around i smell witch haze and wing in the dark vehicle there among hills a friend with the spiritu you dont have a form here oh you know i dont have a form any way. stop the machine. we're here to make a city where peoples unconscious is conscious. this feels good and youre getting it would you like a piece of carriage. its wheels the turn sinks these feet are mere flat tables i eyes are two eye balls i mean dusks. you cant have a different but you can be differ inside start lay fried moths on corner of a dead hat. you know i dont have a form or a former so there were no pied all voice ah the ah ahs and now mute sewnnn i am a large one as bird. liquid previous language secretly compliant

I'm looking for my bird A
I'm looking for my pale body
I'm on the front street of wares, cloths racks of
        jewelry
I'm headed away from and back to.

40

they've cut down trees near one singular tree   i dont know which i im

i am a large one better than an im   im looking for   my beginning my
always   the body in the soul in the white transparent soul clothes is too thick and
older   im looking for my   source of images   cant concentrate on find
because the future time carries me away down the street of wares carries me on
into the more   wares.

i dont know whether to be   with   the one remaining tree   or the
destroyed ones all of us crystal   by the railroad tracks and near the wares

someone had karposi's, walked with difficulty   i had to talk to another in trouble
not him and ignored him one time   hear me now, do you hear me im talking to
you   will you reply   now   in the only dead crystal we all
im sorry for that time and wind in the trees   wind in the trees in another town

where the cars cross the tracks   where trees grow near the river   which the
bridge of course crosses   where my whole school   was sacrificed to a war

i have been a similar soldier   a soldier all along   and will be forever   i im the
soldier   in the chorus of crosses, crystal crosses   near the

new images   we will reinvent our crosses
living inside those doors   beside the magic lights   we   do.

i am the source of images am the cave below the met

as shown by the fact i emerge onto first avenue
from below the theatre its basement, a former school on the corner of
ninth street. if im it why cant i find it?
we buy pizza and will buy beer i suggest dos equis no
he says because a junky he knew drank dos equis too no that
has nothing to do with dos equis which means here two equals–

the doctor has given me the wrong white gown for what   the doctor is always

wrong. the doctor has given me the wrong thin white
momma says he says but hes wrong.

always through and two towards why not different this time through arches pointy
of a shape known. im wearing a top with shorts and a ponytail glasses i must be years
old kid. i could understand the world if there werent cars but now i'll never get it. no
one can take care of themself now and i know it others have to tell them how
others make the cars and tell them how. how to be

I emerge from the source of images into the images. I emerge from theater and school
onto the corner of letter and number near meaningless shops. I come out of it am it.
The long sword has ruined time the quasi feminist says. Dos equals I say different I say
a slavish adherence to the notion the acceptance of dimensions, has ruined us.
No where and outer who
I am not outer who here in declining tree where the forest of loss devastating
So tree amid trees fallen down in a c choose an image why choose an image if you
dont, one will choose you. the manufacture of dreams takes place throughout the
soul encasement of my body throughout me then or of images when I sleep I cant get
this to am scream there is no way one can live in this lower city body images going on
making it here in the corner of my eye to speak of sorrow everyone always
counteracting the requisite with a tear but both must change
the requisite and the tear

in the dream my beautiful mother had a younger sister she was more beautiful than who
died of chrome. the caves never empty the basement of the met is full of presents
borrowed images getting there im getting to the center and receive for my present
underwear white and f ruffled. I wake up feeling much thinner. my father's younger
sister who died, she's the one who died, lobotomized, in the arizona state mental hospital
in her twenties a sometime lovely blond not dark as a witch like her sister another aunt
who got to live twenty years longer than that among images. died in pain too.

im down here young enough to find it the hole im a young young like a witch hazel poke
my image finger through the image floor an image comes up but its an already. already
known and already there. texture of fur its a big long fur arising air. it was practically an
animal. sit sit longer by this hole, in this vision.

now i'm tingling

now thats a different thing, the tingling
                            and its not an image, how its in me
the tingling

now thats thats the name of it
                 but it, its how it *feels*. what it *is*
                                     not
                                     thing
                                     seen.

                           i sit longer here quiet quieter
quieter in this empty basement house this ring of apples because. because when i want
to say anything i say ring, apple, hawk, or hat. its convenient how conveni im leaking
quietude
                   images drown in it. temporarily. its not an image
its more important

thinner thinner today. then its all forgotten. whats the unforgotten for what for what
for.

city isn't tall towers today it is low and irregular
it is these crystals and inside I'm in
a large solarium
someone very vividly joyous faced
runs towards me it is myself.
                   to be
in crystal is bright and clear. a feeling but not as a brash or
romantic thing. this city
is a feeling, sometimes a mountain with its top air

    in the dream both men are using me to say things about. that they have done
that kind of sex to me.

here a voice says here
you can you can bathe here.
being this one, a relief. i dont have to be you any mo. crowded peace a thick sweet. lets
go over there to that party get rid of the war if there is no change was you singing? she
says was like that her people do the demonic party who look like alike i went on further
in or back and it was a body i was in and out of. if they broke it they couldnt exactly.
something still hides there.

come to the place up here where we make the city we just make it.

who   the city   it isn't   just   you

CHANGING TIME BACKWARDS

I'm to make veal   stew   child   stew
eat it and by that process
grow   I haven't even started cooking
it will take until late tonight. so
maybe I wont. Oh, I will
have my children   have children but
won't kill and eat my own child self
wont be corrupted by what happens   which has
already happened   and corrupted me.

Do you understand that I'm changing time backwards?   that this is
one of the things we do in our beautiful city that has no gates
that has no roof   that is only window and   the voice of the mind.

And what of our beautiful bodies
     The body is in the soul   and never dies
What do you mean
     I don't really know   dear I only know Who
the true body
cannot be broken One of the things we do in our city Changing time backwards
is to reconstitute   the body   into its original sense   We dont
know what you mea I dont know who's speaking or if it is true True what's tu true,
is the becoming more lovely as we think about it Who will believe such a Who cares
if Who believe?   believe believe I don't want to have a thing like believe

We have a thing like Think it.

My mother lifts me up
as if I were a child
she is too old to do this
and I am too old to be lifted up
my mother
lifted me up again in her arms at the age of

seventynine I was fiftythree   in the basement of a department store
where I buy toys and later records   everyone is here all the poets   we are sitting
on the floor together. Connie is here   blond Constance and one of the
Calderons is here   another young brunette.   with Lucy's bones and facial
shape   Constance and   Lucidity Luce Light Calderon–
        and Tony had returned
last year with his body reconstituted   from his horrible death   pale but whole
        How can you believe in such

Because I am making it. making it be
in the city

Society Below

It is a heap of
living bodies
nude, marblelike,
attached; perhaps
carved out of the same
marble. They can move, writhe
slowly from the waist up but
are rooted in each other...
Agonized sluggish. In a bare
landscape, black
sky. they are brown-pink

ive caused the flooding of the downstairs apartment where the landlord and his wife live.
she likes me she has three eyes all on the same level the two normal ones are brown and
the central one is pale green. i didnt notice it at first. there is another dream where a face
is a single long metal thing, which is called a 'mote spar': true like a way of brining
bringing up a family so that everyone looks right. everyone is trying to give birth to a
mote spar not me. in my new life childbirth contains all the love to have for them already
from ever future a rose not a line the purpose or center of time so ive put it in backwards.
ive put a lot in backwards. thats why i have a roselike face not the linear mote spar but i
probably have three eyes and what i have anyway is sort of stupid eyes nose mouth the

water is full of rats swimming alongside the cars theyre as big as seals. they get smaller as you go uptown. i sit with a mote spar somewhere and say i used to buy toys around here. because im a lot older. also records.

for a long time i look at you and see the other one you are   who is in another place the mote spar face   disappears   and you have three eyes.

The woman with three eyes said to me, Oh it's you! I like you.

im living in paris specifically but who can stand the dimensions   throw them away
                too old for that heart
                the product of an attitude towards the dimensions viz only emotions can
be broken   they are human the dimensions aren't
you broke me but not the way i felt just what i could do every day what our world is like
only like 'you' not me   you broke me but im   breaking dimensions

its time for me to choose something, how old am i now

i dont choose
personal
characteristics
but i choose
three eyes.

It turned out he was quite young. He was a bum on the métro yesterday on a 7 bis line train, the Louis Blanc line. Cold; there had been ice on the pond the ducks and geese had stood around on it squawking. So he was wearing a Sherlock Holmes hat with the ear flaps down and bundle-y clothes a too-big coat from someone else. He had the slightly dirty tough lives-outdoors complexion, he had moustache and other facial hair. I think he was about thirty. He was an alcoholic, of the hallucinatory world, all on his own, he made unpleasant grunting noises–unh! unh!–incoherent and inarticulate. He got off somewhere like Bolivar or maybe as early as Buttes-Chaumont. Walked off all by himself and looked like he knew where he was going but he had no friends was my impression. I found him admirable because he keeps going, that's your definition of courage. He doesn't seem to see why not. And why not. I think I liked him better than anyone I actually talked to yesterday, he was doing a fantastic job, I nearly cried. I believe he is already consciously in my city. Why else is he still going, what else is he going towards

if youre afraid to have children have them anyway I dont see the point Why do you want points It isnt biology you know Its doing it to find out. You find out who they are, everyone wants them to look right and not have three eyes.

Contemplation   perhaps towards choice   among sets of oh 3 or 4 shapes in relation to each other   say, 3 wavy lines against an amorphous flat shape

which might have wavy edge, edges   Pleasant colors, especially blues   possibly yellows but I don't remember any red. They were glossy   or it was glossy, the experience   It might have something to do with choosing Dimensions. How we chose   what became edged

            The dimensions may be emotion-like, a voice says
            That's how you can change time backwards
            But I don't think you can change the planet back.
            You can only change you   and only part of what you
I was going to say "did"   but that's not right. One   person   hardly   did   a
thing. But they did it with things, like a car. You can't change how you had a car
You arent explaining it right
            Its how you act the same way all the time that creates a
dimension. Puts fist through window. Creates time as we know it. Sits still in a chair
a lot. Creates another kind of time or   maybe you don't even have to say time.
Everyone knows this   No they dont   Or they wouldnt be such shits

Theyre not all shits

A young man who must use   all the space of the métro seat
intruding slightly   into my opposite seat space
because he's delicately tearing out   a precious clipping, small
from the sports pages of Le Parisien.   he accidently touches my knee

in the process of placing the clipping carefully   into the zippered pocket
in the sleeve of his down jacket   I'm thinking he's asking me to help him
with the awkward pocket   and reach out my hand towards him   but he was
apologizing for   touching my knee   he touches my knee, again, in order to
explain. Then gets off at Opera, says au revoir.   That was a crystalline happening

El Amor Brujo. another young man

is listening to that score, in a dream. it seems to
be an opera not a ballet this time. love is a witch because its both invented and not, and
you never know which part youre in a witch is a way of manipulating both
without acknowledged power.

one version of el amor brujo takes place in a trailer
park i wanted to grow up into el amor brujo so i could do that dance that music not be
in a house-y house. gypsies live in caves too

the small figure dressed in white small
and smaller is entering the cavern of myself again and el amor brujo is not especially
sexual why should it be it is the gloss instead on the world but which can also be in
sex. i want to find it what.

now the figure in white is smaller still and the cave larger a
cauldron of love a maw of glossy reason a cement mixer of mattery images an image
an image an i mage el amor brujo an oh fuck a stuff more stuff. stuck with. answer
the life question really the hot trees chime stirring in blood who needs to be a witch i
do to change time backwards.

she is standing on a little stage in the cavern head bowed. she is i, i am very sorry for
participating with you in our world now cant get out except through hard will out i knew i
was wrong all the time i only thought about love, but did it anyway only thought self
scenarios remember in the adolescent theatre o isnt that normal no nothing is.

will rocky milwaukee sit on the grass in the black and talk about maps the map
of the country the world or the stars the map of hidden flowers clovers but there werent
any there might have been a map. you get on that line and you go to the place that lights
up city city you turn to jade temporarily in order to become an object of affection you
become stony to be loved in the world of smoke. no one needs so much love, and it
doesnt have to be people, here is a doctors kit it didnt work. im standing on the stage in
white night gown in the war any war on on the map acting like it isnt who has the right to

there is no right no right to a war and there is no ri twisting and turning beaten by reason
in an old hat. no one has the right to do any thing at all. cant tingle today adolescent this
is the pain of adolescence lasting forever. im refusing to cook and eat the veal stew. i will
have to love some other way this time. im refusing to accept an image

these are the hills of the city but not quite yet   because the egotistical man seems
to want me to have sex with him   and his wifes teeth are like a picket fence they
are ivory mote spars   no he's a bird and his wife is a flower everything's changing
i can't find its sequence i don't know   what order it happens in, except in

memory   my brothers face is scarred as if by pickets by mote spars seared
and he is an older face frozen   in the shorter body of a pre-adolescent because
he went to war and lost his youth his childhood   his time was changed backwards
that way   his childhood was destroyed   by the concept of mote spars warriors

but there are two of him, i know. And really the city is beautiful   high in the
mountains green   there are no cars here the city is named

for a large gentle shaggy mammal my sons can live here when i have them
they will have three eyes

FEAR

what was the use of and here, matted im in it and in no city come out its to be small in the cave of myself and not the cave not the cave walls expanding into gloss of night of cloud pearl light. why am i afraid for you and not myself. gloaming manufact bigger lights lightbulbs so i can see it coming to get me but in the city where our invisible crystal caves our skull minds overlap and theres enough space for all of them fear goes away during timelessness i will never know the sequence of events do you so whe we can know which thi there are no events but a soft cap that falls into a shape of folds why am i afraid for ou you and not myself.

if theres no sequence theres no fear.

A huge and growing light is coming towards me

I'm afraid it will make me painfully different it will make me good or smart or incapable of temper   it will make me see your life as your own and not societys
           a light is coming a growing steady diamondwhite dazzling light is coming towards me   it is hugely a sense   now I see that you are your own and that you owe me nothing   even if I'm your mother   or your daughter

                in this city
                it lights up
                all the crystals of
                which the city is built
                this is one of the
                things we do light up a out of fear thats love though too

                because fear turns over.

i was afraid for you   now i just love you.

These flowers that I can't breathe are mostly red

A large face a female gorilla's was being scrubbed by small people with brushes
brushes on the ends of long handles   she's upset and will take her case   is it the
near extinction of her species?   to the supreme court   Do we have such a
court   justice for such a   large spirit can only come from large spirits
I can't even breathe in red red mums.

a face in kind but what isnt i c recognize i besotted myself in the first life in order to
what to be in a mix a flow an energy of the social but now i am home. in this city i
dont have to to like you or ape you me i am the ape a face as large as the cavernous
hills on which our city has been founded
we are seeing to you we are washing away the veil which obscures you in the face of a
lesser justice.
                    i am an ape and have been so,
bigger better gentler, than you
                                                        the supreme court
would be our own spirits come finally to a   state   where stubborn mental
precisions collapse, like   she is not like us.   then   we are not like her
because we're so small   in spirit.

down here im afraid we will let her disappear. too many knowing, lovely
forms will disappear

i am afraid for her.
am i allowed to change that fear into love? and how would that help? it would

I see myself walking surrounded by
sparkling particles hardly visible.
Another element than crystal
adheres to me in pieces or facets They are "pieces" of
sexual desire these are always about me, as I am always among
the crystal of the crystal city
"These" these other pieces sexual desire are a tingling too   a clustering
Do i know what theyre   for   not just procreation

But why a these?   Because ive been taught that i am physical pieces?   what you
solemnly call molecules.   There are parts to my pieces   which you cant discover
pieces of telepathy spirituality   pieces of love   and pieces of fear

actually i dreamed i was a he not myself   experiencing the sexual pieces
the dream was of i as a he   because i am also composed
of pieces of sympathy   which is not quite telepathy
but very very close. are you listening?

i cant go back to four years old at the moment im experiencing late adolescence its painful
not to be able to go back i must try in this life i must be able to go back back and now i do
i touch a lizard scurrying because i cant bear to touch a snake do you see the scary pieces of
its skin it doesnt think that what it think it whole everything bright eclipse. it is power.
i saw an ant think i saw a i saw a locust think. i saw a moth making a mistake a bad
thought. i saw its fear. these all thought-brains are the clusters and clusters of crystals
everywhere inside the giantest geode of all if it takes over i wont get to be sexual enough
is this a fear in adolescence if theres brilliant soulgood everywhere these these sexuals
attached to my lower stomach wont get to and i wont get to star it. wont get to star it but
what good then i know this is wrong. it isnt just about babies its about impressing people
and taking power its pieces of power over and try to construct a woman how stupid its all
so stupid and then something fantastically sad happen anyway pieces of sorrow sadpathy
have you found the sorrow gene my friend stupid. i know im most afraid of grief. yeah i
always say that but now im four again tingling and wont though im afraid of fire. am i
still afraid of grief in my fifties yes until the fear turns over. into love. grief is love, a
fearful love. but grief loves.

the present the supreme present and his supreme wife are a sexual matter. in their
mansion i get in bed with them   theres no other bed   how can there be no
other bed in the mansion? a *mansion*   Thats because its an anachronism, the
present   Everyone's talking about   the present's sexual affairs   in a
bleachers dotted with blue flowers   blue flowers of reason   Reasonable I know
the present is only sex   sex cancels fear cancels past and future   cancels
doing right   Then in a grimy gray storefront   down on the lower east side
the present asks me for cigarettes   he's thinking sex but asks cigarettes   The
present is a habit   a bad habit in the urine stained night   im looking for a
métro stop that   begins with the letter M   im going to run run away.

i am looking at you real fast. im getting out of here with my
bike helmet my moto helmet my fake head im still carrying this manufactured head
but why? just drop it now i did i dont have your fake present head any more. goes up
on those hills to run run away why why m why oh god mother or something
no its just métro stupid. youre trying to make it be significant but its just what mhat
free free. im not afraid now running free from the
                                        cultural any nationalism children
its time to go and feast on the dead any dead fear will do will stand and walk if we say
so convinced yours pesh pressuring me your ring i meant. im trying to be brave
enough is that a real   i dont know. if time were changed out of sequence
but im only being logical what good that is its, and eating too, time's invention. food
is for time. fear keeps people in line was it invented

algerian women having been warriors in la guerre algérienne   are now wrapped up in
cloth of the law   mister leader looks so warmly passionate, and friendly
proclaiming that women exist solely   to produce sons for Islam   But the algerian
women   whistle coarsely,   with two fingers like   my cousin eileen   and
shout, Not Sudan Not Iran but   Algeria!   they are absolutely right   yet   I'd like to
be a nationalism of one.
                        I feel fear for these women
at the exact moment they say, on my television, one must be brave, and, of the men:
'Why are they so afraid of us?'

        I have no rights
        I have caused everything

leave   me   here   your laws   are   trivial.

the destructive gypsy moth has eaten again, I fall asleep   saying in a plea to who or
what within myself the cavern   'I want to see it
                                        thinking, the dream.'
i dream all night of the woman who has often represented my soul as if my soul as if
that were different from me oh that is when i can't find me. She has a new apartment

with an open window its thanksgiving   Easels   She is making some sort
of art she is painting within small framelike spaces   landscapes   or are they
abstractions?   they are settings   dark and poignant, streaked with colors
        violet   medium blue   yellow.
She's painting my dreams
painting their backdrops
Im supposed to paint some too
we are originating dreams. this is the dream thinking
theres no fear here and therefore no bravery
its beautiful
thinking but not thinking about anything.

all of this is already made this matter we supposedly see
but my relation to it isnt nor mine to you.

these horizon bands that keep me in fetters directions or dimensions
are in the souls paintings but only suggesting themselves   shes painting tarotlike
cards without portraiture or scenario   without love fate fear or death
        without even treelike cuplike verticals and circles   just those same colors that
haunt the back of my mind   those same faint lines the over and over that i here
dont know what

                                yet the stage is so set and expectant of
the usual play inside the "brain"   the source polluted with uranium   for
hundreds of thousands of years   the earth is billions of years old so? you
invented billions   you invented numbers and just because they work
but   i invented poems   and just because they work   this is a sort of spell
but a very serious one   we are painting parts   of the crystal city   on the

cards   because we think there is this city instead of god   low and beautiful
transparent blueglinting yellowglinting crystals in the twilight   in this
dimensionless void My soul tells me she is still afraid   I tell her I'm afraid
too   afraid of you and of what

we've done.

We   some female people go to a wedding in the greater   metropolitan area
I have no sense of who's getting married   We're in a building full of bars and
rooms   looking for the wedding reception   A barman consults his list and
tells us it's uptown way up at   3184 First Avenue   I'm having drinks with a
woman   but the stems of our glasses break off and now I have splinters of
glass in my palm   She suggests we drink the same drink without ice because
then we'll get stemless glasses   Fear of crystal   fear of the pieces

penetrating my hand.

we're bombing iraq today and im afraid   afraid for who dies   afraid of my
guilt, I dont want to be part   of these or any   nations

wasnt reborn to be guilty again the stems of our glasses break off   there is no
wedding to toast   a dream woman said, of some shit in the bathroom,
'Oh X (a man) is taking care of that'   I want to be an ape today an ape   a red
beardlike flame is sprouting from the chin of the ape's soul which is sweet and
almondlike   smooth   young

A stemless glass full of clouds blue sky
A stemless glass full of clouds gray sky.   the crystal city? and these two
intensified, blue and gray might be   brave (reasonable) and afraid   down here
but up there   are only a sense of change.   brave and afraid dont belong to anyone

Objects, in a row, on a long long table   the table at the wedding reception
after the reception was over   covered with emptied dishes streaked with foods.
The room has pale yellow walls and   the objects on the white-covered table
include   an airplane mixed up in an amorphous substance, grounded by it a sort of
lumpy glue or gesso, white stuff–fear?   there is also a stack of cans
said to be cans of "mystery"

CHANGING THE FUTURE/PUBLIC PROPHECIES

some people against our bare hills
are trying to form pretty couples   and trying to be
some ancient corrupt   notion of man and woman   he is carving a very
artistic frieze for her of the socalled world la di dah   no one else here   cares   so
they have no theater   this possibility will evaporate on the nonbreeze.   i have a
case   of earth the size   of a pencilcase shaped   like a long person   a dead one i
guess   image of world down where new catchword   is possibility
          why
is there ever   only one hellish earth worl permeated   with no possibility at all
connected with christmas crackeds channukah ramadan and all the
immoral religio.   Earlier there were seven dresses   thats what possibility gets you
im gettin sick of thes dreams   seven little satin dresses   separated into
three little dresses   and four little dresses   tacked on a board gets you
seven little dresses!   and the head of john i suppose   one john or all the
johns i dont   want to have to think like this drea any mo stop the assembly
line of possibility

          lyric is dead
          she said it wasnt   yeses & nos what kind of lyric
          the yellow one the blue one   yeses & nos
          nothing is dead   except the planet   well the reasoning mind
                                                  is pretty dead
          nothing is dead   except the will to change it
          dead everything   lost everything   should be dead that we make
          make and value should be dead
                    say something like else fuck no nothing right to
to live you have no right   to happiness to self-expression you have no
i havent a right   this world was never possible   so why is it here? so like this
pile of junk suffocat burying   of possibi   Everything they do is invasive
                                        Everything is invasive

i dont know how old i am. i can have crystal stream through my body. try not to be as if
here in any way only there out of it a spirit not doing that my hair is like long moss im
leanin against the proverb oak arent i how old old face like a skull with senses but what
are they they cant count on you. voices say join the voices up here john just the ones up

here they aint doing anything thats my grandmother that which grand maybe the other
too these women whose tasks for love are only belied on earth by the furious men with
their ideas about war or even poetry which is always seen as a war wah fahget it alley
your poems are up here theyve disappear they talk on the wine wind wind dow wah way
way its all a all a And then the tingling gets to start And then i dont have to exist in that
way you you value in which i do more things with matter decimating species and
perpetrate violence upon my own of whom i dont approve on any leve but keep being
How old am i how old is robert johnson now that hes dead with his big red soul rag
bandanna and all his badness where did it go and what what was that only some more
rain of the human kind. he wasnt a car

changing the future and public prophecies   sort of the sa same and so   prophecies of
change are for the future now or fifty years ago   changing the future   has
already not happened   or happened   Depending on how you think   Do you
think?   No. you dont   I have prophesied much more lack of breath in this
expensive city   continuous lack of breath and warmth, of sun   continuous lack
of the color natural green.   i was walking   the breadth of the sophisticated
city   the international   ever more expensive   composite city   of our
western poetries   and realizing i would wear my old   blue for reason suit
as ive called reason blue in a previous poem and now it is   so i wear
light blue and a deeper   blue for reason silk blouse   to the party to the part of this
that   also requires my most expensive shoes   that is my best feet   best soles   but
          the suit is old and no one   has become reasonable in this future.
Later at the party
               Later at the party   which is still the one im going to   not yet
the one ive been at   Do you understand at all?
               Because it hasn't happened   Or has it?   The roseate
woman   is working with   the backside of the clock   she is playing with the
time of this party   which never   quite happens   What on earth can i
prophesy?   When time never happens except now
               Which is when I can't breathe
               And when we're bombing Iraq   (no not now its over)
               And during wars in Africa   in which children are conscripted
                    and forced to be pervertedly violent
               And women   are killed every day
                    every day in Algeria.

in the name of manufactured ideas like yours like yours in the
name of name. people kill in the name of   if you change the name you dont
stop the killing.   And now the color green   doesnt work in my
symbolism   and what a beautiful   cant work in my personal
symbolism   there is no green.   This is my prophecy   can you change the
future? i mean the present Some poet is reading his poem:

      And then, you'll take me down
      from the shelf

      And then youll take me
      down from the shelf

Take your own self down says the crystalline chorus

i was trying to focus on the beautiful green of the pines but only the blue of the sky
rang true
      go back to your embassy   said the russian waiter   in the indonesian
restaurant   in the parisian mall   where the sky was covered over.

There are two
things again
two of those   things
from where?   from dreams
and one is in dissection
cut open with flesh flaps pinned down
the other isn't, the other is large and amorphous. the other is it. meat alexander, the
other is it, you cant conquer it, dissect it o meat alexander
doctor meat alexander, cowboy detective on a horse. he says in this night theres no
room for it. But, it's all that there is! he says its improperly named
improperly named it and so theres no room for it. dr meat alexander never loses

his horse gets shattered but he never loses, his horse of course gets shattered. it has
already been shattered   along with the rain forest this is known   prophecy
along with the cradle of civilization   hes conquered that before bombed a lot

of ants   poured water on an anthill   then they arose as army ants and ate all
the people in the jungle   no theres no jungle rain forest is dead   it isnt dead
yet   its pretty damn dead they give it fifty years   aw it isnt dead yet.   dr meat
alexander will replant it all   his horse is shattered
he'll do it without a horse without leaves without ants. without leaves without ants
dont worry just wait till the time comes

page haunted with zinnia bones. im trying to make us magical we'd rather be robots. it
makes you na necklaces re mem ber, jewels and satin. so so you can be somethin someod
somebody else dreamed up. always be else's always be else than it. in my former life
when i was a you a socalled young woman i experienced various kinds of possession, i
was possessed by states of others. thats why the world is dead now. i had this depression
but that was part of the real the real it i got over it by blocking it didnt i thats how you get
over reality right the reality right is a big bunch of whitehaired guys who tell you you
didnt feel it. after all it hasnt been properly named. i think im going to cr not while im
writing but i feel physically sickened this minute all over my it which they call a body all
over it like the tingling but its disgust sickness how can i go to the city this is part of the
crystal this is when it turns over this is how i found it later through the tingling of disgust.
in a former life. which im in in a state of public prophecy trying to change the future but i
cant believe in that i believe in this disgust and in the fear which came before it i never
want to feel again. ill still try to make us magical. in this old house so scared of myself
because the world in its entirety gos goes wrong out there on the sec floor of a rented
house in the goddamed lovely country where everythings so fucking sacrosanct precious
feelings about customs. little festivals. beer. marriages and births and deaths how sacred.
what the fuck is sacr ive never felt so unallowed as here where the simple things count.
but that was in another, my babies were a lot weirder than sacrality. we are the demons
the beautiful demons. we are salamanders bump bump in the dark slimey water. hold
onto that

Now later in my night

Door opens   a large old blind
dark-skinned man appears
with a cane   though he
is mostly face a huge

face. Glasses   but eyes are
shut. I'm deeply frightened
I understand that he is the figure of
'god' or my deepest soul
I try to wake up   It is too powerful a
figure   I'm still too weak to
face it?   Maleness not important it
is sexless   though not to 'appearances.'

i am so blindworm salamand understand? how you are nothing so thats everything,
cant get and the waves strong powerful time bat the ashes continued ashes of the
stupid world. the wormmoth beloved and the starfresh the starflesh and the soulmeat
so stupendously amorphous and dense one prophesies a readjustment of the
amorphous as in universe time will i know? i wanted to always know it the only
immediate. they are always not really allowing me to think like this. the mesh of
proscriptions has haunted all of first life and still haunts my second. we are keeping
each other from consciousness by owning too much and by following. we are keeping
each other from consciousness. we are keeping each other from consciousness

god   which is not a word i believe   is always the future.   i meet those
girls in a restaurant ever   girls always try to get food   one is a long baby, her
hair is dark and glossy   she too is the size of the   long earthfilled pencilcase coffin
and all her people believe in death   as simple sacrality so she will die   that death
not the fabulous   death in consciousness
                                        I must get to the center of this dissociation of
                                        dreams!
i cant im in a sort of diner dream
lining up with women for humble food of the soup and crackers sort
served by a cook whos a man   next door another woman
tries to get food   from another   diner   she figures if she overwhelms the
place with lots of dishes   they will have to serve her food   Go find me eight
more dishes! she tells me   she and i keep our things   across the street on
the sidewalk   right under the movie marquee of course   but i begin washing

those dishes   in the clothes washer not the dish washer   thats a mistake theyll
break   and now im watching the movie   audrey hepburn analyzing her
loved relation's test for cancer   shes the doctor wearing   a womans
suffocating rag on the head   brown cloth over the head   and her relation
has cancer   in this world everyone has it   so, she paints her eyes red
in the traditional way   for grief   and rides the horsedrawn cart of junk of things
of useless a voice says Its good to paint the whole body red now, red for soul red for
soul   red for grief red for blood red for soul   brown   is a somber red
everyone is ill.   a

public prophecy

i choose more consciousness. can i have more   Go on, says the chorus

This poem this prophecy is   consciousness.
my soul
has a mother   who is darker than she more beautiful
and only wants to take off her shoes   only wants fewer clothes on
though there's gold lamé to swathe her in
near a pyramid a heap of things   in a dark room–what are they?   a pyramid
is just a pile of things   there is no   monument   now i will teach two folklike

melodies of bartok   oh why   they sound right

i'll now silence the western woman in a sari   in order to speak
and teach those melodies

one is the blindman god not god and   one is the mother of my soul
are they two or one

THINKING

I find
beautiful
cliff
again
sheer glass
inset with
rubies
changing
the mountain's
color
lightly
rose. . .

didnt do wrong doing what thinking, it was always a thought can a thought be wrong?
in the crystal city there is only thought never wrong and down here all glasses are
empty nothing you care abouts full.

                      shouldnt ever do, anything but it was thinking
i was guilty of, and changed from being pure couldnt get back.
when the men didnt let you and now think they do they dont i force it. back in the
past

every thought of fear of, thought of fear of, physical violence i might inflict on
another still endures? i thought it didnt i or did i. i thought perhaps i was thinking it
i didnt know if i was thinking it or not the possibility of the thought seemed to be the
thought the thought seemed to be the act itself. or did i. did an it think it. was it
someone elses, always seemed like an invasion. or the suicide thought. can evaporate
how by the facing up to the lack of selfimportance in the final the heart is
selfimportance. as was everything you all said while i wasnt speaking. men who
didnt
       let me speak or act and so i tortured myself with thoughts. can a thought be bad
if it just goes away after all it doesnt go away. how can the crystal city be thought when
thought is so painful but those thoughts aren't painful they are communion and rest,
those crystal thoughts there that mind

Can a thought be bad?

all those hungry scrawny cats out there real cats in the world. we're standing in front
of the fish counter in the covered market. its covered so you just cant have any thing
you want to, just because youre hungry, cat. a lot of glossy fish dead. how can we save,
i say to my friend, all the car colony cats
                    all the car colony cats in the world?
but that is a thought down here that i *should* be having.
                    and all the fish and all the fish in the seas.

and so i was running at the Buttes again thinking   in minor pain of thinking
thoughts of social incidents   careerish slights, perhaps, its my training   what
ive been urged   to care about   doings and sayings, small knots of
happenstance   evanescences   that become thoughts   was that an insult
did i do wrong, myself   by saying something?   Would it be worth dying   to
escape   thought   all   those thoughts   I choose more consciousness but
such thought is not its definition   that is not consciousness at all   Why do
such thoughts last   but   not in the crystal

                    in the crystal we say there is no such
                    frivolous form of memory

Ladies   knights and ladies   lie dead and openeyed
sepulchral statues   lying on tombs   with open blazing lightfilled pupil-less
eyes   They are conscious   They are thinking.   Owls come out of the same
darkness and fly   to the top of sheer cliff   the dark is composed of owls
dissolves into them   flying upward   yellow eyed   Ladies are
lying dead and open-eyed.

was there ever much that you didnt think? everything you   did
existed more in your thought of it than in its fact

you even thought your death with all its imagery thought your dying
thought your loves and hates
waged war because you thought you had to
did you think what others made you do a waste
open your eyes and die   i am thinking from the ground of darkness up as
high as that cliff   if i can just think up think up   just fly up.

flatfaced woman
try to remember a face from the darkness the ship
that came last night in great darkness.
it isnt dark in the city we say in the crystal city say chorus of all the individual
creatures and vegetables and rocks and fires who've ever.
came last night great darkness in all dreams

> In a room lined with
> books. I had wanted there
> to be a ladybug. But now
> are bugs, and bug cocoons
> materializing throughout
> the library, their eggs clack
> as they drop onto the floor.
> 'A bad year is coming.'
> Nothing but bugs. Outside
> in the darkness the streets
> are running with floodwater,
> in the water are monstrous
> fishy creatures different colors.
> Yet there are still cars gliding,
> the waters aren't really deep.
> To cross the street I must
> tell the waters to draw back.
> ... have now crossed the street.

A dream
thinks itself differently   crystal city does too   in neither are your thoughts
bugged
flatfaced singing on the ship   with scalloped hair   around her flat face.

who is thinking these the dreams and the city?

there is such pain down here among the washing machine. this is a basement no tree or wind sound my face has gone flat because im not who i was cant remember my inadequate word, innocent who was ever that. wash some clothes some one else owns the machine some mans machine wash some clothes he always says wash your clothes with my machine. im wearing red down here. im wearing red to assert that i wont be so frightened by my thoughts which you have pushed me pressed me into that i wont find my soul again you are monsters in the water gliding by flattened by the cars wheels into flat fish things we are all flat faces mock entities in the darkness worlds great basement. am always and never down here wash all the dark waters wash all the bugs please. if you keep washing we can keep doing what we want wash it out with the new machine wash it whi wash that little bug wash it whi wash that thought with heavy duty. if you had that thought throw it away and think the light thought think only light think white think wash think tomorrow tonight torm tomo to to.

it is a thought infused with the lines of any haunt. what if i were to kill you—or me— is just a thought. keeps saying its just a thought, because i am trapped in my head with all my thoughts in that life. dont you know my mind is trapped do you know what that means it means that i veritably i am trapped. i have no other body than my mind in this other life it belongs to this house this town. leave that unhappiness now that in another life the deer makes plenty golden grove or lot of the desert full of pebbles graybrown but prettier than rubies all on the alley although i dont want to insult the cliff of heaven climbing climbing up to the unimaginable depths of all your eyes and mind voices i'll never leave now either the alley or the cliff or either or. that wind blows my thought life away
and fills it with the other thought that isnt thinking.
will beauty you in all hat all silver hat.
and rain of it will love joyously
without paroxysm or battle.   but these wind martials down here
                                                a grief of thoughts it gets worse
you can trap a person inside their body and you know this can do it without doing anything to the body there then is no body.

the bugs are coming.

the point at which we thought.
at each point and continuously
in that thought i hoped you werent doing it to me   or we to the sea say or
the air the point at which we thought it was ruined   was   is   its
ruined still ruined   the air and the sea are still ruined

350 migrant workers have been killed in an explosion in a place called Snowflake Hill,
Mexico–not real a thought a thing
that is part of a dream. The thought of this explosion, in the dream
makes one girl cry. She had previously said, that she liked all those dreams in my
poems. Our kitchen is two places at once our kitchen and a restaurant
they have overlapping borders; outside the back window's the river
wide covered with huge lilypads, on which whitebodied couples and families
are living all naked and bathing, wash in the morning river wrap up in towels
they are very white people, and being so white, they can just live on those lilypads
without worrying a thing without a thought. Is this my thought
out the front window of the same house
is an abandoned pitmine
I'm trying to find my place in this house but old ladies are discussing
what a famous man did, during the Cold War Era. Oh now a trunk's carried out of
this house, is it mine I must be moving
All my mail is old things sent back to me old life others keep giving me old life or no
life. Old old life "my" past what a joke and a dream what a thought
old things old things sent back to me as if others had dreamed my life adequately
for me in the past
The point at which we thought, is back in the past of them. A point out of which all
their thoughts come now. The point out of which the world comes now.
The point at which I
am filled with the dream of this present world a vast wound. Then there is the point
at which, all other thought the sky and its fleshless colorless presences thinking
in the way of the sky, in the permanent amnesia of death and its voices its
thoughts. All you can bring to this thought is, it thinks you dreams you like a hawk,
all you can bring to this thought is what ask the voices what

there is no memory here   for what you thought was exactitude
the lines of your life   there is no memory or memorial there is only   the
ability to think   What do you think that is?

this is that other thought, it isnt in the world the a map of the southern world here nearly empty of towns im almost scared on the other side of mexico we will like it where there are hardly any of those so publishable suckers in her glove compartment shes sucking on one before dinner the cleaved chicken. the map of mexicos pale yellow the oceans pale blue im thinking roses there are so few towns people will hear from us from such far places in thought in the mind, thought in the univers side of town or south south mexico or mind. this is never day, past the river noir and all its silly. the moon has been in the room had been in some room speaking of sexism she was my supposed past speaking who said But you'd stopped liking him then. but that was just a passing thought of not liking–what's liking? that isnt true i thought, but its also not true shes the moon. you will say this is all thought, but a whole history has been founded on the thought that i or another woman am the moon and so you can build a nuclear reactor on the river noir and i'll just shine on you anyway what a dream this world is where you eat and drive. the only real worlds in my mind and so i did right to fear my own thought it was all i had it was what you let me you let us. but it was also all that there is. i was disgusted says the moon when i asked the artist a question about contemporary art and he answered it by referring to men only but that was long ago how long ago about twenty-five years, which is no time at all, about twenty-five minutes its not all over just a thing said then fly to that other thought where i live so empty of towns in south south empty. he said it too recently.

BEAUTY IN THE HOLE FROM WHICH IMAGES COME

She gives him a drug   then flies up into a eucalpytus
                 a "hard" woman even icy
became a bird   jewel blue   longbeaked
with long curved corrugated   neck, iridiscent she's watching.
He's holding a round silver pillbox   grains of the drug
he's just taken some of; he is holding a hole or the hole.

That was at night
                        Now deserted white
hot adobe city, so beautiful   against the mountains.
Red geranium petals hanging planter
No one but a voice or two home   the sun's
too hot the time's too late   a century too late, for any
one to be at home. This place was deserted a hundred years ago

        But I'm home, and hard edges are home
      my mother's home
                        and the hole's home.

Later again at night   or was it earlier? earlier
there's a field and nothing else, of white spheres, souls
in the moonlight, small perfect spheres. Shinier whiter on
top–eggs not pearls.

There are mountains everywhere; the hole is everywhere

Beautys a hole   I am it   and/or he is   who has
taken   as I have   a little   of the world drug.
                                        The beauty drug
but beauty isn't stable.

the holes everywhere but matter true matter is disappearing eaten by worms and theres only a machine, grand ugly Are you still trying to find an image or dimension at its source? we abandoned the adobe city of beauty. beauty turns over in the hole you cant find the meaning of the images the ones you live in even on the daily plain. anything can come out of the beauty hole, though beauty should. are you still trying to find the hole the whole hole the bottom finally of the hole of images which are the world and dreams? yes,

i'm tired but will teach   ever, this time teach the Constitution   and its relation to poetry. Does it   symbolize the constitution of everything? No one knows what that is   what that is anymore. So i sleep   and now i cant sleep   i think its morning but my friend says, no its 1:35 a m, there's anomalous light outside which isnt daylight as we know it   it shifts   what is it?   a voice cries Call the

police, there's a goo bai out there a fierce dog...   a goodbye.

freedom meaningless if world a machine the constitution of the composition of the hole is what id try to if a hole has a comp why not its just an image itself the hole what isnt
        im not

here outside the dimensions in dream i'll fail you for not knowing our constitution. our constitution substance's extension shows itself bright orange always a bit of nasturtium pure against the mountain face gray rock or smooth packed beige also constitutional. or a small just-blue alpine apparition flower pale, the light through cut jewel a tourmaline, not quite any other purple shade on a frail, gold, pin. not manifestations of the human spirit as in art, art is not beauty. always dirty in the latenight bar of art filled with smoke and no true warm amber or strange spot ruby, in the nightbar of art all the young men work late in their old army jackets, the toilets are fouled and theres a naked man in one for no reason, nothing wrong with that. a mariposa lily scarlet-orange with three glossy petals. is somewhere. one mans agonized over a death and has found out she had some last words, she asked for a drug or a painkiller, she asked for waldo or marco, died asking for a drugstore wallgreen or walmart not a blue bird this is ugly not a stone shapechanger not a spirit in our grain. thats how we're in hell because now theres no sky theres a huge high ceiling thats night along the cold avenue the ground is ice. a thin longhaired longbearded man not old sits against wall legs outstretched bare feet stretched out on the ice, so youll give him money give him more money thats what they do shameless, people mutter that beggars are asking for what we have. someone convinces him to cover his feet. his name is Lustrous. a voice says Lustrous will now cover his feet. Lustrous is a pearl in a field. we should be able to know and catch the image before and change it.

the tingling could be called beauty or constitutional, it is related to certain images they are so scary and beautiful as if the hole meant to make them and make no others the drug is at first beauty or love or some nearness to the hole but then its a or the machine. i cant make the hole stop have you ever made the hole stop it keeps making the met the world ideas keeps making my dreams keeps it doesnt make time we do invented finity by measure dont say stuff again stone so. finity is an amendment, the dimensions are amendments to the constitution.

in order to go round that curve and climb up i must cross certain emerald sapphire waters beneath a black onyx bridge, entails crossing the shifting jewel in a wooden boat and taking a loose rope which is blowing about, take hold of that. i must keep hold of it for the next part a crossing back around that bend but a newscaster is interviewing me while i hold the line cant lose it, Do you think, she asks, You have more dreams than other people? I'm about to answer saying, 'I remember them more often than others do'–but then I dont know if thats true   but I'm trying to take you there right into the hole or up into the crystal   where youre already speaking where you already are

We're your voices we'll relieve you of the truth We your voices bring relief from fatigue of honing answers We your voices say you can get there even if you let go of the dimension And the living And the rope He

who had drugged himself to death   hadnt died had lain comatose given up on,

came back looking whole and said   they gave up on me but im alive.   I dont trust him   We're embracing but I dont trust   I wonder how his face looks above my shoulder in this long embrace, shifty? but I cant see it—   Ive just dragged his refrigerator   all the way downstairs.   Because this is a dream.   Hes going to take it back   take back his freeze his icy place of no change   Which

71

city are we in?   In the hole things must shift, sometimes   In the hole where the
world comes from   there must be some changeability   which is not the same as
possibility   Its not that anything is possible   Can he die again? must I   still
not trust him   perhaps should destroy trust and not-trust   *theyre* gone
here, voice says, as you know   in the beauty you must both let go of that edge.

they tell me, in the writing of this, i mean it the dream tells me that in the writing of this
i havent taken into account the most important tomb. there it is it is lined with
iron thin layer wrought. but there is no most important tomb. 'i left someone there' a
recurring motif of fear or moral failure i didnt leave a you. even at the tomb. then
who. no one. the lovely addict i still dont trust, no, no one at all. no one left me. i

didnt leave you. what am i supposed to do, nothing   the iron shifts and shimmers
it is a hole or pan beauty makes you clench your teeth and shiver but not just
anything. beauty. then, hello failure no. who cares. who cares of addict who cares
who cares of tomb who cares   stone bird womans edges are shifting
        beauty isnt power its tingling

        the embassy's
tiles are black and white.   im here in retreat from my failure at the tomb, then
my money is stolen in this very room   'i hadnt noticed we were speaking
english'   but are we.   whats the point that it isnt   safe   here?
no wheres safe   if safes what youre thinking.   i dont want to speak
english   or french   or   language

theres a hole in every home
the hearth of a home is the hole   a voice told me this and i saw it   it looked
more like a grave than a hole   iron-lined? maybe   in and out of the hole go
our demon shapes   our beloved friends   trusted or not (who cares about
trust?)   You can climb out of the refrigerator now   because we dont care

about trust.   We care about beauty   and how elusive   it is in a
wormeaten world   There is much thats more beautiful than your image
this feeling for example   gold grit teeth   sound earrings silver and tur
quoise sil ver   tur   quoise   garnet beads beneath bare feet   toes in

the dry white sand   pur   ple   dirt   geranium petal that over
whelming scent   blue   air   slick blue feather   black sleek filigree
bridge   grit   my   teeth.

failure at the iron tomb of tomb. its the tomb of beauty. yet the reunion is everywhere
above our world its days early lemonade and light food mustard Oh the back yard! he
cries–its all cement now. they go for wine, we climb the ropey bridge with claw
carved wooden footholds inside the university tower but the iron tomb of beauty isnt
up there its in the backyard in the hole in the house its an image of beauty in the hole.
died and filled the inside of me with vast wings hah ho buried the buried. you buried
beauty because it was deathy. i buried beauty because it died. its come loose despite.
acres of cement and car roach instead of iceblond changes into a blue bird after having
given him the drug in the worl whol whorl which make me tingle amidst breath out
there out there near the mountains. you are buried in iron but that is beautiful if the
iron is beautiful it is thin hammered and etched like the round silver pillbox of the
hole. grab an image and stop   it. all of my inscriptions are on those vases
now replacing that mans, or am i the inscriptions and not their poet, am i the words
not a person, in a house the house has a hold hole. philadel-phia. i am the
inscriptions im gritting my teeth i am free of the inscriptions i am old or young
enough to be free of the inscriptions as eauti beautiful as they may be. theyre not as
beauty as i two people have gone down the hill behind the house in phil

in philadelphia.   we went to a party young   and in dresses with young men
and one couple is   way down the hill, all the mans bloods coming out   its
leaking out   like straw.   i didnt catch the image as it   war in sierra leone
you didnt catch it stop it in time   everyone there is in that image now   will
become an inscription on a vase   a beautiful earthenware vessel, in a deserted

natural village   time to come is there time to come   depends what you think
time is.   is a jewel or a line of bug eggs   a line of car roaches
Free of inscriptions   would be good to be free   of your
inscription.
Robt Johnson isnt or is he   free of his inscription stones in my passway   i
saw him in a dream   no i only saw his soulred bandanna he was free of me.

Why do you

always name him? Something to do with beauty and the simplicity of a name Like everyones i knew in my beauty youth in the adobe town before we fled it and beauty was destroyed poison One might flirt with poison but it was personal poison not too total cultural Poi son   My teeth grit of the beauty of a certain kind of evil Oh iridisc bluefeather one agai and a tip ri bright red catch   it.

the tomb of beauty gapes open.

the hole is transparent, poetry, an empty room transparent shades of pink and red, bare except for a chair or two.

      white a sand blazing star, streaked inside with orange
      often grows next to a ghost flower   white spotted with red.
      hawkmoths pollinate desert lilies lily lily anemone
      mariposa you are so red

beautys transparent, contradistinction to machine
no, beautys opaque

what we what will do in room of hole. sit down

MUSIC

this small early house at night like that of the emancipator   I my emancipator
will be leaving soon.
      Blue midnight and pines   I'm urged, gently, to disparage it
      I know it must be praised   feel a shock of connection to
      this home with its muted black stove, inside, which is defective but strangely
      beautiful   grayly glossy   like   a black   pearl.

We are now in the auditorium of   emanci   but is that relevant elephan-
tinely large   hall a solemn   woman   dedicated to helping others
gives me advice and a ring
a woman gives me words and a ring I
wont heed and will lose,   the ring is of carnelians   car kneel eons
with cellophane tape around to make it small enough
cannot take advice I
my real name is   'doesnt take advice'.

                  The concerts over
                  the conductor named robert is speaking
onstage to the other musicians   I think this discussion is part of the work, part
of the music the concert–but   everyones getting up now   its over
because music   always ends (not mine)   I have to put on my pants and
leave   a supposed healers laughing at me, for being naked I   dont need to
be healed   I'm always crotch naked during music its the casual music of this

robert somename you must heed, had said the aiding woman   not the healing
woman   why casual   I'm not so casual   why are they here, I dont need
dont need this robert whose music ends at the end   probably like a respectable's
I   only   need a robert like johnson why   he is a johns son

like every man ive ever

known and i need   that plain named sinful person   with his three
brained music   that can be played all night   and in the park, why   and in
what club   the club where the people the park of the crystal city of scars
and the ring changes   to a gold ring   i am bound to   beauty, not a

concert but   poisonous   beauty   all along a life and   the new ring will
protect me   from the disease of help. help and healing   can you imagine
helping either   me or   robert johnson?

it was just so beauty to be oh ten in that empty empty lot nothing there but green that
grows flat to the ground grass and rounder leaved beings small yellows and pale purple
touched whites those were some vines. that was all the rest was spirit even though we
were children. shes dead because people die suddenly, i hadnt thought of her in ages but i
was thinking about the crystal city and falling asleep a voice said in my ear, eileens there
with her husband. a month or two before she died. the colors back then were very rich
because of the greendusty pines the gold light and blue and red things, because of the
large green locusts with their louder music than those in my town or the music is simply
of voices of kids or her whistling through her two fingers. i'd like to send some morning
glories some nightblooming cereus some sego lilies some indian paintbrush all the kinds
of flowers you cant send. they are probably all endangered she was endangered now
shes dead.

we went swimming a lot
i'll dream about going swimming:

we have to take a shower first   and in the shower stall
and in the shower are a kitten and a baby   the mother asks me to hand her her baby
the kittens pearlgray   the babys very narrow
               the babys narrow and slips down the drain headfirst
i cant tell if shes there if thats her sticking out because i dont understand what these
forms are   these images near this   hole   the
babys falling into the hole   of images in the shower   shes fallen in
headfirst i
pull her out and say to her mother dont ever leave her there
                                   again
                              the baby can fall in
the soul may be narrow enough
to slip down the drain headfirst
and fall into the hole from which images come

this is the music my subject   something you are only   in
maybe like the hole   the hole of   images   doctor key is mr leguy
                                                   doctor key is mister
there is no doctor   doctor doctor   there are a lot of keys
all out on the east end of town where the suns always low
im out there again half leaving half staying   where the gas stations are all closed
going to leave you, never goin to leave, going to leave you.

at the bottom of a certain hill   is a large cage i'm in
i'm trying to examine beauty   among the filth   examine the wing of a blue
hairstreak butterfly reason bedraggled among the litter   and schoolboys wont
let me, poke at my body and say their obscenities   caged here   we are the
caged birds here   at the bottom of a certain hill

i don know wha im doin at this poin good thats good. because being here isnt to a
point or purpose of language i am the hole speaking, the mouth itself letting things
come out for no purpose beauty don believe donchyou believe a little thing. in the
ring air forget the ring and sink in me and slide down me, someone will always pull
you back up unfortunate ly. its all black in here like a hawk in here like a hawk i am
circling descending sliding sliding down the drain because im so narrow everythings
glint of red and blue, and i see an emerald too and a topazy yellow. down here wha
and then theres a sudden red sky   thats   ll almost all
above a golden flatland red sky.   you are sleeping with your head
against the mother mountain   against the warm brown crevice   with its
emerald grasses   you will always images   there is so much in them so
much of love in holding the babe or wind in the feather of the hawk. glint on the blue
wing awake   in and out of the velvet of the drainhole alls asleep awake.

it is a very beautiful hole it takes care of you without helping or healing
it is a beautiful hole that is half you
and they are always coming out of you the images because you and you are cuddling them
and you you music beauty color is so clear if youre in it

this is the music my subject
gypsy gypsy ace

a yellow skirt
with an ace on it
im going to wear tonight. yellow is the strange sky background   i havent
learned what yellow means in the yellow room with a large ace
i suppose its a room of soft gold light and a mono thing
the whole one on a skirt whirls to music   making something to be in,
rather than think.
                    i am in it fever, sings the orange trees   snake a sweet-
voiced snake say the masters of intelligence   who and you would never suspect
it are the voices to have no sleeves the naked arms held out   from the top
called a shell   the sleeveless top to the skirt   the top that is dark as the
hole and leaves the arms warmly naked held out to you
i am in it   the skirt and the top,
                                   wearing the ace of aces
lines of electric yellow spark energy burn along the floor towards me and rush straight
up my body   but i dont catch on fire   in this room you try to do this
any johns son can be part of it   playing three guitars wearing three shirts and
singing
the song to have no sleeves   you dont need no sleeves   no matter how old
the sound of things
these are the sound of things first and black down the hole

there are a lot of songs in here tony tony the victory of angels
                              tony tony the victory of angels
the young men are leaving for monrovia, for a year in order to be free
there are other mountains to go to
                    montreal montrouge
                    mont louis

we are driving alongside the river noir where birds are wading in shoals all along
several blue herons and others more exotic others black with red bills and then
i am in the water with fishes   i am with the fishes in the hole
im watching them, spying on the fishes   They are rather orange but not carplike
they come halfway up   out of the water   out of the hole   to feed on a
nutrient which clings to   the overhang of cement   the riverbank is dirty
cement   My mother is missing shes gone   way beneath the water to visit my
uncle   im afraid to stop breathing so long   in order to follow her and swim

away   beneath the cement riverbank   further under the hole
victory of angels you are afraid   montreal montrouge montrouge
victory of angels youre afraid

it said a woman could not have the knowledge, she was it how convenient.
that is the eastern version. whirl around away from it in the ace skirt
i am sitting in a restaurant being talked to   no not again no not   i am a fish and
we are bumping and nibbling filth off the modern embankment we are orange reddish
slithery souls in the hole dont talk to me   i ate it an algae i ate it a scum i
ate ate ate it a piece of the sidescum of the hole   and now i know what you
will never know   con   sciously   there is a place for my pride in the hole
                mount real mount real mount pride

fevered ive come back to the river   in the water near a floating launch
on the othersides a sort of tug or workboat   crosses to the launch on my side
doing that causes an eruption of wake a small tidal wave which is starting to drench
and send me under temporarily
                                        i wake up to noises of ghosts near my bed
am i awake they are whistling past   back and forth they are noises music
a voice says, most people don't have   a high enough IQ   to know what a
ghost really is   little trait

it is like those   why are you afraid   there are effective illicit ways
into the castle for scaling the castle on top of the mount   then ghosts let you in
through the windows   they want you in

music is part you cant see, ghosts let you in. they say nothing changes into something so
something can be happy but i dont believe that do you, thats not quite it. the darkness of
the hole is itself invasive like black sapphire water soothing around curling around. twists
you into sleep again and leaves you to awake into the images of whatever sort youve
consented to by now. many were not allowed to consent at all. but they could find the
music themselves and be in it more than in the consent. if it has to be something to be
bliss thats just another story justifying repressive social conditions castes and
submissiveness of woman so take back your story and and let me be music without it
without any of your stories for the IQ that doesnt know the ghosts. i am reading all the food
in the room because i dont want to eat it

the casual robert was only an idea of something. id rather be in this hole. down here in the pool which is said to be malleable in some way or other, is that how the images, down here the images are on ice, because the rooms full of refrigerators. unfortunately for certain images my fever is done.

a lot of images are in here but still all over the basement toys and records underwear baby clothes dont they ever turn the light off. there may be a sort of music of the nothing state of the black of the hole of the hole itself as the shell the shell the top above the yellow skirt of light, light starting up and whirling light of the ace. there may be a music of the black of the black   a black pearl has to have a little light a little color there thats thats the music   heats up just a little the
        emancipator   leaves?   what does that mean?
                leaves doesnt leave leaves never leave
                this is the song of the dark of the hole
                this is the song the fish eat
                in it in it in the dark
                under the embankment in the dark
                head down the drain in it
                all around my headis a hole   no an
                ace
                of diamond

DOCTOR DOCTOR

i dont know what the doctor is, he says my friend life is riddled with shells cysts probably filled with the liquid first language ever, she has them all over. a blond doctor mystic is there standing by. every doctrine has its doctor, not i. he will remove the shells. making room for the worms? doctor doctor watches tv, i want to tell him about my own favorite soaps soaps and time seen by us as a series of significant gestures like his operations when hes dressed up in sheets but finally i leave in my black younger dress, in my younger body in my cultural body curved like the french weather announcers il pleut and he surely approves yes the doctor shouts after me but at this point i am being him not me. standing in the doorway of the hospital room with or as his look following me in my dress.

the liquid first language is lid slidel slidey
words not quite so   precise   perhaps   no one knows what time it is
or cares about enchainment of actors actions into thee story
it isnt like literature or babies or babies at all its   blue tinged clear joyous
Mind   with a little red tinge too.
               lit by gold
                    its   mind and
from mind to mind   and dreams are it too   its supposedly all frozen up
in   refrigerators in the basement   they are storing it to make brains or babies
doctor doctors   in between soaps   so you will live and have a chance
at a black dress and gold chain belt   or a doctors white uniform   because you
arent already alive   who how can there be   such a you already   as arent alive
they know you already   they   say   but they dont know what theyre
saying   its i who know you already   youre not a cell or two youre expansive
allcrystal

doctor doctors a double person. oh well oh hole. everyones double tonight the man
im with is both with me and watching gossiping about us two, im in a long black dress
theres vodka somewhere icy   and a second man whos called john
leave this hotel circulation in hands is cut   feels very guilty thats another
the first liquid lang ba like bloood cut, for thinking to you that all like rabbit to rabbit
huddled near the train tracks where the hunters dont go. feels very guilty, have not
solve the probl (this lang of thought fast) of eating. i remem another drea in a high

high apt at night she was guilty of food and drink she said she said was alway and
didnt want to. puts face in hands at night so shadow   is heavy with guilt. i
have shoes on her floor the yellow with ties of cloth. everything girly youre so old.
we goss on about someone who tries to be sex still, who always gets up pretends to be
blurred and swaying from her chair alcoholically blurred for any john. so he'll know
she's drunk enough for it.
                                        and the high danger open window. this
age may be a procession of goodbyes for long until more conscious in the crystal. the
contaminated blood still think very clear. i fought you o en em y for ever what w will be
done about that in the crys city
the potent rivalry   you will be more eloquent in this lang tongue and we will
see. hacked him to pieces well then? there ar no pieces here and we're alway to be
here so think. i don know but no one cn kill no one back. grudge mean ing less
hacked you to pieces sexed you or sexed you out of your life? the lon bla dress? you
now only exist in this voice

doctor
          your
               genetic experiments offend against us unconscious you must stop. no
one will remember what bliss is. for a long. it builds there is so much of us   on
planet of dullness you have construct to destruc it became so uninteresting
doctor you have made life so dull

what cant i remember any mo   its a room of women begging to turn someone
on on platforms sexual   beyond that thy lang   spills out onto the ground and
look in
it was colors not bleeding black yellow red   there is a small blue circle
in the midst of each color field
reason is the hole in the middle of
reason, do you love me?
                         tissue of color and space tears apart gently a redtinged blue
unidentified processes   within my own socalled   and doctor doctor
never can finger   what rises up like a liquor clear   and nourishes
the   what is happening within   heart this is heart do you mea
i call from the benign in translation, transefficient cop not a cop   you thought

82

you heard the emotional noun only, "cop"   *then* you hear the noun galvanize the
small words around it "transefficient cop *not a cop*"
thats how language   i dont believe this its funny   the universe is
humorous   but dont tell doctor doctor
you will hear in air the nothing word you will and under stand
under lighn bolt not demon sp face it isnt that   wor you cant remember but know
any how   knows what cant remember doncha kno   if you think in
a color or if you think in a sound or if you think in heart of nothing its black
crystal ring or wake against black go in youre not dead

small figure there tiny on the silver rose was   ·   decorous asian who became
g string procurer now shes now shes returning into the butterfly you i
might dissolve back into the butterfly   you could go anywhere then, now

later and again–she must have become a real image–i say she has no rights even if,
or particularly if, money is involved. because she paid one hundred francs she must
be able to turn him on sexually but i say (you see the whore pays in this story) the
money has bought her no rights. this storys very liquid. the woman who feels guilty
about eating and drinking is still depressed in high building on dark second avenue
feels guilty about two glasses of wine and plate of something one course. i need my
yellow light shoes what a world

this is what someone said, that he thought he was dying and a man came and stood at
the foot of his bed he isnt really sure who it was his dead father perhaps, now he feels fine.
i am saying things to try to find your minds   again   they have recently
felt lost to me "a man came and stood by my bed"   "transefficient cop not
a cop"

i
   i was in a flower   to be in a flower thats all the language
when i look at this photo am in the lyl the lily the other white room   with its
green streak desert lily   and inside it is a you   the seeds always come back
they are robbing all of africa of fifteen thousand years of seeds that come back
doctor doctor genetically improved   seeds which must be bought   every year
will take precidence over lily   any you in the lily.   the indians used to eat the

bulbs of the angelically flowering lily which bulb they called ajo garlic i am in the lily
again   and   again

the language by which we consent to each other in the
world is blanked out uncon how we are   hooked into each other doctor doctor
doncha know   Look hes trying to give a transfusion to a large cooked slab of
salmon   through a salmon pink tube   (the universe is humorous dont tell
him)

oh you will not be conscious of the language there in the crystal for a long
time. if you've never entered a lily   a white room   a pink room   or
red or blue

and spoken it, then   you cant speak lily
we're hooked into each other   flower tissue

there is a non material substance
the white flowers empty but not empty of
rain lily
rain lily
must come up right after the rain sometimes   goes back into the bulb

Unown all seeds

roomful of embryos all night which city.

everything is speaking   ancient phoenician vases   matte mute colors in a gray
light but speaking   you own nothing   how old are you?
escape into the real language   repressed and wordless. moth on a tombstone

roomful of embryos all night which city. there are people who want to own doctor
doctor every cell of you every seed you seed you eat and the embryos you leak too
how unhappy in no air stressed, to sing the ancient air 'moth on a tombstone' is
repressed   and wordless moth on a tob tombstone im sinking back the crystal is free
stared in the mind of

i sat there in my early 40s without any idea of what a life
was there isnt, so i sat hiding   theyve a way to put a seedshell around you
and grow you like a product to work for it theyve always   and make these
embryos and plant them and plant them the human   in the lily, theres no
doctor   is there?   Not yet   i sat still a long time in my 40s so the doctor

couldnt find me. Everyone wants something for you but it is from you Dont leave sit
still. they are gathering up all of the worl seeds righ now you kill the forest and then
you plant your money every where it grows what do you think we can do

Its important to eat and live as little as possible. to live as little as possible is the only
to live

not moving much, sitting on the floor
these two figures are Song and Sex a long time ago   singing and loving
singing and loving   on the steep steep hill   on top of the dirt steep hill
where there was a doberman named Satan   we're smoking grass we're sitting on floor
          high above world nineteen seventy   or are we in the crystal song and sex
          smoking because oh   this is a sort of slow burning time   crystal or no i
dont
          know   "this skinny joints rolled for you"   now Song is talking to me
she has two lovers in two cities   and when she misses her lover in the other
she's somehow already there and   leaves the door of her trailor unlocked all
night   even though he wont know shes there   in case he thinks she might
be   because if you open the door it might happen   if you open the door
of your mind or spirit   the door of change   the door of change world open it
might happen   if we open
                              why is satan there
                              because hes just something
                              hes not bad like doctor doctor
                              hes just animal something
i dont know if theres a body apart from   in this world it belongs to the doctor
belongs to the ice the mental ice its generated from   but really i
dont know if theres a body i cant see it   no one will let me   they hand me
photos instead
                    so i dont look and i can see it   whispering in my mind
which some call a head a or brain   is talki a little or not is transferring presence is
sliding in and a out all over the top of the steep steep hill that its really hard to drive
up straight up   leaking mind again   and my body is part of my conglomerate
but you cant tell it apart   from the masters of the universe from the doctor doctors
would rhyme heart   you hear heart   like cop   i hear   im not composed
of your this world   which is a scream

im in a dark room no im watching me there is this a hospital
im in a bathrobe not mine and my little boy not mine
opens the door and says,   "Operation, do you want me?" is this how we talk in
this world down here. yes
                         theres another womans babushka red for her soul
she took it off so she could be   as manipulative as a transnational   only in
private, man   so it doesnt count, man   No it counts

try to speak anoth. another moth lang flying try to speak flying across the mountains
and desert hills of love where we're conscious im so conscious i dont want to. dont
want to ever
               yes he is a butcher they are at war in thei villages
we are in the wor togeth   as in the room above the steep steep hill hes there he
dont know little satan,   no one cares you you butcher   i talk to people in the
village   have never been innocent we just talk here just in our this is my mind
hes a butcher of you yes yes you are here all here yes no segregation in any way of the
afterlife but there is no after, havent you been reading? youre alive here right now in
this mind here you butcher boudin red red you bring your blood you keep it like that
everybody brings their but nothing they did is worth and you dont understand it you
fucked it and you cant get conscious   try to get conscious Now

MEMORY

memory   was it just shapes   then it was
all shapes slip away slack black rectangles   in a room of a bank
memory bank   im left not substance of memory this morning   can hardly
shoe you are   and a dark   twig earring   a housecar   oh im like
some housecar   in joes johns
air of
     sweep last   black splash   hole square

     co alesce

     and inside a high apt room
     with the figures of love and of glory
the phone rings,   a man named heard is on the line.
when i stop dreaming im still dreaming in this dream or rec rectangleroom
his voice is very low because   his throats been operated on
but i heard him anyway   i forgot to ask him, heard   who perhaps is the
figure of anyone   to collaborate on poems with me, glory, and love
     on some ancient royal

     but now i think i would like to say   that in most dream you must seem to
remember an   entire prior set   of illusory relations which vanish
on awakening.   how are we able to remember such 'never happened at
all'   all along an imaginary past until now?

it only takes a moment   to have been in such a past all along...

im flying over a landscape voice says, "We will have no colors to our clouds"
     no memory?
     not   much, as such

here im where i remember, industrialized but oh so empty landscape the roads are wide
and dark sense of blacktop bits of crumpled paper gas station (remember depressed on
black roof around 1970? having gone up to watch an eclipse of the sun...) so im walking a

long time in this no memory memory space of our social mind in down world, glimpse, just up ahead, something i more really recognize: its the carousel at rue des abbesses have i climbed another mount montmartre? a building where live sex acts between the races have just taken place in empty rooms, two very violent sex acts and the cops and the press are now present particularly brutalized her stomach cut up and twisted is an older blond i want to leave and go home where is that? older like me and cut up on the road of contemplation i cant climb high enough im in down city still dressed in white lace to get to the wedding of what its raining too hard i turn around take off the dress wring it out i call up my soul the dark and she says she doesnt want to go to the wedding at all and will not...

           look at these three-dimensional
yantras roomlike instead   enter these 3D scenes of contemplation
in order to remember, beyond memory, what living has erased.
it wont be like our life that   3-dimensional clue
it wont be a memory
            a wedding   is a memory of   all other weddings
thats why the dark soul wont go to it
im always using a language i dont remember up here if i can be here now above the
rain in the non dimensional allcrystal body of nonhappenstance   red ive brought
my red   but dont remember what it was–my particularity? now its just
red.   inbetween times sunk into a deep groove   of. i cant seem to remember
so much the life of my rebirth any more   i mean what i was changing
backwards. im only reborn.   or is it born

now shes dead i think the same blond, in the same house, of live sex acts
all night was dying in her bed there   its now a hospital
half of her body is changed taken over gone different something demarcated
the half that includes her stomach–is it the worms?
when she dies the words "the frison is gone" are spoken
but one ess is omitted from frisson   frison with one ess
means a little curl or a kind of cow. But I didnt know that
i hadnt forgotten i just never knew
or is it free zone in English?
she is the death of, do you need the blank, or

is death of, sufficient? is that enough to remember? that there must be the death of
but there is no of in the crystal city
she is the death of remembering to be that victim?
she is the death of remembering to
she is the death of
the dream wont tell me   what   she is the death of. doesnt remember

Down heres of   give a reading of
my early poems   in a large loft
i cant remember or is it i cant read or dont have their endings so i improvise
no one likes that though i do. I cant keep my black blouse down it
keeps rolling up   under my breasts.   exposing my own of stomach
i dont remember being this person   this early person or the   early person
i remember what stands in for me

ive rewritten my life to stand in for me   in order to forget it (the life)
since i cant remember it really   any way   Hes come out of the iron tomb
to close the window on that past   the stupid radio keeps playing.

if i ask you are you here   essential you   essential here   i dont remember
who you are   here is the crystal city   dont have to remember such
phrase

          A flat world with three short leafless plane trees late afternoon late
afternoon in winter. My friend and i will try on her   clothes for a joke
but she isn't there   though she's there but she isn't   according to the story or
given   you have to be in   according to the dream. She and i

both try on her clothes, but she isn't there   her husband prefers the way *she*
looks in them   to the way i look in them   though she isn't there.
But shes always there because   he prefers the way she looks in them. he
remembers of course   A plain with plane trees on it or telephone poles

keeps on remembering what he prefers. We seem now to remember we once

committed genocide in Guatemala   while one was trying to concentrate on
whatever else instead, as   In another smaller story   the dead man's
wearing a plasticene illustrated   shirt so we'll remember what happened,   naughty
that he was naughty   That's why he's dead   We're all dead   im
dressed in the shroud of the reaper brown ive walked across

the plain to this small town i dont remember or why ive come here   there are
boxes of people's precious sexual habits everywhere   these folks crawl on all fours
like the guilty like they have to remember who they are how despicable they are
boxes of books detailing their habits obsessions thats how they know

Three three   three what?   threes enough three plane trees   Return the
empty boxed edition box to the university library
ive been carrying it under my cloak but forget it just forget it   the suns going down
on the library and on the three dimensions trees

                    fragment illusion or shock, from remembering this sort of thing
isnt suu supposed to happen–dies right in front of you or something–like the blood
coming out of the body like straw in philly doesnt make sense. it doesnt make sense if
they die you have to remem that thats a thing that will happen. but is it what happens
they cant make you do what they want without a mem. particularly a memory of
what they call death.   do you get much pleasure out of your memory?
sometimes   but its all out there without remembering much
the faces of love   the voices of love   essential you

im four in underpants lift up arms all alive and tingling thats all i want right now
its not a memory its a   its this tingling   find a bat in the heart of it analyze kill so
he pop up disorder. out of ord pants red un all arms mars l la you cant not remember
soet something in order   so? there is no chaos in the universe

does the whole universe remember? remembers enough

to maintain its order. to cohere

in the brown reapers shroud attempted to have orgasm simply by moving. i didnt
forget to say that, i was embarrassed   and actually the man from the iron tomb at
the reading where i forgot my endings   and improvised them, asked me   to read
an early poem about embarrassment. the color of embarrassment   is red the color
of the soul how can that make sense? the   fact that everything thats soulful is
embarrassing in the climate of this degenerate   lower city
                                        i wind up in grand central station
                                        its a honeycomb
                                        of alcoves
the tables in the alcoves have lamps with malachite green lampshades.

i am on a cruise ship honeycomb sailing in void with everyone
the coffeetables covered with large   photo books on Islam
some are thought to be more effective at promoting understanding, friendliness
towards Islam than others   they all look the same. who remembers islam
what am i m remembering momma   all i want is to feel this way now

which   i dont have to remember but   have to be   three, four
theres no door between us   yet i have   my boundaries, what   they
disparagingly call identity   who live to disparage   the green world of rock
lighting lighting its own all   here and here place your mythical cheek against
the lapis inlay   of the identity of lapis.   the identity of dark blue lapis is here.
i remember you

the identity of my brother is here
hes telling me hes still alive. though hes dead but we thought up that word its a word.
hes as thin as the last time i saw him in life but his hairs gone gray as gray as it might
be if hed lived. hes holding a child and there are others, i think that theyre standing
in front of niagara falls.
                              dont wrap me in your torn up implicating sheet says a small
boy to me
              my girl child is too far away, because this house is so big. is she my soul
theres another my soul there the dark older woman   the dreams letting me
know   that im dreaming that my friend means my soul. allowing me to know
this in the dream.   what does this? what there is, what i am

i saw my brother alive in that dream though hes dead   i think it was telling me
that my poem is true that hes there that its there. not   remembered

Hes returned again this morning. he and my father and i were   standing in front
of a wall with a large map on it, plotting an itinerary reviewing an itinerary
something about a path   through the southwest. My father asks me Have you
ever been in Winslow? Yes   Winslow Arizona, he says, city of a hundred hills
(those are the hills of heaven) Then   my brother and i examine   objects on a
table in an alcove   formed by a break in the wall. see   the carved metallic

figure darkened with age a plaque of a saint or knight he asks about   Its Saint
Christopher I say   I bought it for you when you died   (im confused)
I bought it for me   I bought it for Momma...   his face   has darkened
patches of its own   How are you alive? i want to ask but dont   he'd say,
dont you believe in your poem   havent you ever been in   winslow arizona
city of a hundred hills?

I don't want to feel any more as if   I'm being used by something else. I want to be
the something else   Slip out of memory and I might see?
the feelings in memory seem of value but not the snippets of story I.
                                                            Another
a voice says I'm another person   as if theyre very different from me   im for a
moment uncertain   but then it's me who said it. Because I'm four standing in the
sink my foot on a sponge   in the house of four years old   where i was bathed in
the kitchen but   im too tall

CAGES

then why am i so,

forever,   like green or whatever   caged
someone says its to provide   enough edge or resistance for affection   how there
can be love but there has to have been   love already to know that thats
whats wanted   by who what Could go on reasoning like this   forever
too and the wind or something or something
                                                          i lean back against the figure of love
in a dirt lot of tables and restaurant does it   restore she leaned her back against
an oak, so beautiful first he it bend   and then it broke beautiful beautiful   a
mans had a heart attack but has recovered. louis funes the comedian   the
universe is humorous remember
                                                          there are trapped fowls here pet
beautiful, elaborate   guinea fowls with golden ruffs   and red   and green
and black We are stroking them there in their cages of beauty   and love
Cages of beauty and love. the universe is not a cage is it   or is it

ride past the ugly   always uglier   urban suburban resistant to love
ride past the walls resist the surfaces the edges the cages which we have made for
ride past in the train past the surfaces   of the cages ever uglier resist them, if
you resist them youll be inside i mean insane The walls between times
youll be inside the walls between times which   dont exist   you wont be "with"
other people   Time times   will swirl around you as youre dining   on
stupid saint patricks day somewhere in a state   a fixed state   so you think
like pennsylvania
        but i kept remembering   another state taking place   exactly there
        Sure i got scared   no oak but the pleasure at first was intense, of trying of
                trying to remember   what i was dreaming   below our wakefulness.
This is not a dream im describing. i ate with eight women in two worlds or times
i heard what they said but   i was also dreaming that they   were saying other,
dreamed, things which I would almost remember You cant get it   I know I just
cant describe it   There is no such thing as a time zone There is a sticky
nonboundary between zonishness as the sun   passes across the sky The sun
remembers where its going If we stay in one place   we hear only what we've
said but if we travel If we travel on airplanes   across the nonzones we're not in

the same time we were. And so we can dream while awake
Because Im myself and not you   I guess I still had jet lag at that dinner

Do you get it Not quite
I was more me than with *you*. I am more me than   what we make what we
make   together.   Yet I love you   and try to lean   try to lean
on you and on the structures we have made those cages outside the train outside the
plane those   graffitied cages. leaned her back against an oak
first it bent and then it broke

Repeat it more clearly. I ate dinner with some women and dreamed I was talking to
them   at the same time as I was talking to them saying different things, it was a
benign experience. the door between dreaming and awake   was wide open oak
broke. it was jetlag sure but a relief   from feeling more caged in our times than
ever, from feeling that everything we build is worse   than ever. oak broke. i
liked it except for the fear that i   could be locked up for it

Repeat more clearly   I was dreaming while awake both awake and dreaming were
going on at the same time and involved the same people the same table   I
was with them really   and also was dreaming of them.

my soul and i are in las vegas   later in a real dream after   everyones
worried about their lives (there are no lives such cages)   we my soul and I
want to find she says (she says but why) a certain Fantasie Park
in her vehicle   the car/airplane   Speed through the foggy night   (fog in
the desert?) along/above the highway towards Henderson   we've left Vegas
already   and are headed towards Henderson   land and get out at a place a
park a plant its a sewage treatment plant   rectangular pools of the shitty
substance of the of the what we are living what a smell my soul hurries back into the
vehicle   it is now a helicopter   get in she says, we cant live in this fantasy

                              Take these boys to the boulderado   hotel
the place of rock   because its pouring rain into our house right through the roof!

then a man says that im not beautiful enough to be painted who cares who can care
about that, now he says its my fault not the artists, who cares, take these boys to the
rocklike establishment these girls these young   take them to rock. it will break
when they lean
not if its the real airy rock, the crystal airy rock   i'll take them without my looks
What a cage   looks were
dont you ever lean against anyone girl
they are a cage
all the chickens   are now beautiful no one will eat them. but they are caged
wh why   word why   past that word the cage why is a wh wind is a

because the cages have gotten harder. but harder to see as there are more. was you
always in cage benight i find gotten harder harder. they are in category cage try to
make a hard dream this woman says that theres no conscious because b darwin and
buddha because darwin and buddh theres no self the old fall for what a man once said
trick. the magazine likes her picture a lot and she likes her not self that gets to be loud.
i cant remember any more of my times was in order to redesign my rebirth. ive lost
all this memory this morning, march its equinox of no. its equinox of no
                                                                planetary
beauty

steering wheel beneath a lamplight. its going to rain who can live here   it will
rain but nothing will grow. the inferno and the purgatorio are the same building or
cage   with slightly different roofs   roofs nothing will grow i know everybody
there and am in both   still both.   and in the master crystal
where i can let go let go of that cage and take wing   which means

leave cage or named dimension nouned dimension. as you ever do thinking

a childs body again my soul (there are still several ways to portray it
my soul in dream or poem) is it my
Anyway a child's
body i scan it downward i mean look. It is said
that it is poetry The body is poetry
I am that body of the soul I, I

95

the body is poetry   and is there a diff   as long as you dont cage
and how   and how not   but
the body of the soul   I am that soul. dont
category cage cat   the boundaries around any   posited body
as he would dream
the doctor would dream your soul away.
So you can pick up her remains and put her in a box when she's dead
caged in a future cemetery like any ghoul.

he cries out how there shouldnt be a phone in the country
there shouldnt be a telephone in your home there
hes the theres-something-wrong-with-the-way-i-look guy, and its my fault,
and its my fault that i want a telephone in the country
so i can call up the world the heavens the inferno the purgatorio the cemetery and any
posited any posited body who speaks as an i I want to call you up.

try last ni to break out anntisociial telephone telephone. if you throw all the chairs across
the cage. i only wanted to break down the borders between countries nightmare blue this
is the threebrained nightmare on my passway momma bare baby bare m am a bare bare
way a sure body. i was so bad i was trying. try to get through or out. he look at me and
try to read me as if he were a freudi hah how can you read a mudscuk mudsucker bump
bump i cant wait im in the mud is it hell i cant wait for the heat cant wait to be left for a
hawk. and the eyes looking out of all cages fly into yours caged i am the sun i am the sun
and i know what im doing and remember where to go i am a rock and i know what im
doing i remember where to stay am not caged. why all this mud emotion in my hell heart
volcano i am a volcano and i know heat bumping up so the red salamanders bump bump
again i am pretending im a salamander so i wont feel guilt im pretending there is no past
night and that no one was there or is ever here because i am damaging my cage so i can
get out and the doctor dont like it What are you doing to it Being bad To damage your
cage is to be bad. they say. I threw a chair across the room and broke it. Because my
opinions werent allowed.

whadi you mean by love   and jonahs in the whalecage again   why if no one

asks what meaning means mean by love what is i would say why say   its all
rooms here the whale ribcage the whale shape dark ive been swallowed again by the
cage. which is not our city our citys love and so is the body which is not a cage.

there is no love when there are teams factions sides countries   they wont let
you talk unless you scream. there is no love. its in a cage want you in a cage so they
can stroke your feathers from time to time your smoothed and colorful ruff your
collar of sex your owned appearance your characteristic manners your sound of voice
and little scratch of nail. you are all owned but not if you scream. you are not loved
or is it love you are not love unless you scream. they havent listened unless you
screamed no love in a ca cage   put on these bits of colors and leave this house
this morning go out into the wider cage of plenty   someone is trying
to OD out of it   and leave and leave that room. put on these bits of colors and
shape up   shape into cage its all over the papers   this years clothes for women
here is my pluvial heart rain blood outside the door any door just to get there get out
outside the door.   keep trying, often go backwards

These three girls are trying
to get back into this high room. they
are holding onto the windowledge legs dangling down over airshaft
sense of belatedness young men help them up
one woman tries too quickly before anyone takes her hand and she falls
down the airshaft onto the ground blood organs crushed

call the ambulance too many minutes we have failed her
opted for out tried to get back in because out there was a cage
as small as an airshaft she was a junky
maybe call the ambulance call the doctor   give her some love is it what kind
the kind that isnt a product of   you but just is   the way that my anger isnt a
product of me. its been passed to me, it's *the* anger   she needs *the* love

the tape-recorder in front of me explodes, concertina-like people
        reading concertina-like newspapers
        about the bombing of Serbia
the tape-recorder in front of me explodes like a lightbulb   what was i recording
how to be a person here.

97

inside the tissue of the diamond there is only diamond and certain white lines. it is my body and my soul it is my mind melting with all yours. i am here again finally the cages are tiny specks elsewhere dont fail those girls why we will fail someone you dont have to you dont have to fail the chickens all you have to do is open door open door. throw things out let things in. theyd just put money on your horn making money. so dont. whos spea it is i the actress of the mother no bra the young man says ill be penalized for drinking coffee before rehearsals i have to play the queen hah im not going to. there are so many things im not going to do.

open the door between times between cages
the queen thats the story war men story
time, sides to have opinions such as i prefer the lexical cage and the, the living
building but what is that whats the real building or cage? why the crystal city of course
all my love to where even the most monstrous leader (arent all leaders monstrous)
blindly amnesiacally even his unconsciousness. is there. there its harmless how
because weak and under tended. barely evident but here in our

and the weak down there are most manifest here, because this city is all theyve ever had.

having having i am having. turning it over and having diamond
the white lines in the diamond are the lines of the cages demolished

CITY

we move back into a damaged city   figure of love and i   near the
entrance from the hole of images, that old theater.   they were about to throw out
a box of presents i left here when i moved   still wrapped in silver foil   i
choose some and scoop them up   and one of them is perfume, and heres an old
checkbook   the same old checks. old checks   when you move back
into the damaged city the old apt doorless with ripped out floorboards   a rat
and a cat to chase it   a skinny cat with a patch of   blue coloration a reasonable

cat, the mice are pissed off at it chasing it   next in the store, going to the store
oh i never wanted to do this again buy pasta and a pasta pan   listen to the
ignorant young women prattle in hero worship   of a heroine poet, amid sauces,
while the proprietors wife   it was supposed to be her all her in an apron she
got stuck here lost and now im looking for drinks that i dont want to   drink,
i want to be in the crystal city crystal city   i dont want to live in the damaged city
amid the same   stop off at a different apartment   to get cared for

No not me.   this tall herb this light colored grass   protects you from
AIDS   a couple says   i am walking out the door now, going home where is
that   in the wrong city no i am walking out the door now going back to the
ghoulish dead of the damaged of the city of worldwide   spread of the damage of
the damage No. im going home to the crystal   where you are glints in the
pearl   your eyes are light glints there

light glints there.

will the secretary of state ever take you home to such a place, she is trying to shake me
as we walk together from the drugstore on front street towards broadway but i wont
leave.
            you are using me again you dead men, that's why i shatter   all your empty
bottles with a hatchet.
                        all of this anger was given to me for use   where did it
come from   it first appeared i believe when there were different rules
for male spiritness. then there were always different rules for that and for his hat, his

political ideas he would always be the expert   no now im in the crys im going
there ive broken all the bottles and ive followed albright to the all bright city where

she has disappeared, because she has no distinction here, as my prizes dissolve and
your expertise. here, there is no. you and you have no charm here, and your loud
voice cant prevail because a voice isnt a voice its a mind you might say and all minds
are working all the time so no one mind can prevail. im listening to the whole mix
speaking colors and shapes dissolvable tendencies no bell rings how can i find you not
walking exactly because my function as use for as use for a previous definition of the
animal kingdom is defunct.

                              tony has shown up
at the conference at the womens college   he   shows up everywhere,
though he looks lost.   he has stayed young, around twenty.

        back and forth i go   between the two cities
pain of the damage down here, in me, because all the facets are joined. down here, up
there,
                    tony doesnt know what to do at the conference at the womens college
        they arent going to discuss how he was used, made into a soldier and killed,
before he finished college   because the bottles are kept separate
and the facets and the facets
                        are only realized consciously in the. so you see

me, breaking and breaking with an axe all the bottles you have emptied
destroy use it is sinking
                        because all the facets are joined. cant keep him away
        is hispanic minority   no he is tony twenty   no he is tony
whom i have known   since we were six.   he stopped having an age
at about twenty-two now im fifty-three   he is tony whom im known since we

were six
hes here, looking lost   at the avant-garde conference at the womens college.

every night i plead i ask the veritable air   for a vision of the crystal city   and i
get another dream of   people i know and have known, of course   they are
the city.   Last night the crystal city was down in the métro down among staircases
where you catch the Balard-Créteil line to Invalides   the city was young male
lovers who say, why dont we use a sap or a knife or other object in sex? because this is
love   we dont because its love   And that is   an answer, o philosopher-
scientist, that   the skin of the body that the flesh and muscle of the soul   are

love   its your procedures are foreign knives and clubs   in the holes to the
soul   the crystal facets which open   in skin   In the lower depths
a hassled thieving life   of an unmoneyed sort   is transpiring here mirror of
the corporate, but with love just a little more love   spills out in sloppiness of cheap
alcohol vieux papes the mentally defective   transient we used to see around
is back climbing a staircase Up   i guess hes supposed to be me because   the
others say theyll find him anywhere, writing a poem   and there, a

waif   is   old friend whose name is now   carol nadir Yes
this is the crystal   city   i know it well have always known it thus

i must enter city right now wings of dew and hawk eyes i must fly right in through the
blazing clear light of your voices vi the strong we pouring forth in individual
consciousnesses talk talk like li stream of the ignorant man laughing at him hes there
but hes still susc unconsciousness he'll never unfortunately because he decided we
were a weave a habit a concatenation   of evolutionary scientific trick so now
hes here but not not really hes about   as here as milosevic who is, is here but will
be mute soul for eon. too bad you   splend in the night and that dead man
was there i was talking to him next to where the train come in a slab of pr pork a slab
of cold prk station next to the métro métro to the tall the building where im huste
hutl hustled in so someones old wife wont see me, oh you who care. i enter
into the middle of it the building of facet for tricks beyond wives and habits beyond all
trick of con of scientific   conning. but wouldnt you like to be conscious? but
all those whims of yours   pretending they explain this thi blaze blinding voice and
you cant even expal explai the liquidity of the voice that is conscious or uncon
because   explain   is   a con a con ah riv

101

you are as here as the dazed dead is

I saw them all as equals
in that moment it made me feel as if I were standing
up very straight   everything else was wiped away.   to see
everyone as equal to one
and all accomplishment erased   is the most mystic of experience.
destroys science there is no fittest

and all your wives and husbands are there   and all your rapists and your victims
and every bit of difference from you   what you werent born and didnt become
are there is there   being addressed by you now   truly now murderer
in its or your state of splendor or mutedness Thats our description?   Isnt it? Wah
what is important then nothing nothing at all Thats why I like   this is the ethic of
what matters   the exact blazing nothing you can be   caring to be but not
caring about thing at all   caring for but not caring about   to careful like
a hawk, an apple and not a hat
                                        i saw her throughout last night
young and alive and i saw the old ill dead man the night before. slab of pork
slabs of pork either they or the métro platform   and she was at the college and she
was there all night city of women   but we are the city of no one. drop of a hat

the fish in the foyer are overfed he says i can smell it when i take off the top of the
aquarium. let them out to cry from scum from the underside of the riverbank let us
out so we can eat scum   let us out so we can learn to be the nothing necessary
to survive in full consciousness in the crystal city we want to eat scum and be scum
let out of cage and be as good as scum   be as good as algae if you dare   have
as much soul   as a bacteria if you dare know as much of crystal if you know how

i dreamed i was that small in the black black ocean of all   swimming towards the
awful shore that we had created   out of our manly arrogance. in the city of crystal i
am all of the crystal   all and one   one facet   all of it and i

i have to have the key to the himalayas by tonight. i have to get out of here
i have created a diagram or picture   that allows the woman me in the picture to

rise up riding a skeleton-butterfly   butterfly with skeleton body blue winged
with gold light bars on the blue   riding a skeleton-butterfly to the very top of

the himalayas   the picture is of an indian   woman other   nationality oh
what difference does that make?   none of that matters, you   and via the

agency of this picture   i have the key to the himalayas   red dinosaur
laughing   red dinosaur soul smiling at me.   there is the iron rose

and there is the petrified vaginal hole   of images skeletons, there are all the
nines   of competition and rating   im flying up above them riding an

image   an image riding an image   in a diagram   of how to get there

no i have to go back to school first he says. hes a hard man a middleclass middleaged
school administration man says i have to go back to that same womens college theres a
darkness to my right in this room, this room which is at the same time the outside campus
and grounds of the school as well as a piece of paper hes showing to me, telling me id
previously achieved a score high enough to get in go back to school for further education.
this paper says. i wonder whats in that darkness that school wont ever tell me because of the
bottles and of him, i know the city is in that darkness the city i am in keep entering
and leaving keep describing but not and thats because. the door of reason. thats because,
is in that darkness the city and not the college tony the highest of mountains a darkness to
my right in this room. there is my anger given to me for use but hard to control where i
have unwrapped it from its silver foil what do i do with all these things these perfumes
and further dreams? i have a new blue book of reason in which to write down more
dreams. the crystal city's towers never shatter are they a learning denied will not be tried
by you i wont be in keep ive shattered male bottles we're entering the city through the
darkness the crystal roads and streets not walking at all not used by definition or
evolution breaking the heart tony and i. are entering the crystal city bright blue sky
throughout the body we are of reason not of use we will not be of use. and if there is no
use here what will you do. that is for me to find out that is the new knowledge youve
never thought before.

the poem says 'we have finally found our house' and is presented interlinearly in a different colored ink with the accompanying letter, viz there is a line of letter followed by a line of poem then a line of the letter followed by a line of the poem, and so on. the poem and the letter clearly different but can not be easily separated. as each beings two lives cant be. the figure of love and i are standing reading the letter across from the park which is two parks in two cities. green trees it is spring. then we will enter the pharmacy while i am young as young as long hair. as young and long as the long skirt im wearing here that i once wore. this is the drugstore of my youth drink a cherry phosphate red like a thin silk blouse with short sleeves a soul red blouse.

ive forgotten that man is dead he isnt always dead

this is the song you sing when youre dancing with a ghost i dont mind, this all this is the whole song you sing   when   youre not being used

who invented use and all the schemes to justify it that book gets published endlessly, we're not being used now, not being used here

A DAILINESS

i would like you to know of the opacity and
transparency   of our   transactions
all day   and not just night.   you may be almost

airlessly evil   as evil is a person   acting   now

and we use soldiers to kill him   so we become him vi evil
eating at a long table
                         in the suehiro restaurant near   the airport at
Vancouver.   at one end is a family   at the other myself and the figure of love
that is   what are we   figuratively now,   which is other than what

we are,   as defined by sight and tradition   What we do to others do
we do as figures   of the valued   (and would never   want to be a figure)

but youre flowingly knowing more than see or say, or what i see
or what that family there   or the chef cooking our food, both
theirs and ours at the same   at the same table

he looks tired.

oh my dead beloved you are still trying to cure your liver and this time its with the large
liver of a philosopher i'll never read everyone talks about this was before leaving for
vancity tried im trying to show you the dream in the day this time my dead loved holding
in a dream the large square liver like a mattress almost but red of the most ren trend
philosopher of this fleeting fraction of an era. always a real voice downstairs staying up
all night a real dog a real a dream is too. 'he's trying to get well' i think but why should
anyone bother to think like that sick and well support their vision and i do but dont want
to through the bars this spring. the gold ankh poets are being valued against whatever so
recite your old poems, what about this new
                         A woman leads a small girl by the
hand up some steps to a door, that means that shes the mother of her soul of her own soul
          a better thought than the bitter mattress too and the voices are you and the
voices i value while i am hating are right now in the world you love so are not voices but
nonetheless your voices you cant hear them though   i can hear them.

winding sheet and wrap it around the steak the shitake mushrooms and the green tea ice
cream a cloister near the airport. the japanese restaurant was better than the philosophy tent
        at the summer poetry school in the park at invalides inside which was kept
the liver you could cure your own with supposedly your liver with anothers   touch a
philosophers liver and be cured.

       hes back i accept that hes not dead
       hes going to write lots of poems
       hes saying that if he gets enough pasta
       into the pantry he can stay up and write all night
                             i'm
       starting to get clear that
       he didnt die but was ill and then?
       i'll ask him because i'm sure now
       that something very simple happened i'm
       reconciled to his being back if I can only know this thing   as to how
       he didnt die   how didnt you die

Wake up and hes dead its hot Heres a book with some poems of his
in the mail.
        do i understand?
all night thought of the baffling of time in poems Do i understand?
the crystal city is like poetry   but there doesnt have to be any baffling
listening listening all day now for voices
in between the daily, the shit daily
Others are telling me   put in baffles   and yet
and yet this flow are telling me   i dont know that other thing a
baffle is, a device   to create an effect Why create an effect

riding this train you can ride it both dreaming and awake youve done it so often both
crystallized and in aging flesh   youve done it   so often.   any it   The

transitional moment where everyone's still in their costumes the shoes they are

wearing for the   about to be but not this moment was discussing tarot cards first in
life, then   in a dream then in life again.   the men say in the dream
which anticipates subsequent talk (in life)   that is, after ive said, im showing

you how poets think,   the men say that actually   im just using the topic of
the tarot   to talk about myself that   the word is out   that thats what
i do right now as in this poem,   though they dont mind and i say and i say
nothing but on this train   where the lowly howling voices of all

are in my ears i say that that isnt true   that im talking to you about us but do
you know youre talking to me on this métro car in this poem too   while
whatever war the aids in south afric etcet speaks to me   opacity the evil one man
everyone is   fixated on why politics his voice in the crystal a is milosev

bluntly a mallet of mute air but down here he says i am having my   effect on the
world of your thought   participating in his thought and in the bright jay blue
make   a new world with language? but the language   the real language isnt
words this   is only figuratively it   as i figuratively sleep   through this

train   ride to the buttes

golden light in a cave again, there was
golden light in a cave   in my mind   i can get it back
only sometimes, the exact   experience of it in my mind. I saw
the gold light then in a thought or
image but cant see it now Why

after i dreamed the tarot card conversation, i had the conversation awake   though
a little differently.

wake up and hes dead and alive at the same time as all former marriages contingent
are, and dead people are alive this society only   believes in the visible so fucked
as it is with war wake up and a cat   is both alive and dead   Wake up and
you are part of war and a local peace in spring Oh, no, doctor, no one tells me anything
but you, oh he must be reassured that only the tangible as hes defined it, is

and war doesnt take place in the thought air nothing there except the air in molecules
policed   as to their stated randomness. Theres a kitten who   that
was a dream a kitten who (no, doctor, a kittens not a who) im made to believe is not
there with   one eye larger than the other   because hes my former cat, in an
early time in his life as im a child often in this middle age (no doctor i am never) But

in this dream   im made to believe hes not really there so when he leaps onto my
bed, and i cry out as if threatened   threatened by the spirit of that cat?   why be
frightened ever, i wake up in terror but then im not a part of this later war   two
men pursuing each other, no matter   whos pursuing who: it changes   the
blond one hands me his ninja star so   he wont throw it at, kill, the other   i toss

it into the gutter thats wrong the wrong action he   picks it up again   i was
supposed to keep it hold the weapon myself Someone must keep the weapon not toss
it away Why Someone must have it must possess the weapon why No reason so far
theres no reason   for anything thats like that   We are all speaking together in air
how can we deny it everything   it wasnt a ninja star it was the   curved

blade   i saw on a sign–please declare these–   at vancouver
airport next day

                                        tells me to keep   the weapon but there
                                                shouldnt be one
                                        if i throw it away someone like him will take it again
                                        this is   insupportable

its a book
of drawings
of costumes of medieval
knights,
i want to copy the only one thats a
womans
but
theres something wrong with the
drawing her torso is wrong i
cant copy that

So i can keep his weapon next time?
defend my possession of it in armor?

Nothing ever dies. everyone denies it nothing ever dies everyone denies. cant
change cant city
                    Any time im talking to you im talking to all the living and all the
dead Thats why i try to talk to you in the city instead where we dont have to
remember and only crystal itself will leak down seep down and seep down. there was
a beautiful gold light in a cave while i was conscious its the only clue that ive had
lately that and the commonplace   iridiscence of the stellars jay.

theres no reason for anything, still. i'll never find it the reason, the men stole it a long
time ago i may be in a past of mine now they stole the reason and hid it throughout
the oppressive texture they created to stifle my thought to stifle the voices of the dead
and to construct a life dedicated to rhythms of war why in that past life i find this out
and am devastated to see so clearly i find it out all day while i walk to the store east
village and am never deprived of anything except living wholely without kissing the
male ass of violence because youd rather believe anyone than your own mind full of
voice. *he is trying to get well so i can finally hear his voice*, that occurs to me as voice
          last night i was in a bed of women two of them went out for dessert and i
noted the late time four thirty a m then when i woke up got up a few minutes i thought to
notice the real awake time it was four forty a m Do you understand? i knew
what time it really was while dreaming Do i understand Its not that im not here its
that here isnt here something else is Do you understand Do I understand Youre repeti
Thats because you dont understa The apartments full of swarming bugs again which
are worms supposedly lice they are eating our life and our time There is no life and no
ti theyre eating theyre stealing us Tries to suffocate me   with a pillow again and
again
Because i can dream
the literal time or something

how didnt you die

isnt going to answer because i should know   but i dont know everything in words
          he didnt die because   hes always in the crystal city but thats not good

enough as words its even sentimental and though my poem wants to show that, its
not the truth   as those words   he didnt die because he keeps coming
back to me thats better   but i dont like it why   the secret of the iron tomb
the secret is that he comes back i dont want him to he didnt die he died he didnt
comes back to be sick again is getting better so he didnt die   how is he like this
how is he   and the dead cat and the dead cat   this is too personal the cat
i remember hearing a voice say that we would meet again my cat and i   its not like
heaven but its like the communication we were born to   I   was never born
its communion and i mean communion thats a joke The jokes personal
is there a personal   thing in this crystal   yes and yes
if crystals a persons home here   and a cats   Because i dont want him to
come back as sick   i only want to communicate with him as crystal as crystal Can
he be   crystal

DIRT

lets call it permanence, the crystal but
we're about to call it   dirt

my mother my sister who leaves us and i
are approaching a town in the desert   whose real name is...ive always

known it but now   i cant remember.   my sister says before disappearing
that it is, in one aspect   an ugly industrial town, fort moabi   with also a military
guise   But thats not its real name, fort moabi   its really a beautiful town which

we've always loved built to conform to the desert landscape as dirtlike
structures towerlike but low   my mother and i are now near it but
crawling in the same dirt its built of.   this crawling in the dirt is a greatly
          pleasureable   experience i can scarcely describe

as we crawl towards its main street we see a couple—the mans in a cowboy
hat, cotton shirt, belt and jeans—fall into the dirt fall down, the sweet dirt
pulls them down.   oh i keep trying to remember the real name of the town

crystal is dirt matter the body dirt is crystal the bodys decay   is crystal is crystal

he didnt die, because his story only   exist in your eye. the story counts for you, so
im trapped in it too.   decaying into crystal sand nothing is happening is it
these illusory stories of ours   make a separation of the two   there
is that past i am still. story   In a small countryish town   im admiring
the drawings   of someone in the past who didnt finally become that great artist,
though the moon and others praised him then   and one was told to
admire a man   Thats not even the story if a story of many i see you there and im
admiring everyone but myself then.   Figure of loves lost somewhere in urban
figure of life arrives with her baby   figure of mainstream zips by on a bike takes
a book from my hands the short version she can have it, i   dont believe in

these stories i only believe

that im enclosed in the large feeling each story relegates to back looming night   the
veritable ground that both   life and art find irrelevant. is this a dream
im looking for that figure of love   in several hotels with blatant bars but he
turns into a past man   its the past though the setting is paris present   all the
past people are leaving an   arty event, and across the lake, a border   is
past love talking looming from his fragility

          go on past most story to the place where crystal and dirt crystal and matter
coincide   and death is a beautiful pleasure not the cursed ground and true night
how died didnt matter nor any other nor any story any story there are no store
glistening crystal dry goods and basement young department store and someones
chosen a defective baby thats the kind of that we.   its like all those clones thrown
back into the sea of crystal dying and deformed have you heard of   all the
cloned animals dying and deformed? they dont matter they arent people they arent a
real   story at the park of the sick   i always see him at the park of the sick across
from the tomb of the depraved conqueror everyone worships with his gold dome and
preserved   body whats a body   dont know how to look or see

i dont have a body. i have this   all my loves have one

read about the choosing of a supposedly defective
baby, a few days later, in a magazine.

she stole away the short version of beloved on her bicycle. i thought it was better than
the long one because there was less room for lies about love its not the book youre
thinking of its simply a book of be love not like it it keeps coming back and in a sense
which thats love. its the fact that everyone is in permanence. he says a star not a word a
burst small of light trying near the flowering tree glass basin of this world so get the
mattress out of it and wake up before it dies, the world. and now i'll have to do it crawl
all the way to maybe hope arizona to tell that stories are all that decay. nothing else
disappears, though stories have a half life of length but length is meaningless here and
what decays is the human made story of the body not the body it is the same as crystal
becomes and becomes crys s or some not all the way to hope or in a glass basin. its the
babys bedtime in the theater where baby lives hes absorbing stories through the walls the
floors and the ceiling people are standing in line to see the movie thats playing in his own

house and life his mother is standing w around in her bathrobe about to fall asleep and
dream too. i still havent figured out anything being too much of a figure too figure still
yet. shedding figures and stories, except for how didnt you die. that isnt how did you die
and that keeps mattering. when the body matter disappear into crystal all the stories
stores the stored go simultaneous

walk through these beautiful half lives of leftover stories
they arent quite the ones you tell
they are stripped down to figuration and the sequence
trembles and collapses—in the day here
in the lower city because you know this story,
walk through parts of the hidden story which tremble and exist as
separate parts in no order   in a strange gold and black
or unearth blue   light
these stories are decaying are decaying. their parts are statuesque sometimes true

so the very present bursts   out of his closet again
in order to keep a sexual assignation,   he will leave his administrative offices
disguised wrapped up in coats and scarves a big down jacket and a wool cap
clutching a poem.   the very present is trying   to keep a date in
the present   he should be faithful to his wife constance, but
he needs to keep this date   Is it with me? no   im watching from no one the
times gone by   of my unkept date with him   theres a goddamned marching band
which   has marched all over the city

                              it has arrived in our neighborhood
                              it will play then be done marching
                              its male musicians and its majorettes
                              in short sexist skirts
                              my dark neighbors and i
                              are glad it will be over soon
the story
its not dirt its the story. dirt is soft and clean   such   pleasure

i can only know these things this way, a sentence not a thought not a complete. why
again did i have to be   reborn as i say and change my times   backwards? so i
could be in   my past as differently as time goes on,   entrapping me but
A dream is a thinking   backwards and forwards a way of getting out of the
present,   the present tries   to get out of the present the poor trapped
indescribable present   how didnt he die is he dream dreamed out of the present
and in his dream speak dreaming is talking it communicates

                    Tell me something city
                  wild grow wilder grow. time plate tem plate
the real template there is no. i   is not from a template   I saw you in the
counterfeit store I see through, you see through plates of glass, reason   grasp
sensed air dirt the body matter crawling crystal across the desert to wickenburg wickiup
maybe No, now i remember   it must be winslow arizona   city my
father had said of a hundred hills the point is, you cant hear them the voices you
know them   being a grand unconscious   be that other   Know now dont
put on a muff coat and make an assignation in the illicit illicit world. because theres a
real present of voice

Scared myself went down into cave of gold
light during the quotidian afternoon yesterday
        when i came up the world
threatened to be different Its covers were coming off
it was pulling apart it was opening it wasnt
going to look look like you say it looks
and it didnt it looks like a feeling It cant be seen
seeing is only approximate location i calmed the feeling
down and away because   i had to go out and be regu
the world doesnt look any way any way at all   we dont
originally exist   to be looked at. but
we cant bump into each other too much bump bump though our voices can

now all the younger poets will slide across the country sitting on their effects their
basic pared down possessions   as if their things were sleds, they will slide across
on the map on the dirt on the map   and   the dirt   im going with them

114

as an older   but am saying goodbye doing lastminute vocal   tasks talking
tasks while they leave, so i'll have to catch up   a young womans drawing a map
of how to catch up with them   Traveling with them   better than feeling
excluded by man in a large room doesnt like me,   and theres too much blood in the
toilet there   and the mermaids hair on the cruise ship way of traveling a

moneyed way   is blond and long clamped waves   i will slide across america
with the young   slide in the dirt on my ass protesting   war and leaders
protesting leaders particularly   we wont be led   and i am there to show
that i am not leading   leading them   In newspaper story corrupt the old man
one i often dream of as landlord   is abusing his political office, get rid of these
offices we cant be elected to   destroys the lives of woma yes again reading the
sunday paper in my dreams because   theres no sunday paper awake in paris Start
over   wake up and start   seeing else the chapters are scattered

                    it isnt   the   dirt   it isnt   shell of you
left   its what there is   is   The not being of use
Am both the cave and the light in   it, then   i know i am home   we have
trained outselves to make and see   sequence and position. strain should be dead
visual pile of papers look at the plastic wrapper trash   its composed of the light
in or on it and the cave and the cave the light comes from   the plastic. is a story
What parts a story? the plastic and   the cave and the ground cave and the dirt
the any   dirt isnt use the dirt so soft and beautiful soul-like free unformed
light all around me in a ring in cave   image i was in   but try i am trying to see
what friday i saw yes sequence day on sequence day i saw a how the space between
position wasnt made   by position wasnt that and so the objects around me
werent fixed. they were better than that   they float, anchored

one leaves   present time   in dreams and enoc encounters the jumble
why images it has to consolidate into one pla plane or assemblage If all time is at the
same time   and   consciousness is continuous   and simultaneous,
not being used,   if consciousness is whats not used   there is no then.
If consciousness is simultaneously   all worlds that have been will be   if
im trained not to see   that,   im crawling in the dirt towards seeing crawling
towards a slow win   a din window town a town of dirt dirt sparkles the cleanest
dirt in town

always in the train station again then. uptown el

breast hurts last night because my brain is lactating. the milk leaks down the side of
my face, toys in this house and a sort of toy-child, a girl who gets put on a certain shelf
to sleep gets put like a toy, i'd nurse her but now shes too old   in the old part of

town, near where i'd once dreamed there was a dirt motel composed of mounds of
lovely adobelike dirt with lamps outside lamps sparkling outside each door.

crawl slowly into dirt chamber   and know as much as any
have a door and have an all   and are crickets inside theirs yes heres a picture of an
orange jerusalem cricket chirruping in my head   voice voice voice   a snake
a   sideblotched lizard lizards many in the white in the light dirt can yon
i dont even know what im saying   saying word voice cricket dirt door town door

long hair the milk i was leaking   was mixed with my long hair so the dream was
in the past   past body   to which the figure of past love was faithful
he died   he didnt   how didnt they die? dirt is crystal   crystal
is   crawling   dirt

CASTLE

school the junky students desk in an alcove near a stairwell near the brightness of
windows   What an elaborate syringe you have whoever you are so that I, passing by
get caught in it a hook there,   sprayed with bloody water there is so much of this
weak water   made red by red the souls blood or what i still dont understand. such
diluted ruby I summon   authority an official woman to unhook me   and am
chided by this junky   How dare he   I   want some order, I say   I need
order in my life,   and you should think about it too!   So, now, impressed he
asks me to be his girlfriend   His out box is full of dead insects. dark and dry with
their excrement

what is it of, an order of what, too many images? but in fantasies   where the
world gets changed, but   must fantasy   be ordered?   as i am saying who am
no particular   respecter of junkies.
                                        We must, I once wrote, Change
                                                    the forms in dreams

in this room
a city   a search for it and being it. order among the images
which im addicted to but dont approve of, exactly   i have
abandoned beauty time after time in order to get here, have abandoned
beauty subtlety the outside   in a principled crawl, a slow slide. Because the
crystal city seeps between the images   between the threes the given way
of ordering time into three   and through the bodys porosity   and
through the souls own body And through   this lengthy process

I am a capital or capitol

I am order among the images.

if you could understand and change them, looking for clues not to conquest and own
death, self interest but to the way world is working as a set of stable images which are
then translated into the fluidity of our thought at night as our minds go out above time.
we are in charge of the stable world but our vast world of image shared in the sea of the

medium of mind is likewise in charge of us day and night we can have no thought that doesnt reflect from this sea of telepathic communion. but the image hole is now always open mouthed crazed street person babbling and crying. everyone and the past asserting this world and our way i was an old person and with old people about six like french in trenchcoats light we entered the butchers at night near the périphérique and montrouge near the périphérique we entered through the front door and left through the back i am watching us as well as being that one that old not-me everyones putting on the costume for this except me and will they notice all the old ones are putting on their costumes for this except me. just some costumes, be images, its our way.

i am merely asserting we hear each others all other too and if we were to change the images in our dreams we'd hear those changes. every morning i realize i have dreamed a little of the future because theres no sequence there are items laid out actionate objects on emotional counter they are practically our thoughts though are not thought. the hole the hole back to the

someones stolen our model castle
because we left it on the street. but we live on the street and leave
everything there we can make it again by piling
the same materials cant we on top of each other?
we can reassemble the materials ourselves
we can remodel our ideal though the kits have all been
sold from the newsstore the thai man owns
the hinges the glue and instructions are in the kit
such a fetish about known form on this street on this street divisidero,
that means border avenue. When we havent yet perceived the worlds form

I dreamed I was vindicated as a writer early of essays on
poets wrote a booklet on three of course men in my dream youth
wake up and this is somewhat the case because
a womans said on internet that i was early on, in my career
an essayist, this morning. But thats a time The booklet of the three
of the three essays on postmoderns but post mod thats just
a time. In model castle time in crystal city time when
somethings stolen its a shadow

                                i'm afraid i'll start seeing differently and be afraid
i'm afraid i'll be afraid
I fear that space the emptiness between things will grow and visibly flow.
the substance of space seems to flow through me too
we're going to different events at the same time my friend is already
choosing her dress to impress   who? probably some bosses
if we could unmoor the bosses if their bossform ceased to be attached
if it all came apart since you die before youre born something like that like
to be on right on doesnt have to be time or timing i bet I
bet it keeps it keeps time without it the castle holds it as i am order
the the mind is not what you call brain now choosing the dress
time an organizational model isnt itself like one is. a birds eye is supposed to be so
different from my an organizational presumption wildeyed oh you dont
have to think about different

some old men sometime invented time to keep us in line
some old aristos once invented time.

this is my fathers world but not that model of time its a hum hymn associated with a
street in light not in time around the corner from four years old and where the methodist
church is. its either the methodists or the masons in this life which well but im only
thinking about a quality of light in the mind so i sneak back around the corner from the
church the white wall of it and am now in tree shade along the dirt road lacy chinaberry
tree with purple. space go crazy on me again space between these supposed things all
nature sings and round me rings up dome blue. i get there and hear how clamor for. in
heav the counter clock

rejoin and a woman is there a figure who is lamenting how
when she lies in bed with her husband, shes just supposed to be There
they dont make love. the other woman blond says thats the case with her too
this isnt the case with me but i'm just There in their story
there are a lot of books on the shelves to get such stories from

having isolated self from the eroticism
of thought sheen of the world as not just seen but

reflecting thought. bursting open slowly a pink flower i have been in
near front street at night   across from mohave park a pink   room with no
chairs, because it was a   flower. you could be in and outside at the same time
someone with a plain name was there.   the pink room meant now as of flowers
the dark blue room referring to the fact that i had known not quite consciously
my brother would die of the past war, finally,   meant that you could   know the
future and prevent war.   the white room was a destructive   dark father a
revolutionary   with a gun. really the past, he never changes his violent way
And time had created the world as a slow   suicide pact   the suicide
pact of death in time   you can die now or later now or later junky ruby flower
dabbler isnt this a gun   order a model castle

as i am always walking, and is that use by a force outside me, i find a large white or red
flower in the pines and is that flower a castle i think it is it has order and room and is
pierced by light but it grows and dies yet its body is clearly spiritual and it never leaves
us it is always subtly speaking once seen. you have seen its i and it never leaves you
can you reside in such a castle do you yourself the order breathing thought breathing it
in and out.
        as i am always walking i have again walked the arduous nighttime
walk through the desert to topock the border town the small city on a hill at the place
where two states meet a town near a bridge a town near a river a small group of
dwellings with lights on at night found after the fifteen-mile walk along the river
through the dirt. i have no money and i dont want anything from the cafe i find a
dime on the ground
        and a small lost thing to glue   onto a collage. I will now
walk back but this is what i do at night many nights walk there and back because i
have to though dont know why searching for order or the or the order which must be
perceivable near this border between what and what the road back the dirt road is
marked by tires and is gravelly goes all the way back to a city where i feel i may be
neglecting someone. border at death or border at knowing in life. ive been making
this journey for years back and forth at night. i often thought in previous years that i
wouldnt even make it to the border that town there but now its easy enough to and to
get back.

        twisted up inside tell me theres no requirement for being here let it go free.

one dime the sense castle stock im here but i have to walk back because the border
hasnt told me anything again one dime and one small object to glue onto this every
night every night. standing at the border between california and arizona west and east
and a one hour time change the time changes here so they say.

        border
        why didnt he die?   is still a question

        border and order

     dont know where am nowhere
     is nowhere
     sit down in front of light
     inside self it is the space
     between objects maybe

      dimensions are   shoe fits
      I tell you see   castle gate

       see it its between because you
 made the other stuff   but its in me
 & out   what happens at
 border, order am not used though two legged   walking lily
 sleeping tardy. dont sleep

the buddhist monk is a double person he is he in his robes but his double is full of
steel parts that is he has constructed another over time, as i have but not of steel, i
have constructed another, real, body   sometimes its me painted white and
sometimes its my baby, remember? but i didnt construct her really. i found her and
maybe i found my other body. now f planes fly above which sini signify that the war is
over, the boats back from africa only half full though containing survivors my babys
onboard she has a fever   my babys leg has come off does she want the pajama
outfit in which she can pretend to wear her own leg or the other outfit? she wants to
pretend but she doesnt need the leg or legs she isnt being used well doesnt she look
better with the leg she thinks so when her friends come over Dont sleep any more

these dreams are ridiculous No, they arent Theyre all about clothes   just like
everyday here is what outfit to wear for the second time godawful white as to a
wedding wedding again i only want to stand at the border order the castles that
mountain maybe no but its a clue im sick of clues im feverish fro from clues and
borders maybe i should have constructed t some steel parts i dont want them i dont
want that male that. a steel other body.

these giant sequoialike trees   are thousands of years old, one   fallen
has a new redflowering tree growing from it   that other over there is covered
with lavender wisteria   a soul guide   in a ranger hat a ranger shirt is
explaining things in front of the tourist center

                                        red flowers or purple the model castle
used to grow everywhere but find it only here now.   there were all those
antarctic penguins last night on television hundreds crowded   can find each
others voices   after a split second almost telepathically   like alls
mental like the all mental that sequoia fallen with the red flowered voice
Grows out of the oldest   you are, Im old and old.   And the junky turned up
too in daily life. and in another dream someone wrote, "I know motion will be
needling   my san franciscan knots"   if time is more like knots, if you can tie
and untie your own time   im trying to take a bath in a house and i cant lock the
door of the bathroom   the adult and child say dont, its better if you dont in this
bathroom,   down the hall from the useless party, so i got the mattress out of the tub
Your definition   of the natural world is wrong because it doesnt include
telepathy and the invisible   Nature isnt just nature

COVERED MARKET

in a bank a man a tall man, in   a memory bank? he stands in the bank in a
trance   and we're–   for i'm somewhat though not entirely there–
looking at a very past collage   of a man shaving   the image is
surrounded by white   'i love that white space,'   the tall man says.
then i'm writing the or a story   i finish it at the bottom of the picture: 'And that's
how i came to marry   a one-legged man and live in a boat.' there's one star up in
the dark   That was a dream.   Later, awake, i'm working on this poem
and i need more material, so i court a conscious   image see myself, in a tee-shirt

old skirt old   haircut   in a boat, in a boat ive strayed too close   to the
white moon, but isnt it cold?   ive wanted to contemplate existence prior to
images,   is that this white light?   And i sit down at the bright
computer screen to type both   the dream and the waking vision,   and find the
previous poem's words, 'in a boat with soul on water...'   i grow dizzy and fall to
the floor.   i later remember that there was a boat, too, in the picture   of
the shaving man.   Not in the dream but in real life do you follow? the
picture   exists in my life   was being remembered, seen   partially in

the dream   in all of this is involved the word Chicago–the collage
was a cover for my magazine Chicago   on my teeshirt in the waking dream i see
the word also–   but thats too personal o my soul (she doesnt care)   In Chicago
was where i first   fell to the floor like that   27 years ago.

that is how its serious thats how my lifes not divided. how did life originally become
divided. i hear two voices
                        "ive got to get you off my back father"   "i have
to get a message to you" he replies
                                agitated writing again this morning.
                                        unsure of what crippled
means now. in a room with an audience drawn on a wall as background, the figure of
love and the figure of life stand near a horse which lies on its side. love is describing a
cruel practice in which the horses torso is cut from its legs and haunches. life

intervenes and says no the real way a horse sacrifice is performed is that the horses
legs are cut off from a little below where they join the main body. the siberian horse
sacrifice, i recall this morning after the dream, is often prelude to a shamanic journey
though the shaman doesnt ride the horse, he conducts its soul to a high
heaven Do you know the sixth heaven is the realm of the moon,   it is a
somewhat high   place but there are many many higher

                                                            in siberian horse
sacrifice the horse is killed in such a way as to keep it intact to prevent a single
drop of blood from leaving the body
this is opposite to my dream   my dream of the crippling of the horse

cut off its legs and it can fly   i fall to the floor, not being used
only i am doing this to me. disabling myself
trying to approach the moon with a mutilated horse which can fly
im older now and i can do it   this dangerous thing shamanic

then it all takes place in the covered market again its all covered over
what im thinking is hidden from me again   except for there being the almost
inevitable sexism will i ever cease to dream such She and i
my blonde friend and i are in the maze of rooms   in the covered market
competing for, its a contest of thought, of essays perhaps   and we
are two of the finalists   we lose to a much younger man   maybe the one who
was a junky in a previous dream   he's presenting a chart of his ideas
oh the form everyone prefers, a chart.   i have comforted my friend and then
one of the organizers says, hes even forgotten who we are,   says to me, i assume
you are his—the winner's—sister!

                              no recourse but flight, there
was an old woman tossed in a basket/seventeen times as high as the moon
In the rhyme she sweeps the cobwebs from the sky the top of the mind they will never be
swept clean perhaps only in ones own ones own mind or of course in the city itself i
am trying to take off in a plane in a couple of hours but must cook forever dinner in
the covered market according to the prevailing time contingencies i wont make my
plane im somewhere in the center of the market in my own apartment in the market

among the vegetables antiques and hungup dead animals rabbits and lambs i suppose
but im wearing an ancient twopiece outfit orange dress i wore for a job interview
when i was nineteen and a dont want to finish that story. seventeen times as wild and
fleeting up and up singing the song of the horse whose legs have been cut i am
leaving i am arriving i am leaving we arc sailing what is your message then what? it
is to true it. it is true it is all truer and truer across the border into land. moonlight all
over the landscape the gravelly pearls and the river of malachite azurite now
blackblue and glossy and white near black mountains over which creatures fly creature
souls fly so im tingling im just tingling again. wobby wobby you are a mess but true
Am i willing these words the word true true keeps coming through. hes telling me its
all true   thats the message he must get to me

        this is all true

oh LA a tangle of trees and houses
why be here or anywhere. the terrible thing that happens is that the
figure of love, walking too fast for me not looking back we get separated
i dont know where the car is i never do   im   lost in LA
people drive me to a beachfront motel room   a kitchenette and two
grandma crocheted tablecloths hanging up for decoration, terrible twilight
young people hanging out outside and inside a fat one wont let me find my own
phone number so i can get   the message through to love   all night and
a witch, or is she, is there   black rocks and blue twilight beach
and all that ocean what happened to the boat and is the moon there? all
about a car about a car again. a witch is waiting.

i have to get back to him there had been three possible divergences of road
back at the beginning of the episode
we had come to that neighborhood in order to leave it so i could get lost, that's
how the dream story was working, it didnt need everything
it didnt need the event we were there for   it led up to it and away from it
the true present was the future of loss it's   never very important what we   do
in that social sense

on and on thus the need for the white moon a stillness a monolithic   order

that i am.   if you sail or fly too close too close to what you are
will no longer move at all   i sent out my voice no words just sounds Ah! Ah!
when i fell to the floor   when you fall down or otherwise
nothings going to happen nothing of interest just the painful or uselessly sensed
that sen that, remember
                              how you can fall asleep for about half a minute and its an
endless   chasm of time i did that repeatedly yesterday at around four fifteen   in
the afternoon i thought the clock had stopped would sleep and wake up it hadnt
moved finally it moved a minute.
                              if you dont walk or some thing theres none same
stuff same stuff thats time thats why theres none, war and holocaust same stuff or
deliverance of self to the time of day there is none there is transformation of bodies
called aging but isnt that transformation and if thats it the evolutionary answer is a

male sort of answer a convenience for the boss of the. thee   an antlers kind of
answer though   the big useless antlers are a stickler
made a little mistake in the socalled   paleolithic there   in the far times
when animals were so artistic in their presentation of their furred   and baroquely
horned souls their voices of keep going there is none keep going there is none
the animals deny our time sense deny our time with their short   lives
with their large   clockless   moment   of beauty

back in the covered market amid the display its fish today   theres the kid with a
john   theyve told a little lie about the size of the flying fish   the flying fish
are small small things   silver with winglike ridged fins but short   i gently
remark on the lie   and the kid says looking ashamed, 'I   just dont know what
the imagination is.'   shapes our dimensions   shapes our obeisances
all of our notions of value How much for a flying fish today in the covered   twenty two
hundred and fifty   that number just popped out   of my
imagination.

    the witches on tv say a spell those words will prevail over those others the
words love gentleness and faith prevail over the words stab her   why should
there have to be a spell i keep resisting this dimension of just another fucking die-
mention   of the poem the pompous the poem. we are in a car crossing to

other side of the bay the saintly poor side once again the kid is there another kid gets in his father has just been slagged in a journal he wears his hair over his face i cant remember his name he says its ille that one, we pass a truck off the road in grass a chinese man the kid the original kid says he teaches his classes tonguetwisting rhymes involving the names of people who died martyrous deaths as it turns out as it turns out this man in the truck his son did he was the martyred fred wong, cross over into the sainted city i will be very very quiet i am waiting with those two kids for whatever they and theres a bit of sunlight there to lie in lying on the sidewalk i slide over and place my face in the light the light and warmth there is just big enough for my face. im saying a spell for poverty its blanket and a square of light.

i dreamed of the kid and the john while they were together in real life, in another time zone. i found this out today.

near the sea again all night because   i must sail too close to the moon again soon though im frightened i dont know what the imagination is except perhaps the origin of the real the who the hole of images and the ground.   out over the sea are little cafes   built on the old wooden uprights built on the piers.   you can buy any fried fish that you want or a sausage   a sausage sandwich some fries a cup of coffee. there is much   social happenstance on the side roads   but i keep longing to eat frittura or a sausage over the sea

fright frightened all week the moon the screen very white i am stiff i am frozen at this time in a suppression of terror and moon. but it wont come back out and get me and make it happen its there underneath the surface mind see i'm it is e me and i'm flying however lamely on the h on the horse without legs up over over the sea and up to the moon of this is true. as im talking to you.   i down by the sea i say to the proprietor of the fish and sausage cafe that   i was recently kept from drinking coffee there, he doesnt seem to mind.   that means thats about how i didnt really

go out to sea   i ah had a lot to do involving the young
                        but he means by not caring that im already there. the sausage and i keep being there in a fear that   i'll leave others if i do what im already doing its probably a sausage of horsemeat   from the horsemeat butcher in the covered its all taking place in the covered in the covered covered sea below the covered

covered moon i am sailing   seventeen times as high. glad i finally fell down on
the floor   frightened enough to fly.   the   original   technique for ecstasy

h has become fear we are sailing   this is what now this is it and has always been
has been going on for non-years

for a long time i didnt want to but i have to.

i keep a kid from doing something only social that doesnt make sense he couldnt
know what he wanted because everyone told him what it was, what he wanted. why
should he want anything choose anything i just take him in. take them in. no one
has to choose anything. choosing to be good is taking too long he says and hes right
nothing should take long at all. his father is a misshapen sound engineer what can he
hear the voices i presume

                    i presume you are talking to my friends. the souls of horses
and others. we are sailing, anyone can do this.

COR COR

if youre falling asleep almost asleep and you almost dream and you   see
suddenly a dreamed picture,   then pull back from it,   of a wooden ruler
laid against an envelope with flap open   and projecting upward so that the
rulers at the base of the flap   horizontal to the lower edge   of the envelope
and there are colors nearby   though i cant remember what theyre part of
saturated red and black,   how did you do that?   what does it mean?

Still   struggling for order perhaps

i am the teacher a lady reason tall in a blue dress
and high heeled strong knowing shoes   i am also watching this woman
the students have a doll   a male doll with its own semen   which it injects
into a female doll and they   are only interested in that, she must put up with
that, teaching   Walk walking home in the crowded streets a yellow sky   a
yellow sky covers this earthly city i try to get home   from my dreams to my
dreamers bed   most of what ive done   where ive been
is hidden. i cant remember the crystal

the language of nature
it has sometimes been thought   that theres a language of nature,
that all animals speak and maybe plants and rocks do i
speak it is it the liquid the liquid lang
it sounds like sounds li what i say sah chiiiirrrp   and   voice vo   says that.
arose in a bo boat and went to take you in a blu dress you can take your semen too if you
know how. all of this world coming out of the mouth   there are these you
can call them words or sounds but theyre neither one nor or the other or thoughts or

thou theyre not even thou too one theyre not even one theyre not eve thing. going to

on the not even wind of the horse or the boat, which are the same
the moons in your eye and throat so you can be there
tingling all up my legs now legs theyre just nothing   in front of a machine. dont
have to but do keep do keep this natural speak ing   is it a time   bird of
leg and sexual part just there li delicacy you can talk you can talk the dead through
your mouth if want to. or a dream   of an envelope and a ruler   how is
that   you

maybe there will be some order now. measure, order
at the border of the envelope, container of images?

so i float back to the classroom again   its always potentially satanic it
seems   even if lady reason is teaching there
or is satanic satanic
i always float near the window
the focus of interest this time is a gradually emerging wolfish
face in the air of the room. everyones waiting then its there the
face is young a young animal face imbued with the very air and the airs own
delicacy particlelike   perhaps boyish   sweetly made
the hair is soft and delineated   this animals so beautiful, because
the body is in the soul which is the air the untainted air of a third-story classroom.
something satanic is always there

i am climbing higher than the classroom
i am climbing climbing a dirt path i must use my hands too to pull myself up
in the soft dirt of this path   ive encountered the figure of Bliss
in order to reach lifes enclave a high   high mountain city a bus is here there is
public transport   up and down the dirt path Love and i are
staying with Life   there   in the high mountain city

but we have to go   back down, go back down to a party   what can i wear
will the dark blue velvet   shirt   do   again? its like the old house Her house
is like the house i once lived in   a long time ago, of particle waves
          The body is in the soul?

     You are my soul   and you are my soul   but i am
     my very soul
               we enter each others souls, with our voices
     and dont hurt each other   we   enter and leave   enter and leave
     we   talk to each other

     dont need our legs our arms and legs for that   we are like babies
     like old babies.

there are three paths up and none of them work. thats today. Ive missed one turnoff
and also the steep one   are three paths up   and also theres one thats
blocked off to the right, so   there are these roads up   amid desert shrubs
and none of them work   How can a road not work   It just doesnt take
doesnt go

                        i am always trying to find you but you are there   so
stop trying. it was a message from an asterisk, didnt even mean.   are shiny
people earnest   even ironic refuse to sing but are interested in being the
coupling dolls

                        and how to organize the coupling in new ways called new society,
without having children too to couple so what do they know? i will have to teach
them without letting them know   im doing that thats down here
where one has to be

lady reason but   often in the guise of hilarity. its all figures and roles. this is now
and the recent past and future   where is my own quote order?   they want a
sedative it seems   they want a sedative and a drink   it is making them very
excited   to think of being sedated   young and blonde in their cutoffs
running all over the lawn. the sort of young   to be sedated enough so that sex
can be all.

up in the soft dirt d town the crystal dirt ville   among the speaking waves which
are sometimes not waves   are we   our voice voices and we and we
i have ever found without particularly knowing a particle   because
identification and description   rob us   and demonize us do though we mus
be part demon that how the language turn from halfway there into   the very you
follo   we being it then hafta be we im dizzy dizzy again   right   now
when i write like this   right   now   when im really   inside it right
now   you are a glittery   beak   or fur wolf face   lovely
little demon red sl salamand   or a skink   just a voice   up   talk to any
flower   talk   talks back they talk back   the ruler supposed to keep me from
getting diz zy

a voice says the words cor cor heart heart of the core.

i open this book ive never read says that in yoga and in certain
primitive initiatory rites
a new body is formed   often figured as a baby and a rebirth is said to be
accomplished I still cant remember why i began in a rebirth
began this poem in a rebirth as my child self living through my life again
changing it backwards
i just knew i should
                              Tony was there last night
as a small child and i was as small   i taught him how
to place an embroidery hoop on his head and so
crown himself. He is now crowned a crown or a halo the wooden hoop
was actually within its   hoopshaped metallic case.
in a house i didnt recognize   his mother too was there Marcellina who is now
dead too i had just dreamed of the letter M again   are you two talking to me
in some way, in some way?   did i change both of our pasts Tony you
you are now crowned

four children and one who died the story of four children one who died
everyone knows this story   im not sure which story of that this is   theirs or

theirs or theirs   Hes opening the refrigerator a dead man my love, hes embodying
another poets story of four children one girl who died but   its   his   story
its almost my story, too
A blind old man with white hair and cane being led through our old apartment why
why and who? He must be one of several i know   all our stories are merging
though   we arent   we arent the same people   but know the same stories
cor cor core of core
old man whose eyes dont and whose legs
                                        there are the hookers on parade there in their
white minis
same old stories. Do i know you i do now
she was a mess thin and with tracks all ove stumbling dizzy in front of the church
no she wasnt a hooker or a mess a junky she   i was a hooker and a mess i
you aer you wer the same   Sings me to sleep in my dreams   better than a
poet who only   better than a poet who only tinkers with some letters like M
she is M the hooker M   says knows how to say Not Mine and so Mine
your Mind is Mine   but not you youre not Mine but your Mind is Mine. sings
that to me   and the song, cor cor core of core.

two men dead but only ones dead but two are dead i encounter a dead one who tells
me about his dead brother but awake hes dead and his brother isnt two men dead
but only ones dead. hes standing in front of a machine a robot machine a large robot man
a thing which makes him be dead or alive in our eyes? the machine the machine, the
machine that takes into the future dreams which emerge from the hole and bore into
our corcor like bugs? it must be our machine we must own it as we own. i neve knew
wha that machine wa or is it or is it he shows me he not the robot a poem by his dead
brother marvels at it nearby is a poor deceiver i know at a table of conning magazines
why is he there, because everyones like that a con, we're in a startingover house, me
and love but there are too many bugs here these are roaches hatching while i bathe,
with their long reaching out legs. i dont know if i believe what im reading that
                                                                              spirit the
reality permeates this profane natural world but we can only know it in isolation and
will never with each other, no i dont believe that thats not what this poems about i
dont believe in any of the worlds great religions including science as stated for one
thing they are sexist and for another are partial and overly developed in their own
long directions into the images the images they have each generated too many images,
and the cor cor and the cor cor is right there losing its images and doesnt need a
religion or a science or an isolation not if everyone gets to know. no no more
definition have some experience, poetrys like that now so overly defined that you feel
that you dont have to read it but this poem by the dead brother whos not dead is good
because it communicates from death like a voice like our voices like our cor voi

at the edge of the gully and down in the gully are buildings   it is all one
childrens center the toilets in that one dont work right because
theyre newfangled and contain no replaceable parts   so the whole things broken
when its broken. what does that mean. means
you cant have any old parts   you have to accept the new entirely so when it
breaks down theres shit everywhere. theres shit everywhere.

back there at the other   part of the childrens center a man is a young
a man is a young child again ive healed him backwards too
and theres a girl baby climbing a pole up and up   her mothers outside
but im lifting her up and holding her   she used to be an old woman.

at the edge of the gully and down in the desert gully theres a sort of a city
that seems to be for children and me   and some others   im a sort of a child
and this baby i know   used to be   an old woman

you cant leave this city to go find your old best   friend but your old friend is here

you cant go through the back door and through   the garden in order to
find her. everythings in the desert here there is no garden   there is no human
made gar den   though there are humanfaced or is it voiced
wolves   or is it coyotes speaking   to you like your old best friend in the
language, is it the language   of nature (is it that) Someone in the gully told me
my   poem some poem was no good an i tol her if that was the case i wouldn
have let it take up six   pages   in the selected extrusions from the envelop
the envelop where in the desert blank in the hole near black and red will never explai except
goin on with   is it it isnt in the what   ba ba   or is t is it the lang
that   there the   order is in for no reason
i am order and reason a new   body   a   body

PART II

A LENS FOR NOT SEEING IMAGES

oh, late, at one of the many   corners on the prime avenue   who
will go home with you in pizza stand night?   too many people are out late
and on an avenue further east   an elementary schools letting out at eleven pm
my own little girls going home   with a woman whose name begins with M

Then heres an adolescent male   a murderer, with red hair, in a
building on a sidestreet   My own room here belongs to the girl he has murdered
while hes talking to my neighbor in the hallway, whose name starts with an M
I quickly let myself in and out   of my and the murdered girl's room,   so he

wont know that I have her key, that her key is my key
who is the Murdered girl Me?   past Me that I carry?
or a me   once forbidden   that I've become the soul that I become?

once more i am in it the hole of images,   it itself is an image a house.
but i know its the hole awake later   in the dream i act accordingly without
knowing precisely   that its where images come from,   not just an
illusory   house to be described,   a house with lacy curtains   vase
of flowers, bookshelves   there is a woman here whose sister was murdered
at some time in the past   blurred photos of the victim are shown to me   but
she, the live one, keeps her baby locked up   locked in a cubicle in the basement
in the depths of the true hole of images   Because i will myself down into

the basement   i wilfully crash through the floor   to stand here, which is
here, this poem and here, not a house not an image   the infant girl, who grows
lankier   has a slight moustache: thats one reason why her mother keeps her
hidden   her mother is me   or the murdered sisters me   or the
infant girl is me or all three, all three   now bring the infant girl up   the girl
tells me that she wants   to come up.   (i was so gleeful when i crashed
through that i laughed.)   the womans husband tells me   that he asked me here
to free this baby   i have

recounted images but also what happened. which is
that i came to be now

the transparency of the city is in one respect a lens. for not seeing images.   not just
seeing them   not just saying the outlines between them   not just connecting
them by story   whether   theyre in the dreamed or waking world
do i have to wear my underpants again   because its different now Momma
different,   just   is.   no one knows where our world is. look
through the images, its nowhere

                    we walk down into the maw of dirt under the blaze, sun or star

                    your new body is a   your new body is   not a form you can
                    describe

                    you call me to a place, it isnt what   you see

yes I really believe   that   all life is a telepathic field, how else would you
know   anything?
                              I said,   and that our unconsciousnesses are
interconnected, creating the world as we want it   transcending it too
by being so constituted   by being everything, mind   open to images,

ultimately bringing, as it were, demonic red   to the crystalline   the souls
individual taint, still dont know why

                              I had a dream last night that happened too fast   its
middle part happened too fast   for me to remember it   faster than my
own thought   It was about a man and how he was funny   and he too
was amused   but why this was so   was so speeded up I couldnt catch it. it
wasnt important   but perhaps it was red

                                        the road is lined with young men
on their way to the crystal city   they are being counted one by one
they are an each   each is an i   each is all i, soul

some of them are sleeping on steel railings   alongside trees   in this very room
the fact is they are waiting to be counted

im here in the same place i was, being here is different. their tops intermingle tall yew
trees, two
                            under the moon at night and a yellow bright owl is roosting in one of
these trees which are glossy gray and named after a goddess   whose name ends
with the syllable -is. the red berries have been thought of though they arent here. this
is what its like today, and the cabin between the two trees is very neatly made with a
cabalistic design of small rectangles cut into the wood for its windows. a lot of people i
know are down in the town.   a bright yellow light is in my
head, i am sending out a voice   and you are sending one back

                            down in the town lie down. there is a place where people
line up in order to try out a special action, any one they think to, in this exact spot
behind the shrunken shack bookstore i am just lying down i am not being used
neither leg im lying down though two women are in line behind me for this special
place i'll have to get up soon. when i do one says i should take the scarf with me what
scarf it is a dark dusty blue from while i was lying down wasnt being used by peoples
legs for they are everyones my legs the way a body by its similarity belongs to every
person in this world, there are other colors in the mind dusty dark dusty blue. here
like legs is the head of alice long, who is a young man a long baby on the way to the
crystal city stamped on a coin just like legs everyones legs but this world im in is not
that one of a coin minted rather it is glossy very glossy and things float because we
havent agreed i havent agreed with you as to where we are the gray is almost like
being in an owl i mean that light of not being nature but being mind as the bird is
quickest mind these yews are different they dont look like they do in this wildlife book
how are they in the room anyway   if not by telepathy and floatingness?

the eighteenth century ladies and lords   dance back and forth on the métro
platform at poissonnières, telling me thus that time goes backwards and forwards like
a wave, the very last time they dance backwards and then disappear   they leave a
little girl   dressed like them   we know who she is we just know

       we know who she is   i am am constant in her and

she is no image at all. though dressed in image and small   in the same stiff

139

purple silks as the ladies and lords   purple trimmed with yellow

the scent of these trees which arent here is most overwhelming, summer in the heat
gray the gray métro of back and forth the glass gloss of heat there. i ride you to the
mind and back to the mind

                          this is scary
                                        from the souls nervous system which is
mine she is scare tonight shows houses laid out like in a past theres a violent
atmosphere there are corpses, but there *are*, arent there and someone who is *with* us,
but he *is*   a young man who will kill oh anyone and then write on their body in
red paint the spanish word CUTANEO   my soul nervous system is telling me
through these other means not cutaneo. down the street is another   creepier older
house that my mother who is old and young is curious about theres a small box
attached to the front of the house an image it the smaller image is like a mailbox has a
little pyramidal object in it which my mother who is both old and young fingers
curiously if these are images why dont i know what they are soul the soul is showing
me something which isnt like the thoughts and things weve invented oh so clearcut
its a a small pyramid which means nothing and is not an image its a its a. soul shows
me things dispassionately. a voice from the house warns my mother away or she too
will be killed and the word cutaneo written on her she isnt afraid though im afraid for
her, Oh I get it! she says, it's Freezer Johnson. Yes! says the house   (maybe
its a frost bitten fingertip   the part of Johnson that was cutaneo has
become an object of worship a frozen obj

nothing of him, robert   he took It to the crystal city as red. this is not an image it
is sort of the liquid lang i am trying to get to you who are not cutaneo which is your
image rather i swim in and towards you whoever you are

we're left with it variously called mind or reason/love or the real or   beautiful
hole which can fill with floating images.   The my soul the my nervous system
produces the dream full of images because theyre like what weve made awake.
i am the I am the soul   I was thinking to myself, you, without interference. I was
thinking that dream to you or you were thinking it to me we   are not so
indivisible. Im talking to myself and to you, and in this form to all you. You were

younger but not so much younger wearing purple and younger hair   lying in a
bed and fearful because the windows exposed you to the sidewalk street, you were in a
basement raised up to up to almost sidewalk level. and you were fearful that a man
would stop and shake his finger at you in a sexual rhythm a man you knew to be an
exhibitionist and brutal. you and the figure of love had just been talking about an
article, written by male art critics, about women in the art world in the 1970s in art
criticism a certain period has been called The Death and the subsequent one The
Burial—then he went upstairs and you were alone in purple in bed afraid presumably
of being only cutaneo though I am the soul but you cant seem to know me enough
that is to believe that i am what i obviously am and the world is full of exhibitionists
telling you you are what a man says has been saying since the enlightenment one is
cutaneo therefore i dont exist but oh i do thats why another person stands against a
lilac tree as if part of it holding out to me masses of lilacs, just a little later, because i
am.

holding out to me masses of lilacs from amid   lilacs   what does purple
mean   its red and blue together

The soul nervous system is well attested to since   no scientist will touch
the problem of dreams.

i see myself at a desk *the* desk with the crystal puzzle a rectangle almost completed
the jagged crystal pieces have been made into a smooth crystal unity, except for the
lower righthand corner as yet undone   then some moment later after an
unimportant lapse a cartoon baby a wrong one, with a screwed up head, says 'You
don't want a hole! You want a thing!'

i have come to this festival of artistic events today on my board on rollers im sliding on
my stomach. ive already read my poems part of the afternoons unprestigious roster so
presumably i read like this, on my board on rollers, am i the soul i do as i please. im
urged to attend the staging of a current fairy tale, said to be very good and i roll in but
dont stay i dont want to a mans making a speech again like one did last night in another
place where it was supposed to be a streetcar named desire but it was speeches speeches
by a man, last night. todays fairy tale is a man speech against backdrop of some pines and
mountains the woman who urged me to take it in hates me for leaving wont give me any

credit for not walking for being on a board for doing what i want for being being the soul that is she should simply let me go without a word because i know, know what im doing. the more famous rosters coming up though im not going a lot of guys are studying that list and also some music ahead a dead mans scheduled to sing hes not dead i guess no hes dead because hes a skinhead hes lost his big head of hair thats what that means in this context i figure out later awake but in the dream hes alive he is roy orbison a skinhead actually king the son of the beautiful sun or moon and will sing one of his beautiful diva hits here why arent you dead. because no one is

TWO PULSE POINTS

her name is M, a voice said

                    white fish had a long spinal chord   but that
wasnt it was only an image   of the one i am using, the souls spinal chord. I
finally knew it You are finally   paying us a real   visit, said my relations my
familiars   but I think they stood for everyone   everyone there is,
in their basement   We were speaking   in their basement, bicycles rags

Oh im not there and Im not here Im not inside it its a bad flat day   Yes you are

Lying there that i would open   to all other one or ones, that i was past this
illusory storied detail. that keeps us from each other   open to the world im
talking about, that you might not see but i do. these bushes near home are
thousands of years old   theyve become more beautiful   down here
down in this gully or basement or place. down in the valley other low place i am
open to them and   they dont look, look like   In my mind are creosote
bush souls

        any
        have made it
        into the basement of all
    relation. steps

        final corner   me or
    any johns son
        come over
        to relax into the grand
    musculature nerves of sea or dirt

I cant concentrate You dont concentrate Dont have to concentrate here

this is a fishing village near the big biggest ocean, it is named after someones son or
after a large amount of something worthless, thats only its name i am just walking
around here eating, eating fileted fish this is the world but then theres the ocean out

there. then im walking in the urban part of world its a crowded street its a green gray
sky a dark sky we've made with pollution or is it just a sky in a room in a room of a
head, in a room of my head. I'm walking with short hair with a band in it a headband
on to keep thought down im walking with someone else and behind me a round
whitish-yellow brilliant light not so large perhaps the size of a fist is following me
specifically. so i guess i dont have to follow it   so closely, thinking about it
it thinks about me its me it some mind part of my mind
it thinks about me it dreams   in me   is it in me

      Now these are the skeleton charms or pendants
      hung together on a chain. it is said that theyre very effective
      because theyve been touched to an actual coffin

              though i cant remember
what theyre for,
      what do you think? i dont know if theyre for anything that i care
about though they look great   nothing ever had to be the way it is except for,
you know, consciousness my mind. or maybe theyre soul skeletons
theyre soul skeletons

There are no demons   thatve become monsters
except are made by all of us   though one says thats what
someone did with his life became a monster made war or just plain
killing, tyranny, ran people ran us around   thats his life thats what hes still doing
as the story is dissolving images he died   in 1253 BC or AD and we talk to him
up here   and talk about him down there   in our history   Down there
hes a monster up here in this air hes just a peep another peep   We are all
talking now. instead of anything else to know and be

      instructions to the insurance company half a page long   see that
the grave is kept clean, of. not the grave of light   because we're down below in it
(up above in it)   the only place left to go where theres space. grave for all the
soul skeletons

the light trailing me is keeping me informed   in formed second body its me
we made the grave there the grave of species down there (right here) is the grave of

144

species   up here or down, in our grave, are we light and all the species here
talk mind nothing disappears in the grave but youll never know that never know it
consciously you may be unconscious though still peeping to us for all of your death
peep peep people unconscious you

        yes that one you used to hate
        you have to talk to *her* here. shes talking mind
shes over there Is this true, in the sense of owning up
in the sense of owning up the victimless state you lost we all lost we dont even know
when it was that we once didnt lose in the life part and the life part didnt
have to separate from the death part from the cave or grave of light   part
What makes it go We're all part of what an imageless encounter   in these pines
in this pines of tony and bobby robert also myself in our
children of the second bodies   this is the crystal piney second world the city
and we are talking though not exactly but i am with you and not afraid of any or to die

for example theres a serial killer over there peeping has to be here because
theres nowhere else it doesnt matter now at this moment at which down there he
may be serially killing because he isnt anyone in this death or life we cant define any
more what we hate and love what we do he cant do anything though   there
he may kill me or you   still in the false sense of now without a crystal
he has never had any   power nor have you there is no moment to refer it to it was

all your or our idea it was just an idea this structure of a world its just an idea walk out
of walk out of this idea. he will kill me Walk out You are a crystal and he is too and
now we are all here he is a peep he cant remember that hes here and you are a
beautiful crys a voice a container of the embryonic universe which is small compared
to this or you Maybe he'll remember that hes here some time

theres nowhere else it doesnt matter now at this moment at which he supposedly
he is killing a country   we have all given him his power in that world dont
give it any more with my mind. it doesnt matter what you do you dont have any
power over me   you dont have power over me.

        the blue light was my blues
        the red light was my mind
the blue light was my reason the red light was my everyones light is a red

145

light   everyones reason is the same blue   in the sea of crystal
where blues forgets to be blues is only blue where red all that red is only red.

two dimensional white bird Then   a black one. Someone is a killer
in traffic   im in a car with another whos driving in traffic The killer   is a large
man   white membranes over his eyes   like an ostrich's nictitating membrane
why not? an ostrich is like us why not Whitish membranes   Hes killing people in
traffic   He kills them in their cars, their small community cars   I shout
that hes a killer and then my driver   tries to kill him, runs over him in traffic but
then I say, "He doesn't die!"   The man attaches himself   to the back of our
car   splayed out around it: "I dont die!" he says

Later trying to help someone
a very large man in a coat. Perhaps the
same man, the same killer
he needs to be helped Hes a killer He needs to b be helped He isnt
conscious standing there in his coat isnt conscious of crystal

we are all red the color of our soul of our mind blue   is for reason which is blind
the blues reasons the way the way we just do   A mesh slide triangle   allows
any johns son to slide back and forth between the two worlds as in a guitar playing
playing. So it was you I dont care about the blues   as   form. form form
hole of images I am sitting down here looking through a lens a membrane blind I
guess I must be a killer, and   I dont die. What does that what does that mean?
Oh, mean   I have touched my soul spinal chord and my soul nervous system
to a coffin I am a killer killing my idea of myself   your idea of yourself
killing killing the dead world I am a Killing the illusion of our justice I am killer.

          i didnt care which one i was you or me though i was me
her name is M because shes me   her name is M for metrics
her name is M for the same kind of metrics as any johns son might also use
as complicating to linearity as true time is   as complicating as being bad
because you cant stand the prevailing   M for metrics ma ma M for
the red light was   i am the Ma of my baby in my left
breast and she cries out to me Ma Ma

when you change you change. now i dont remember who i was
i touched my spinal chord   to a real coffin

in a context of being moved   emotionally this man always   chooses the man,
Oh my father! he says   He continues to be the son any old son Why are you saying
Why am I I told him he was a sexist, in an office where a so woman sat behind a desk
but there shouldnt be such a   bureaucratic place in the desert in the car on the
way to las vegas my breasts are a couple, that is, a man and a woman   not just
a woman not just the ma voice or M voice   not just

"You need two pulse points now."   not for the two   breasts but for the two
the two what?   maybe they dont stand for maybe they are the two   the two
Im working on it   the two and one is the soul   the two I and I am not
separated
              in a closetlike room off the big room
              im puttering with the

machinery   But I think there have been two pulse points   all   along
Cant you can you hear   them
metrics and metrics metrics two Who cares what it says   now
because Im different who cares what it says   now but now having come here
not before But was there before It was contingent upon this moment now
of two pulses One for and one one for and one   the two and one is the soul

i touched my skeleton to a real coffin and now my soul has a blue net of nerves a
white spinal chord and a pulse, its own pulse. it   she, has a red haze
and a yellow-white ability to follow   and help me catch up by showing me my dreams
This is all a story
it doesnt and yet   my soul has its own pulse and i can feel it this morning
inside me
I have nerves a spinal chord and a pulse a second pulse
have always but am conscious now

and in the bone   house   giving them their time
refuse to recognize me in the new   a hes been asked not to know me though
im wearing my soul as a white slip and a she has left the room
without saying goodbye as if she didnt know me
the train had derailed at louis blanc station   but i   didnt derail
time and progress had derailed together but i hadnt
yet im asked not to be recognizable
im asked not to bring my own book along
im asked to read from an anthology of some 'school'
theres a table with candles on it near the derailment people sit mutely there
as if they were running things
thats all down here

And in the bone house I am here here here
your pulse is everywhere the doctor said after my dizziness

the universe is shrinking inside all space it is part of the derailment   a concept
dictionary in the bedroom. near the bookshelf, room shadowy
what kind of words are in it   langel langage
not in alphabetical order   how do you look a word up it isnt a word

DON'T STOP SAYING CRYSTAL CITY

in a small ship at night myself and the pilot. I guess I'm the captain   I see myself
next to the pilot before the dark windows then hear myself say, 'I want to go as far as
possible, because   I'll have to turn back soon   but I want to know as much
as I can since I'll take this trip again Oh, its getting dark.'   Now there are pictures
or windows   as if those basic determinants, sometimes painted and sent

by the soul to try to show me the structure   of our all identity, but

I have to get up I must wake up and   that frays them around their edges. Later
when I'm asleep again   there are up ahead, in this large room   cafeteria trays
with whole fish on them for everyone   they appear to be incomplete fish
incomplete meals frayed around the edges, but   it turns out the fish are whole
the parts are there, all the parts   of the meal. nothings frayed

though each thing existing stretches beyond its borders

this childish swimming pool will do for purposes of purification and presence of sea
though it contains no fish i mean this childhood swimming pool heavily chlorinated
blue stings the eyes i will be purified here because the collegiate pool of later   is
roped off into squares for men, men only   competing with each other,
who shit into the purifying waters ruining them.   this small   childhood

swimming pool will do   because im ageless   and later older but not my
age now i tell john i only need   small change, ones and fives   to pursue my
acting career. my other friend   the other john tells him   because the
first john'll give it to me, 'Youre   a sucker!' then   at the border, just a room
the borders just a darkened   room like a stage   with a car a state trooper and a

bad smell in it   but its the mexican border   some action at the border   a sewer
smell

        I only need small change
        to pursue my acting career

theres a strong smell of sewage
at the mexican border where

i only need small change
dark room highway patrol
i have my change but can i cross
the border with its bad smell

Everythings going on in that same dark room it isnt a room its a space, is it a
space it doesnt have a floor or a ceiling its lit like a theater but isnt there, it isnt there Is
that where my acting career is taking place?   the hole of images nothings there.
'you must act soon'

they were a group of people, next,   religious aspirants of some sort   led
by a woman whose name means beginning   they had lost faith in the person
they   had aspired towards before   had lost their faith and were trying
to place it in me How stupid   there isnt a person involved, there is nothing
to aspire towards   does one stay a person forever I would say no o shape of the
soul an amorphous embryonic image doesnt have to be a thing a thing at all
except in this void of a theater
                                        was all night again in
that theater
that space   but I cant remember what happens   and later

stare at the floor thinking   im not really here where theres a floor
(theres no floor in that space)   thinking
it takes two people to create time. one person   isnt in time by herself
(there isnt any person   or thing to aspire towards)
but no one   is outside of time   alone   no ones alone in crystal

stare at the floor think im not really here staring at the tiles lit warmly in the
afternoon rosy brown with lines   The soul nervous system amorphous am I
who knows the shape of who knows the shape of the world?

Then all night and for several nights   in that space that theater but i cant remember
cant remember events the   border or the hole is still going on
cant remember cant remember at all

takes two people to make time   two people being same time
takes two people to make space,   does it
but it only takes two pulse points to make me. does it does it
thats my own definition
thats just me thats poetry,   not a tyranny of imposition

there are two there are

             everyone boy stands in front of a church door of
             course
     maybe in Rheims   pulse   points
I have two   choose your own   pulse   points
you dont have to be like every other soul   you dont have to be like
pulse points dont have to be like the universe   young   men   stand
in   hall or hold of images Sing
             Im going to find this leadership that leads through
             Im going to find this leadership

        Its only your own
            That leads through
        you dont have to be like you dont have to be like the
     universe Its our creation as we understand it Dont have to
    be like that The second pulse point is telling me
        that   Say   That
        Oh
        Im going to find a leadership of   white insectlike
        legs
        small sticks of a, possibly of a soul   my   soul
Thats your own image though   Yes its mine

Her name is a pretty bird
I find a dollar shore   That was the kind of thing an old pulse said
    to the young men

My mother is holy Jerome
Washington DC proved my legs

Young men say that but they have no legs
Thats your image though Yes

You dont have to be like the universe its our creation
Im walking all the way uphill pushing a cart an empty cart towards a door.

church of rice. small rice. the smallest grains you can swallow. or the church of one
everything. what do your think? standing at the crossroads I mean the border there is
no universe nothing is here nothing at all   I dont have to be the supposed fact that
Im alive like you   I am in the crystal and thats all the one everything that isnt
a church.

These arent   the bodies
This isnt the signature 'He made me' or
'It made me' (evolution say)
There is no signature

There is proof we are we   there is no proof we are here

Yet   isnt the crossroads a here and now isnt the smell at the border? I
seem to be ordering the largest   coffin Ive ever seen it must be for everything.
Soon Love and I   are standing by the highway at night   across from the
crystal city as dirt, across from a clifflike formation   a rearing back frozen dirt wave
unscrolling from the top but dirt just dirt   here in this desert   Love

says At least thats still here. he catches a red kite   which belongs to a man
running along on the highway   catches a red kite blowing out into the desert at night

        And someone had said a male friend had said to me If you make the
coffin yours   it wont have to be anothers How can I do that?   the soul
keeps running away from me, in my dreams, so I dont know   what anything
means   oh means   It is a huge black coffin a big black square or
monolith a big black block

                                the coffin of the dying planet which is the

152

same as a specific person anyone you love anyone you love is the dying planet
the sewage at the border   There is no sewage and dirt is clean
the sewage at the border the smell of this world as we've ruined it So
crossing the border is to take that smell with you   with me   oh means
I have to get into the coffin too
I was always in it   In it   out of it   two

the cafe proprietor downstairs screamed out twice last night long cursing drunken
sentences   he is brutal and hateful   he is here ever here, unconscious and
doesnt know   His long sentences I couldnt understand   coursed through my
dreams all night he was who was here here or there In what place or moment of time
None of course   he was there and I and others   were possibly in line for

some food   in one of those void rooms then outside   outside the void or
hole of images there was a seaside setting   with a beautiful young frenchlooking
girl   a brunette with short hair and bangs, one of the usual french haircuts
who used steel crutches because she was crippled   because she was the soul, my
soul   we sat and visited awhile   dunes small plants a gray sky

she had
sticklike legs

I wonder if I can stop saying
Crystal City now   Probably not until all of its pieces are in place
then you can stop   stop saying an image name

                                        I was at some point in some
sequence some piece   looking down at a man
whose face was like a brain   lobey and wrinkled   I felt repugnance
the brain isnt anyone or anything This
part of a complex of happenstance
                                        taking place in a porched in house
around the corner from another house   both dark in a place that was both a city
and a small
            town. the house is very close to a former clinic and also a desert hill

Cease to call it Crystal City but then what will you call it
Various things happen in the house around the corner, then I enter the second house

around the corner from the first house and I am told Jackson is dead well he is
obviously the same as Johnson   so I am taking place in his ceremony all the time
some people think all living is   a taking part in such a ceremony
I dont I dont think   in that way any more   of honoring something or
other   some john or jacks son has said I must honor   honor honor
This is   the only stop on my trip.   I mean living has only one stop on my
trip   mean, mean   Ill come here any time   to this dream in the
middle of the night but I am at one stop   Ill come here any time   to
the same old house around the corner from the house around the corner

nothings frayed or blurred. we are at the seaside and things we dont really need
keep falling into the water such as plastic packets of   eight rolls of toilet
paper   except one is missing there are seven rolls how   significant an
aspirant to   religious or gnostic status would say, seven   seven rolls of toilet paper
or whatever   whatever falls into the water either my soul or I

must rescue first   she does and then does again, then finally I do   I dive into
the sea for the   insignificant package and I wonder why Im not naked   one of my
breasts is uncovered   the left one which contains the voice that says Ma
oh isnt that significant   stop saying crystal city Then what would I say I have to

say something what would I say

CRYSTAL AS SNOW

we, the figure of love and I, are shown
an expanse of gleaming white floor
it is impossibly clean and smooth   with nothing whatsoever on it
there are white walls too, but it is the floor we are concentrating on
its so beautiful, a marvel
                            Upstairs my father
another   dead man whos still alive   says he will tell us
exactly how much that floor costs.

have I said that here there is no fame   the concept is forgotten. distinction
except for difference   between entities   is gone, up here or down here
you have no effect on me. there is no effect

                                        your history is broken, scattered

this floor costs a major
overhaul, a
maneuver   as of turning upsidedown,
going antarctic

put it in the place, he says
in the place right there

we are, love and I and another, in the antarctic at the bottom of the world. the third
one of us has flown us   here to this white land   in an airplane a small
dark plane instruments dials steering wheel. he   represents loss but so do we as
anyone might the figures of loss but the concept of loss is gone
in the crystal stop saying that city, no one is lost there   I mean here, down here

or up here depending on your orientation. he says we have all three together
discovered the auk, which seems to lie dead   on the floor of the cabin its downy
wings spread out.   perhaps its the extinct great auk
but nothing is extinct   down here, up here where   it is so purely white.

155

now elsewhere in time and place I am wearing no blouse
in this party in dark rooms   with red and blue lights its
important to be that naked in front of these–
but this is later, and not antarctic exactly–these   fame seeking poets.
this is later in the sequence of the night but
earlier in my life
do I have a voice in my left breast

there must be snow outside all over the ground because its iowa

and because the soul has been painting white frames all white pictures for days

everything that ever   comes from disappears to   this white, this white which
represents crystal so unrepresentable   it seems to be
benignly consuming my life

then I dont stay with base white the world we live and dream in is   unstable I
want crystal but   the dream frames are out of my control   though   I am my
soul   and I make them
                              when I sleep I am open to all that can change and
she/I changes   the story as is necessary   so that I so that I   can know
know what Im knowing asleep, know what messages what thoughts Im
receiving From where Oh you know, the crystal set

                              on the west end of hometown on the river road so
overgrown it is vines trees glossy green and inviting some of us are walking the sky is
odd with a new purple cloud formation in it a shape almost like a letter though I dont
know which it isnt threatening to me but the others exclaim and point. I first see the
strange boy here walking through the overgrown vegetation for this is really desert
country and has never been like this but he is walking towards the road and he has only
one eye it is slightly veiled with a membrane and where the other should be there is none
just the shadow the suggestion like absence of an eye. later we are in our house and he
enters it innocently looking for elsewhere everyones alarmed but I tell them hes a
classmate of mine then I wonder I wonder how old am I. how old am I

how old in another part as I scratch at the cheeks of the figure of life but her cheeks are
only or also the pages of a book   a book of life written by everyone imposed as
rules and dimensions   she had denied   that I needed relief in her version

Let me tell you how much this floor costs it costs you approval participation in the
book itself it costs you an eye it costs you the fact you cant buy it

> woman in a dress shop
> in front of racks of them
> measuring me for clothes
> with ribbony tape measure, says
>   "not for a bought...
>   for a winged part..."

                                                                how old am I? as
old as the white of the moon and the snow as old, older than the book. still fighting
live phantoms

Veinous a soared floor
Venus a sored floor
Thats simply another song that comes through in the air
a dark little man with large ears   so he can hear such songs? from wherever they
come from,   scrubbing the white floor.   Then Im awake but close my eyes
and see an eye looking at me from within me   I see an eye looking at me inside
me   its surrounded by short blondish locks of female hair.

yet Im still involved in my young and old life in all these other stories why
Im wearing with others in long skirts a long skirt   and an incomplete necklace
black with some beads frayed   it's seven thirty the events at eight Who shall
we honor, says the arts administrator,   shall we honor you?   Its a little late for
tonight I say and anyway, why should it be me?
                                                  As it would be, I think to myself,
a repetition of the same event as has always occurred the ceremony of honor   its
the same occasion from forever, oh whats the point? in other house, man wants to ask
the parents of my friend   if he can marry   my friends sister, How boring!

says my friend   why be the same thing again do the same antiquainted thing
Outside in the night hear cops arriving down there in squad cars in order to make

the same old   arrests as for thousands of years Back at the party   Is it the same
party, where I finally wasnt honored   and where theres a small caged rabbit
its time to leave along with the prettiest woman and her children I'm taking her
home, to the east end of town she wont go   all the way to her home at the border,
shes staying elsewhere   the little boy says Oh how pretty she is!   she's a
honeyblonde wearing pink lipstick and   I know its the lipstick he really likes
I look in the mirror Im the palest   of blondes with no lipstick   Because
she refuses to go home, I must drive her cart all the way to the border myself

it is drawn by a rabbit and other small   animal, take them home.

lets go home to an old apartment where all our dogs still live even the dead one. so
we, I and other one, go home there, and in that bed oh no is a child whos effectively
dead but isnt at all he lies in the dark there covered with sores his eyes are crusty I
wake up from this dream crying. I dont know who he is, is he the auk
                                                                                    I fall back
asleep asking for this dream to be made right. I knock on the door of the apartment
again and many many people are inside I am formally introduced to them all and one I
think is the boy or auk made whole

it was the door to the city but it is a possible place in this lower world a healing
compound a lodge in the woods. the auk isnt dead, isnt ever dead in the crystal
but we could in this lower world heal ourselves of our lack our negative our blindness
that comes with our two eyes   heal his sores by healing us, inside this
building in the woods the remnants of the wild   how   by changing
by   rubbing salve on each of his sores   and feeding him making him whole
whole in death yes but whole. that would heal us to heal him   its snowing

on the pines now   though theres still a dark formation in the sky, a figure or symbol
if you think like that   but its indecipherable,

in the liquel ladl in soun in sound the bab babe a baby
might understand it lodle ga

there is this language you speak but dont understand you dont have to its white its crystal but its white its squiggly and purple its blue and red   it is a condition and contains other textures contains this whole imagined world it is white and it is crystal its thought its glue there is nothing but glue   How does anything happen? 'pattes marchent chez push'   says a voice but where does the push come from come from from us?

                    all of the women here are rushing to catch a train with a ghost on it a dead man whos still alive,

then then   im riding in a van with a dead man

                    whos still alive
                    driven by a john
                    and all the land is covered with snow
                    i think and now hes *driving* or is it *hes* driving
                    we're past all the parts of the landscape, he says
                    that x (another male poet) has covered in his work
                    i dont care says the dead man alive and
                    i think whats the difference its all covered with snow its
                    all blank white then
                    they leave me in my mothers yard without even taking me
                    there   i am left there
                    as if i were a child   how old am I I think
                    here are all the flowers to winter with
                    my mother brings them home in pots in the car
                    they are pansies blue pensées and mums
                    they all says my mother have to be kept inside even the mums

my rage is white too white and crystal   cant you talk to me now that you dont own anything at all now that theres no territory?

i am in the crystal he says and you can finally see me there without my care for personality i am my shaping hulk see its white with patches of ruby on me youre still seeing me stop seeing me then youll get it. i didnt die. its moment here and we talk that and we dont have to talk either because that language isnt a tongue or a set of symbols or anything but communication like with animals who knew it better all along little roaches squirrels and codfish. so we. and so i. His form stretches that is the outline my sense that its there stretches until it isnt until its everywhere I still hear his mind, the thing I did to

you how I died and then stayed alive wounded isnt a thing it is a story and nothing I didnt
do it to you leave you there child in a yard its only a story you lived the vast emotions of
because those emotions not the story into la lodle long cant ever explai. it dont explain
these configurations attached to the emotional wind with its purple signature out of the
white and crys

they are going to hang me, I dream,
for nothing for doing nothing,   me and two others Im not afraid
but I dont want to die I say, I didnt do anything at all. there is the
noose, this   is how it works the lower city, 'the thing i did to you,
the thing you did to me'   this is how it works a grossly imagined
trial come out of white long ago   the great auk is dead because it was stupid   stupid
utilizable and guilty thats how this lower city thinks   I am healing the
boy on my own.

UNREAL FLOWERS/SONGS

a boy dirty and appealing
   house in woods contains
everything including   food counters
     and display racks
   boy wants to buy these socalled

   yogurt sticks which come out of a tube
or is it a can like whipped cream it seems you
     squeeze out
      this white
      which
     becomes
      yogurt
       sticks

oh, one way to get your white   crystal   death   beauty

Sitting with women in long skirts again, discussing awards that we almost win
outside its those woods   shes wearing a blue   shirt, a black skirt. boy who
eats yogurt sticks is around somewhere   not quite the same as the one-eyed
boy or the dead one still alive   hes just the dirty wise boy   I dont have to know
if same or one if theyre the same as   each other or oneself but one of them must be
healed by us and one the   one-eyed one is probably I another figure of soul as is
the third the dirty but   maybe they are all I.
          Ive been so many others lately colors
Ive been wheeled in and out of hospital wards in tents in my dreams only because
someone I love was hospitalized   the figure of love   but we are all
everything together in a field of mind

          I have HIV I said to an impossibly
     young version of a friend who in life had
     died of AIDS   He said to me, in the dream,
     will you die of it? I was being him, then, now
     whereas in life when it happened I was far away
     had been unsympathetic to his other condition of
     painintheass which I was always more mindful of

mindful mindful You cant cross the room and talk to
me without anticipating my mind even if I dont
know you the proper name for this is telepathy not
social conditioning which simply means a
subdivision of telepathy–knowing what others
expect of you is an aspect of mind. is telepathy too

no time except made by   all of us and all of our times. All of my times
are any story   but the emotion but the emotions are anyones constancy.   o he
wants the white yogurt   which comes from deep in the hole   where
loss an overwhelming emotion takes you near the source of loss and all emotion

face it then you   might not have it any more. blue   singer plays here
I get left like in song   if I choose for myself the story which the song only chooses
from possible emotion to go with the chords.   blue reasons it without emotion
precisely, with music precisely instead. red red   is the true instability of our
condition, generalized   the color of insta and why still down here in hole:

          searching for
          the source of instability.

     These are the flowers Ive damaged, no they are works of art   sunflowers
yellow Ive forgotten that color again   I open the door to the high ceilinged room
where the men who are estheticians live   with all these flowers all works the
works owned by everyone, but   since *they* judge them, *they* have them   they
have them in this room, and my sunflowers are here, theyre theirs too

fashioned by an artist

whose name resembles mine.   all my artworks are slightly worn by use
damaged   by the very fact that I use them for art   these flowers have
missing centers now no theyre just blank   blank like the bottom of the
hole   like an eye that isnt there any more   Im happy to see them again
now Im on my way to a hospital   in a wheelchair   carrying art flowers

made by another friend who died of AIDS

turned to art who cares about art, they were already beauty If you died but didnt die
why not be beauty in my city   like the young one the   impossibly young
and beautiful one who asked me if I would die of AIDS   because he didnt he didnt
die though he died but he is beauty thats what the dream says says,
Red

                                        is the instability of what we require of each other down here
to keep the flowers of loss inside all season till they turn to art   I   died of
your illness but dont ever tell. dont ever tell that there is a corpsechild with oozing
sores still alive in

                                my own death room, or that the eye I dont need is becoming
covered over with dirtlike flesh dirty boygirl that I am

                                                                red is our blood but it isnt blood its red
                flower of the sun?

I stepped inside an ancient dungeon where political martyrs had once been kept, of
various persuasions I didnt respect them or the building beautiful   lasting stone
with gothic arches everywhere, lit by discreet spheres. a splinter of the true cross and a
queens napkin   when I left the sky was moving across the sky in purple
formation it was raining and cars nothing was in its original language nobody knows
and everyone speaks and, in fact, nothing was red. a stable artificiality had been
created
                I prefer instability
                                        I have strung small flowers on a flower
abacus, become guitar songs are sung or spoken. you dont have to know the language
to speak it
                in the hole of instability Ive given birth to another baby named jade or art
oh why   endless endless.   the ignorance of humans, a phantom in the
whole of the infinity outside this universe, is a marvel

                                                        "I prefer

pestilence and drugs" says one youth

Bless your heart yourself
Anyone want a cushion
I got blues on my,
Blues on my mind

                          thats robert entering a bleak latenight university

I am robert and Im I mean my soul is making up the song but then my soul whos a he
this time   very like robert pours   two glasses of milk onto the table,
       creating a smooth white surface

bless your heart yourself
anyone want a cushion
i got blues on my
blues on my mind

one of the men who died but didnt die returns once more in a story which is the color
of pale instability   we are still not stable in the crystal almost but not. this is his
new small chapbook   and all of its poems are torn made by tearing out of else,
tearing words away from the given text of the world and finding a poem. he shows it
to me the last two poems are about his relationship with a woman which transpired
after hed died you understand and he is still dead though hes alive This is the poem thats
the second-to-last

                At a pile get a gent's rose
                    thema
                    thema

          do you know how much money
                    can bring?
       it brings you will.

And the last poem, made of pink paper and ragged like an unsymmetrical
                                      paper doll:

All the
             poems
                            are torn
from another
                woman's
                               heart
(they aren't
            torn from yours...
                                or mine
I didn't
         die

(written on torn pink paper

        the color of instability

I say, "none of these words would matter if you'd go away." But I dont mean that I mean if this if these if stories   would go away away disappear and leave the crystal Then the soul as robert returns and tells me more songs:

Blue is unspeakable
blue is unspeakable   a single golden eye
red is unstable
so you can be shy (why) . . .

In the hole begin to grow like a broken baby
in the hole begin to grow like a broken baby
what they call the universe is   a broken baby
it was broken long before it was born . . .

The beautiful one-eyed sun
the blossom of the sun
a broken conception
My mind is not broken, ever . . .

You were bad because you were clever
ruthless and seeded by others

165

I am seeded by myself
any true eye . . .

The universe is hollow   *absolutely*
you put it there
you put it all there
except for our beautiful eyes . . .

in this tent which is almost the covered market thirty years ago in this tent where I am being willed to marry an adams son but I wont in the past now I am not I have married in another way than yours thats all I have married no story it is piece of crystal not cake and Ive never attended the wedding which is a story. stories we thrive on I renounce and also your heart in the pink dusk poem so we can meet I renounce our hearts so we can meet. I renounce wounds

a large expanse of rooms on the top floor of a high building they are schoolrooms as I pass through each the teacher is refusing to teach them the speech or song they will need in order to perform when the time comes. the teacher says I wont tell you until the time comes. this is the postponement of knowledge of being itself throughout life that is practiced in our times this is our sin but I know the song and I tie a string around my finger so I will remember it the lines from Granada about the snow-capped

sierra nevada

SONGU

I descend step step into   crystal canyon of vastness   here people are inside
crystal their souls, the body is in the soul   and sometimes the body the image
shifts and   becomes one great eye form,   amorphous   natural
it isnt clearcut and I accept it

                                           There is the dead man in his crystal or eye Why didnt
he die   and he as if says, 'I love you and can say that, you   cant   forbid
me to   even if you have your own system. your dreams about me arent true,
I seem to have to say it again   theyre stories. arent true. they flicker unstably,
emotional creations, but   your poem is true'

                                                                              theres
red through the crystal a shifting coloration a light or tint Oh its all an image   Im
still trapped in an eye   but when Im   all eye like you that will be
another thing

                           awkward image   opens my mind   to outside the
broken universe the broken   baby

                   are you conscious yet are you in this city consciously yet   or
only still unconsciously,   all of you?

another some mans son, says, "I'm finally going to take you   to Grand Island this
weekend!"   Im excited in the dream but awake I think,   why cant I go
on my own   and arent I   there on my own, we   listened to jazz waiting
for the weekend a beautiful   dark singer with bouffant hair dressed in orange
or red on the covers of her albums   Outside on this smalltown street, a
litup truck drove by   because the highway is everywhere now, everywhere
yet, Singer you are the splendor of the album I   by which we escape the
highway though   the sky is purple again. What is real in the corrupt world then?

the timbre of a voice
the timbre of a mind
                           of   any old johns sons mind   not   much else.
some strange luck is real?   'She calls herself baby john...'   Who?
just a voice in my head which   said something realer than a truck.   The

universe is a broken baby but the crystal city never breaks and we never break, never
break   in the crystal city we arent grotesque No one is grotesque   even a
broken baby a broken baby like this universe   I see lights everywhere dotting the
crystal canyon the grand   It isnt an island Thats how he was wrong
and I didnt go, dont   go to an island

he who died but didnt die meant that I   wont allow him the 'I love you'
because its too much the worlds   Id rather be a bok broken baby   in the red
break   in the red break inside crystal   the red light is my baby and the blue
light is my reasonable   so the trucks go by in front of the house and someone
says that momma   momma'll be okay because of that big old monolithic
air conditioner   on the front lawn, now what does that mean?   it means
that science will take care of the air, honey, with another machine it means   that you

can go on breaking it break the air yourself   remain unconscious in the crystal,
everyone I know   you   islands

songu metapills
someone sings

I believe this is in re our illness and treatment

heres a lot of separate crystals   together with a blue border
there is an implied other plane of crystal from or in which we'll begin treatment now.
take your songu metapills take your crystals

                              on the lawn of the childhood house Im watching
those changes to the house across the street   where the woman with a
romantic name the former name has died. her house is now compressed into a white
boxcarlike prefab   with no windows open though theres the sound of music from
inside, banal rock. I say to my companion,   I remember when she was still alive
and one could go over and see her sitting absolutely still in the silence of the room.
that was in the 70s wasnt it, says my companion, even in the 80s I say, as silence was
song in real air. they are excavating the yard there, next door, I am standing on the

edge of a ditch

I think we need to know the language just a little better, the one everyone speaks
though nobody knows they do. a truck doesnt speak it a plant does How do you know
how to be? They are forever telling you you are a machine set in motion but you are a
broken baby you know   the planet is covered with sores, like a boy dead and not
dead with crusty eyes

        the new disease that strikes down the young
        only the young who have come to this
        town   catch the new virus when
        they eat bacon and eggs
        because we broke the world for them, but
        they do what we do they break it too
        the trouble is that everyone is traditional
        I have never
        known someone who wasnt in some sense
        so I have gathered some young men
        together in an old apartment
        we are trying to cook something else
        at the windowbox which is a stove
        at the windowbox where plants are
        burners but the flames   keep going out
        boiling water spills on the aloes the aloes are broken now
        without them we cant be healed not without aloes

this avantgarde poet is so traditional
               hes stolen my earliest work and wont give it
back says he wont ever give it back to me. But this other one is so traditional that he
has stolen a later work of mine
            and wont give it back either. lovely blue books fragile
oldlooking   handwritten   the original language isnt written though
or even spoken or even
        We approximate it in songu the language of poetry cum
dream the u in songu stands for the goo at the edges of a perceived thing.

outside on this suburban lawn theres something wrong with the birds assembling
here vireo junco kingfisher theres   always something wrong So I will
become a snake for awhile Im trying to assemble my length and I am inside the long
tube of myself but it/I wont quite get assembled   a short part of my length
is composed of a different material   I need something. I always need something

I return to the bookstore to get a paper from the owner with his writing on it it will
solve it No,   writing from a man an owner wont solve it the problem of songu
No   I have cramps and an old   brunette double awaits me at home No
the its in me all along my length unlike a brain its all one oneself   on the other
side of the snakeskin or the other side of its scientific   analysis.   here it is

no old double   insideout I

inside the dream or   insideouting the dreams or the uncon where we   the
dreams lead to where we   lead to dissolution of stories in the crystal they are
dissolving around their edges and into their and on and so as they go away
in songu in some no-language   in some   we are left

          Its this apartment again
          which was never mine
its all rotten wood theres a bed and perhaps some kitchen equipment
all blue rotting wood in the dark a high window opening into an airshaft with ledges
and angles of wood I and the figure of love lying in bed. there on a ledge in the
airshaft a beastly or beautiful man long hair blond long beard and body hair he is nude
hes abject hes possibly a murderer the perpetrator of a grisly murder in the past he is
tall and stands straight as he always did

                                        at the rotting door
is a dark scruffy clochard who thinks he is helping by warning us   about the man
in the airshaft, wants to be invited in because hes warning us behind hims the voice of
a drunk we know that third mans out there in the hall   In this vantage the
crystal appears to be rotten wood and a city of beasts beastly men well it is This is has
always been my real   welcome home everyone   all you who
all you who know songu the monarch of real the lang of rot rot dissolute people and
words aloes know. there are a lot of broken babies in this dark room floating a horror
cloud everyone projects here welcome human horror you never knew anything
though you speak the language aloes know   It isnt a language it isnt a known it

isnt in any way visible   the way everything is in the same. fish in the night
welcome home   illtempered pigeons and gulls   mosquitoes and rats

I pick up cherries in the parking lot
pick them because theyre red and neither natural nor artificial they are the
songu anything cherries Get in a car with a lot of these women The one who's
supposed to be a healer Shes wearing an awfully elaborate headdress to which she
keeps adding just one more thing dont do that dont need to do that Its just a
cultural that youre making up

right now on your own but its
                              still just a cultural Constructing an attic or hierarchy on
your read I mean head and now a cloth like a curtain all across it so I say something
but that doesnt matter Where are we going in this car
To the store or something To an event to a workshop   Id rather go to a stillness
you cant run a culture on that I dont want one a politics I dont want one   I
am a broken baby and I just want to think about that
                                          So I wind up in a room
with a lot of these guys as I often do
I call some gays "power queens" then embarrassed I say "of course Im a power queen
too" all the guys who are also gays laugh this is a cultural this is a tiny its an almost
story   dissolving at the edges   its almost a songu song   power queen/
power queen/I am a power queen too/in the crystal, power and queen are melting
/until you until you/until theres nothing but you   its a little bit like the tune of
spider man he says

in life is anything interesting   thats why it isnt life
thats why people invent their myths   which so lead us astray the phone the
endless cord of we say

                    Crystal is a
                    condition and it
                    contains other textures
                    its actual topography is imaginative

171

but in its center
the imagination
tends to cease

below all of the this the edged world
as we've conjured it into existence
haunts all our days
I will never change it it is hopelessly
broken
because of its measurability

songu was never a god or queen or even a story. all of the goo that comes out of the aloes would be like crystal healing liquidly I'd be covered with it you too as if newborns once again but this time really with nothing to do because finally no one would make us be in a story your name not son and mine not nothing both of our names are fish head I saw several live fish being chopped into thick   slices at

the covered market

and one was only a fish head its body had been chopped off and sliced the monger was going to do further things to its head tear out the brains keep the ears or was it not keep them under directions from the customer an exacting women but not just yet she had to tell him what to do first tell and tell the head just lay there gasping the fish head so I mean the fish the head was still alive and gasping without its body a large-eyed carp it was dying it would never die and in the crystal and in the crystal was its one great eye

which you

FATE

'I would like to dream
 bacteria down 'cause I can
dream it down'
                              'They   too
are people, people of the crystal'

'I would like to dream
the crystalline bacteria
down   see them as their crystal selves
down here'

What else did the voice say
that sang that funny dialogue   about disease
in my head   it said
                              Fate because its so good
and I answered
                    The only good
and it said
                    Fate is an adjective   of crystal, a handler of space.

Fate because its so good
its the only good that isnt
the crystal

fate is red. the red it just turns to red.

the key is in the strafing house, said a serious chinese man in a plain red shirt. we are being strafed we are in a metropolitan emergency ward which I recognize as crystal because present are a bleached hooker a probable junkie some poorish people and some people following aged parent on trolley   and there is also an old woman here who is only alone everyones body in the soul is in trouble everyone is in a state of connection with each other without troubling to speak of it being elsewhere and here, elsewhere and here. no thats wrong being here which is nearly the literal

crystal everyone in this room knows theyre connected to each other in some sense of
fate the red   one woman in a trolley is splattered with small ruby spots. this is
not a dream

        the key is in the strafing house but you wont find it because theres a boot on the
law or is it on flu law Im having trouble reading this text which is a translation from a
translation of our original. some rooms are full of corn and some are full of grits you
can guess which is preferable in the corrupt world always corn of course nothing but
corn is respected in this world down here corn and opaque boots elsewhere in my
consciousness is a newborn baby remarkable   in its nakedness and cleanliness. I
stared and stared at   its nakedness and cleanliness anyone.

        fate isnt chance which is trivial   or greek   which is
superstitious   it isnt an image and doesnt come from the hole of images.
it is a sur movement or sous movement of the imagistic surface it organizes that
surface once the trivial images have gathered, it collects the shapes of past and future
into a coherence a strong   shade which isnt ominous but forceful and it is
spoken for in dreams by the soul interpreting it as anciently fate was called that which
is spoken. that was correct but the soul speaks the final version herself, or himself the
boy dirty or the one-eyed, it is spoken in songu know it dont know it. there didnt
have to be it except insofar as there had to be something I   suppose

so, said another more aggressive voice in my uncon just about conscious, take your
religion our religion and just ho ho throw it away. the voice added, I don't want to
talk about any people because   I don't want to talk   about *decency*.

then fate isnt death or class or sex some colossal aside in a book. bad ending, that.
fate is the only   deep part of time
the voices speak   'this defeats blue ink'   is said in a room among columns and a
mosaic floor with bits of red in it and broad windows   somehow like
the entrance to the gare de l'est   That is is fate stronger than reason? I dont
think so, voices   I think it may be part of it   as it   reaches outward
        towards the others in corruption, because it, can only love them   Ive forgotten
what *it* is here fate or reason

defeats blue ink but not blue light
the blue light   was   my   mind
the red light was my
what was left of my fate.

                                        And then a
more devilish voice says: 'what is this the bottom of, the top of, something you said?'
          But, what Im saying is as true as one can get   with songu, in
translation,
am I speaking the language or not?   in translation

      The figure of love and I are having therapy
inside a room at the dunes by the sea at the bottom of the hole a person who is I is the
therapist but I, I am really   watching. then we are waiting   and the
therapist I and I are waiting for two different things two different outcomes which are
both therapy or both the therapy. one outcome is fate   and one is crystal

meanwhile a large two-dimensional but freestanding outward I mean artwork has
been accomplished by someone a man I know but really its a copy and when he
explains it hes explaining the original and how it relates, the original, to the other
work of its time. I despise this but then the work changes so it isnt anyones, it is there
and since I dreamed it   it is mine in fact though I dont need it as mine the colors
are clear beautiful   in one place its actually a cliche about   two spiritual
looking hands   everyone has hands   not a bacteria
I hate those hands

      now this is the walkway through the gare de l'est, that I am taking instead of the way
up and out. this walkway is called   leaning the leaning walk. I am leaning
on the crystal as crystal others and as crystal but not as anything normally religious
like the cliché of two hands praying or working. there is no image of a man or a
woman as a god on which to lean there is only the gare de l'est its walkway which is
fate and fate is the crystal friend. here are two men and in order to know theyre in
crystal they must touch their foreheads to each other they are now able to speak
without speaking they know the language.
does fate relate

does fate relate
to bacteria

the other species would seem to
have come to understand fate
sooner and better than we
and shape it
to suit them better.

this is a pearl again and then *its silence is gone forever*   *Fate*, says the voice
(hear voice speaking again) *is a miracle of justice. don't go to work*   Whos
speaking? I ask   *your fate*, says   the voice   So he says it and says it, the
voice says,   *he went to the sea and saw*   *that theyre somebody, good me, and*
long (who, voice?)   all in a tall white pearl   You really are speaking to
me now, now now   No one needs an angel   or a god   or an image of
a power   because one has always been, then, that, the pearl   whose silence
when known   vanishes   but we know silence cant vanish   I

am rushing through underground tunnels of

Paris beneath the Seine, was that the   quoi la, the louvre or leave   is a stupid
place.   fate is the only *beauty*   *When the wind is rushing pain, the body is*
in the soul but   *it cannot happen it enough*   the soul cannot
happen it enough   voices, our subject is fate   a voice says, *the*
measurements were: *cared the whole world*   cared the whole world
those are the measurements of fate   your fate is comprised of the whole
worlds measure and thats why and thats why the world   must be cared...
no matter what else   is happening to you

I'm trying out for a play part
                in a gymlike theatre of bright blond wood
another actor is trying out ahead of me. but I begin spontaneously
                                to bleed at first from my

hands and wrists, someone else says that will help with getting the part
It's my turn and I act I recite   everyone thinks I'm so good and I'm still
bleeding but then I begin   to bleed more its so uncontrollable

                                                          bleed through the
skin of many different parts of my body, it wont stop and I cry out that I cant stop it
stop it fate stop it soul stop it blood

                                        then there are two ways ways to
what but I cant remember
                    I only remember   the song:

                    the shade bird
                    the after bird
                    the dead bird
                                  flying
              no it wasnt with any-
                  thing but it gathered
                  and that shape
                  but why
            I didnt see it so it would be
                  because
                  some things
                  arent natural
                      and
                  are real

              I didnt see it so it would be, why should that be
                  and be the good?

fate is required essence of particulars Who required it You Or else you wouldnt
                    your blood fate was
                    leakage beautiful
                    beautiful of soul because
                    you were a spring
Tell me why The voices are telling you *You are lucky to bleed*

I am bleeding white flakes on the sheets mixed with blood and with a certain shading of blue its all over the sheets Im bleeding snow mixed with blood and blue Im bleeding white now. someone is faithless near a window do I care   and someone refuses to share   but what is it there is no it   I need so why do I care? she has gone upstairs amid this garden-surrounded house carrying it all for herself shes wearing a lank cotton housedress. There is no it   Now this is a book about a rowboat in which thomas jefferson capsizes he shouldnt have been just another son of a son   She   kept it for herself   he   capsized with his lover in shallow water well that was, the founding fathers scene, always a matter of shallow

water wasnt it. here is another man who wants to tell me something another woman shes   waiting for him actually near a carthaginian baptismal font because she waits for dido because hes a him his last name ends   with the syllable man not son so he leads me away from her to show me what he knows its just some food a bit of mozzarella cheese another useless it another image held in two hands the cliche body which bleeds blood and doesnt ooze soul ooze red crystal red is the only beauty I mean fate is because   it isnt   always him, or is it   tell me voices
You dont need anything, they say   *fate will supply it*, forget the housedress the son man the boat the baptismal font   You dont need   anything

PAIN

in the bright eclectic sun
that is, in the dark sun
     that gives off light a gold
     rim that I
     remember from

          No no you mean a beach   with   dunes
          or antarctic snow   you use too many images

          There *are*   too many images
in the hole
in hole
where fate coalesces too
(I am   *any one of us is*   *dying of too many images)*

I'm not remembering my dreams because I'm in one every day. I'm in this dream it goes from the gare de l'est, near the covered market, to the canal over the bridge, to the l'hôpital. I enter a green building take the elevator to geranium and among warm figures am accosted by fate in the form of change to the body in the soul of the figure of love whose soul doesnt change isnt changing at all in the crystal. fate in the changing shape of this dream. it isnt a dream. it is it is. (but physical pain isnt. or is it even if it hurts so. yes)
        because   I   am a dream when I go anywhere as someone who goes, as   someone who does but   between   you, love, and me whats between you and me (in "the air") isnt a dream

what goes on between us isnt a dream.

          I went to the gare de l'est like any hawk hummingbird or fly it didnt matter going there through   one of the gates to the city   but a between thing a thing between   two beings mattered when I left the gare and crossed the canal entered the hospital and   it was there the between us

what goes on between us isnt a dream
maybe the only thing   *that isnt a dream*

nobody wants to sit beside the bad child struggling with his parent why not there was a middleaged woman   sitting there but she left, and after she left a silver ribbon remained in her chair. the silver ribbons a relief   from her   What kind of dream is that It wasnt a dream it was a little vision Any silver ribbon is better than a judgment of another soul Why did you see that I dont know She left her snake there She left her soul. I dont

understand that   there was the crystal   with a messy other and
she didnt know how   to take it with her.

in the hospital they will tell you theres no silver ribbon. We all know that Gate or Gare is to the city how many gates as many as you have pores of skin in the body in the soul but the bodys in pain as gates to the city think of how many gates there are in the skin of a river bullfrog how many gates breathing gates to the crystal city I am entering it I am letting it in again ribbon is left I am a ribbon the snake that can tell you that all you do is dream. you dream because you only care about objects and not whats in between   all that matters is whats in between   and even when you are in pain the in between is let in   the in between is stronger

you exist to let it in
you exist to let in what happens in between

you arent an image
and when youre in pain you sing or cry out make songu an in between

but in the heartblown
industry I fade
in what they say every day   denying that being is in between, is crystal and not the isolated objects the isolated bodies they analyze.   Is pain the passion of an outside choice something that wants outside the crystal that comes in a sort of jealousy of your soul to try to create   another body   one it can own?   And bodies taken as all there are have always been subjugable So   as youve been subjugable to   certain   other   people concepts and structures   you become subjugable to pain   But you can use it to make yourself   more translucent

I have seen this translucence
I am who sees it the hawk the hummingbird the snake the too many images

I have all
the parts of my snake and now I can see   Im the snake in the tree   with
large eyes that cry   tears of no emotion that   has so far been listed and
described   as in the heartblown industry   These are tears of reason and relation
tears of no dream tears of crystal

I have found my entire length   Now no part of me is synthetic.

I awoke crying from no dream. I had been in the bottom of the black hole   the
dark sun with its flame rim rememorable from. I dont believe any thing they say
there is no purpose to pain though you can probably use it you can use anything but
why use things   I had thought it might be useful as a gate   away from the
banality of the lives we are forced   to lead   and there is probably
some use to its travail   but its one that we have made up   like everything
else   and I dont believe   that it should be honored in any way
though it make your face more
translucent   so that your soul is evident both   within and without your body
but I'd seen it like that already   and I myself am simply   bleeding through every
pore I have painted my   entire body red though my body itself has done it for me
by bleeding, bleeding   my name in this old dream means burn and I am wearing a
brownish sari in india   that womans cloth that stupid rag over my
head remember that dream in which   I am also a physician   and have
diagnosed my lovers cancer, on christmas eve of '98. In the traditional manner I have

thus painted my eyes red and large just like a snake in a tree the snake who weeps in a
tree (*you use too many images*) I am riding on a cart which is horsedrawn and heaped with
objects A voice says to me, *It's good to paint the whole body red now*   I
wear a red imbued brown and I am burned   *you use too many images*
There are too many images   the mind is full of them and   we live in that mind down
here.

there is no purpose to the body we are forced to live in
have forced ourselves to live in

it is the wrong one because
we have reinvented it and done that so badly
but I have another body
I dont want another to help me ever
they will try to make me stay in the wrong body

my feet are wrapped in rags or sheets all around. well Ive been becoming legless
limbless   or is it simply that Im shoeless   having nothing though I must
once more walk to the hospital   how can I do that with these   hugely
wrapped feet   Now I am standing on a quai where there are sailboats, where there
are myriad masts   all night I try to remember this simple scene since Ive been
unable   to dream for days.   but if I say Hi Mary would I be able to walk
on wrapped up stumps   Cramps in my feet all night the "real" feet   I will
never pray for anyone I will never hope I will never falsify the mind. my feet are
wrapped in awkward white rags so be it I am still covered with gates   I am all gates
already who needs shoes whats the difference   between being dead or alive I
dont know any more

          there is certainly pain but
          it doesnt tell us about our bodies we
          dont have those bodies

at the hospital bedside there is a blackhaired blackmailing woman who gets patients to
tell their secrets into the bedside telephone while her coconspirator listens hi mary im
in distress, oh then i'll help you. not sure if the secrets are told by the patient directly
into the phone or are somehow told by the patient inside the phone only in the voice
that is heard inside the phone by the voice on the other side of the phone if you get
what i mean though no one has any secrets thats invention too but you can also get
someone to do one of these worldwide things that arent true like make you think you
have secrets bedside secrets confessions places deep down in the body soul which
someone must help you release why you might become better in the sense of good or
the sense of healthy so so you can either say Hi Mary in heaven or come back to life
here. She the blackhaired blackmailing woman has walked away from the bedside
and Im now confronting her for being a blackmailer   but I think the blackmail
the crime is simply her pretence of spiritual authority. I have known about the crystal
have been in the crystal consciously too long now to care   there is no   there
has been pain and it hasnt seemed reasonable blue it may have become soulful red it

hasnt been crystalline though it like everything else has transpired in the crystal and
will convert to it or has in the future

some thing obscure like anger is approaching in the form of a woman who thinks that
only the shape of her life is important but that isnt fate thats trivial. its the herself
song I remember her it isnt about the in between its about the her. another and
similar woman approaches they are both blackmailers, with their apparent goodness
but there isnt goodness only blue reason the bloody soul and the crystal. she
advertises her blood in fact but you cant advertise it or advertisement begins to
destroy your lovely your crystal consciousness and you become unconscious once
more, thats not so bad no but I dont want   to be unconscious Id rather fly like a
fly into the gare or walk on my tied up stumps than to blackmail you with my
goodness my understanding my virtue shit

my other body is so beautiful you
cant see it or know it Ive only known it from
waking in the middle of a dream
though that dream of course wasnt a dream
(and Im still not dreaming at night
the hospital is my dream)
that dream that wasnt a dream is all that I cling to besides the in between

my other body will never know any pain.
I remember my chest was painted white in some few simple stripes to show
that our vision of ourselves was not valid:
we arent skeletons we are locations
my daily body was asleep beside me on one side and the figure of love was
asleep beside me on the other. I was lucid awake between
I was the in between

Another time I requested of sleep a validation of this previous experience
and sleep allowed me to awake and arise ever so gently from my daily body
only for a moment   I only needed a moment
but you have to stay in the pain body in order to talk to others
who all and only live in their pain bodies the ones that permit others
to enslave them in

the millenia long agreement we honor
because we love so to honor agreements
I must have a dream a real dream at night
I am weeping tears of reason everyday now
they squeeze out of me the essence of
those stories those dream stories which
are preferable to the world
they only squeeze out the crystal
they squeeze out   from the hole its simple
crystal from which stories are made
but no stories get made
they squeeze out the knowledge of fate
its the same substance all the same crystal
my soul wont tell me a story she knows Im just it

SECOND BODY

the revelator (as in a john   a john the revelator)   is really a johns
revelator a   transparent   glandlike   small organ we all have
But we know that fact   in the language   we can speak   but not know–

        tell me about   the revelator
        We call it that because hes singing
        What does that mean
        Hes getting to   go Where.
        What does that mean   hes getting to go
        where hes at   in the second body
        You do you believe that   Yeah
        but its not always by singing
        its by being   there in the crystal and whats
        revealed is us there   Al the revelator
        I'm Al the revelator   but   I only mean
        I have a revelator too

dont let the doctors find out   about the other organs
Never   I promise not to tell, ever

Pain   is not the only   It doesnt have to be physical   pain   to make you
sing   but it has to be pain Which kind   the hardest Why   I cant answer
still   Use it but
        dont use another
        dont use another
        surrounded by silver
        in the gold market
        to get a gold tooth

gold   dont mean a thing   and Sing doesnt mean sing

        I know theres another body   because it cries out to you all night   while
youre away   its whats me   I know theres another body   because its my
mind   I know theres another body its writing this Some wont accept it because it doesnt
come from the body they know and approve It comes from the   johns gland

185

from any whores gland   from the revelator

               I now dont live in the body they know and approve.

I'm always at the hospital   thats my dream awake or asleep   and certainly
last night I was there for awhile among the beds and windows the smells then
searched for a place to pee   but there was a man asleep in or on or curled at the
base of every toilet in the room, because there was no place   there is just no place
to sleep   in the uncrystalline crystal down here. this is my world this is the part I
accept   all these poor johns like me looking for johns for any   revelators to
sleep near and find the truth from

i ant to b want to be in the other body knowing it right now i dont feel a think or even
i lay me down snake burden or bird because there is no die time i remem pain a little
it was burning away all the gates to the west east tout south north and the yous of use.
i suppose they wants n so they want some nouns so they can ignore the crystal
between the bedpans and towels and nightingales only i see. yes i still have hands and
feet but have you noticed how snakelike they and i really in appearance a digression
weep crystal yesterday reasonbl tears walking place vendôme staring at rubies and
emeralds and i never never st feel any more a feeling described in prose or poet
                                       take a
stand take my sta is this another body rising up lik a mind u above the uses of these
keys there are keys to all the gates there throw them away no need now and every
time has simply gone awa he said he wasnt sure about the second body but i said its
the only one that knows thats why we jus dont talk brain here we talk the whole dam
length of the spine the snake the time as a one thing as those red eye tears that know
what a san snake does these are those tears but i still want to dream. too many images,
a gland or a snake   who cares   how many image

                            and so then I dreamed the old dream of
the bugs. the walls of the hospital room were filled with large bugs the same color
as the hospital walls   the walls were bugged to make sure   we didnt talk
about the other body but   Then I am walking down the highway where there
are all alligators or crocodiles   al alligators or crock of shit crocodiles? I suspect
al alligators   al the revelator me the violent gates of my suffering self to the beauty
all the way to the city that very city.

False song: *All you got to do is*
                do this oh do this oh
                do this it has stopped

                the blond woman
                with gold tooth
                who sang it grins.

has anything ever started and stopped has anything ever

Has there ever been anything you had to do   That was only the gold.   fuck
the gold fuck

The shoes walk up these stairs
the shoes walk up these stairs
this is a truer song I saw them
walk walking up   in their daily shoes   their any sons shoes
like angels
            I dont have shoes
I am more like the staircase   closer to the staircase slither I snake I snake I gland

on a bus we are stopping for a peepee and caca break in the beautiful French
countryside everyone says it will be better staged later in a certain way by someone else
a nurse Sure why not. Why not write about this my friends? The johns son in my
head this morning these blues was on my mind that is the second body all that I have
sun those blues is sun Go look at that go read that beautiful memorial to the dead no
fuck that I have to go peepee and caca sorry Im in the hospital not the museum
                                                    and why does someone
else always have to stage the toilet break and say shit here exactly here in honor of
your live or dead love why am I being led about again i will snake away then and
leave and leave this world needs a devil this world needs a large weeping awa eye eye
needs this world needs a serpentine mine with a tear   sorrow will have a name
        and it will be the devils
                            because hes good limbless and good

187

what people do to each other I saw it all
day in an emotion, someone trying to straighten it all out so that she has done right
how   despicable whats burning are not the leaves but the cards theyre burning
but they had no use they told lies to broken   babies and now burn in autumn
no sparrows had approved them or had approved other useless dice she was writing
this letter in the hospital twice and she said she couldnt come, where, but she wouldnt
I dont know to where I think it was a place where she couldnt become large enough
very large like the largest tear. couldnt either come to the hospital or to the official
deposit repository of all the worlds most worshipped caca and peepee maybe it was a
museum or napoleons tomb or a set of tomes by a man

But I am now so large if you

entered it the tear you would get lost the tear crystal I am   and I'm of no use to
you I'm glad learn to be your own. I said I couldnt come but I wouldnt still dont know
where though I seem to be getting on a bus at night any old bus some old second body
dark full of people who cant afford nothin else but the night bus in the unbeautiful
destroyed our landscape. I go with you

in the second body i sleep and act awake i mean i sleep and dream and dreamings like being
awake so how else can you explain it

except as a second body?
except as a second body

its like everyone thinks you have a television implant inside but it should be obvious
that you have some sort of second self. second body that the souls in being visible.
and all that poverty age and sickness all that sorrow: the dreaming bodys never ill or
poor never the same age. You think its a hallucination, my dear but what is a
hallucination, a word. darkness baby dust baby reasoning which as he say soon be over
and have a so ro have a name. he doesnt mean a name he doesnt mean that sorrow
will have a name he means in fact that it wont exist anymore thats what have a name
means, when I have mine I am never existing thats for su answer thats for sure.

This body
rises and goes to you where
Im not allowed
you are too pale
theyre drugging you so
because they started
and dont know how to stop

                                        no one knows how to stop
                                        anything

old clothes and cardboard boxes all over the street in daylight, print dresses and shirts a
lot of red clothes for everyone. everyones afraid to take them why now theyre just
some second body clothes go into the store of frozen food the frozen food locker
bringing things there bunch of food to store for everyone i too am taking things there
but im looking for a particular thing and find it a black steak. now i have a black steak.
ive forgotten what to do with it. why take it back onto the dark black bus which is
really the same as the hospital and the mans there whos the one who scrubbed the
white tiles a while ago I now know hes both a man and a reptile he has very large ears
because he hears what we say in the crystal all the time. some stupid john, some me

I wanted to leave my body last night because it hurt it ached a lot I had two real dreams
and forgot them.

I had another one last night and forgot it too. a deep dream but I had a shallow one
also that I remembered   a game of squares or tiles   in shallow box on a
table and all the tiles were set edge to edge and each had a word a word printed on it
and four of them said the word "sun"   is that because I said the blues is the sun
is that because four is the blues or is it just because

                        sun
                        sun
                        sun
                        sun.

in sco second body without dream i ca still cant drea twisting n and multiplying like
snakes of crystal reason like wires to everyone i cant remember it thinking too of you
please dont be violent. this w what i thought to d to you oh dont be violent the wind
thats crystals blowing through of all the uncon we are not cons and it isnt that its love
its reason its is accepting you as we accept ourselves i am having not no arms legs and
singing like mad to the everything silver silver ring because gold is corny money is a
corny thing. sun sun sun sun not a metal but a john a burning caca hole the light of
the unnatural all my peace. all my sex was so the crystal could flow fro t from the

pores from and to and the revelator my revle v revelator always there revealing too, everything that is known in the language of songu.

there was a dream there was good i dont want any look into the crystal its right in front of you and I meant to say food now i know that the crystal means good there was a dream there was good i dont want any look into the crystal its right in front of you you dont need any thing like good because you have a second body it wont let me dream because im walking it walking it everywhere. i said ti befo said it before Who care sun sun sun sun the four gates to the city the body the crystal. i have rage and vanity but i also have second body and its absolute transparence i have grown so large and clear that you are inside it all the time look into. its right in front of you the pronouns are meaningless it might be you but i have grown grown so large and round like a crystal tear or ball that you are inside it all the time look into. I am that non person nondream the tiny litter of the planet of the all over it is burning from the light the combustion through the crystal of the sun sun sun sun the devil is our mother the creature who has no limbs for the making of technic. when the snake was our mother but that is just song or sun or like a crystal tear that you are inside all the time you dont need to look into it

LAW

The tall blue skirts song:

> *pants in a range*
> *they will steal your pride*
> *and make you strange*
> *they will steal your wisdom*
> *and throw it away*

I'm in an official room   full of wooden chairs and women waiting   thinking
          I thought the favors the favors the favors   The favors are not.

                                             favors were invented by men.
I'm considering a court order   against in this dream a man who but I
cant say his name or his crime in the dream it wont come   out of my mouth
except as *indis*   *indis*   indiscreet?   not allowed to say it

Made the laws and have done you the favor   of extending small portion to you
In the crystal only the law of wisdom is conscious   huge   the law
is all I can see up here   while down there   some man helps little john
to his perfect cheer   laughs while J eats and drinks at a cafe table telling stories
fascinating anecdotes   of bar-room pugilism. the john nods to me in his good
humor.

          they will steal your pride
          and make you strange
they will steal your wisdom and throw it away because youre a woman or because
you have weak arms and small feet   or because you have no arms and no feet.
or because you thought arms and hands feet were of the unit of your wisdom
a snake all spine all wisdom all of the law it cant be   enforced it can only be.

          More shoes on the floor. boys and shoes I wasnt good enough with the young,
something about their shoes Is this a dream I still cant have dreams   its a
split-second dream   I didnt buy the boys whom I didnt hit   enough   shoes.

          ...will tell you how much one needs

It is important   to live in affection
but it is really important that people have   things Favor favor favor You have a
beautiful diploma   You have a clipboard. you have a garden you have a library you
have furniture even a future. you have.

changed into a tear   which is the largest most rational   crystal of all
not sorrow but sight (*and sorrow*   *will have a name*)
Look at yourself just look at yourself Look at what youve done
Look at who you are...lies

the blue skirt of rationality all around me, in this crystal I've been crying because
everyone can only see   themselves. but theres no one to see
unless you look for the second body   theres no one to see but the diagram
handed down through millenia clipboard clipboard clipboard You look like this.
a page in a book.

                        He got out of his hospital bed wasnt supposed to supposed to walk
hes walking around the hospital in his dressing gown, says "There's an owl" and I
know he means wisdom "There's an owl" and then "I don't want to use courting"
wisdom is never courted It isnt courtable or couldnt be wise.
                                                it will alight on his
shoulder when he isnt looking

lie down they told him as they tried to make my father lie down   he stared at a flag
flapping outside the hospital window like an owls wings it was wisdom it could have
been anything (what's a flag)   it was wings. it was wings it didnt have edges.

in the hospitals everythings white considering i might remember this dream but now
of course I dont there are a lot of beds in the one white room everything white except
for the doctors clipboard. Im being *told*
                        something   of course

        In the rocky canyon now though dont know for a while if its me or the figure

192

of love touch the rock the cool rock remember the natural. I am he   its light
in front of me strangely again in a cavemouth. I was him for a long while now I am I
in a wool skirt why   then walk further in and wear refracted light not a skirt.
there are people here, light through their
                                        second bodies

                              the world because of a hardening into ignorance of the first
one the first body world sees only the first   body there are agreed upon images
because of this hardness an attempt to make thought hard to make action and
knowledge hard to make law hard: people did and do. they insisted that animals are
hard and plants too

                              the material universe is not a fact its your choice your law
                              you do nothing but define the edges of this unreality

cant change collective choices but can try to see to be own body the law. the doctor can
only do one thing manipulate the noncrystal body til it ceases   I saw you light up
yesterday   anyone has seen such a thing. they dont call it light they call it you,
or your face   and act like thats a logical thing part of their idea that you come or go
like a machine. your face lights up no you are a machine. the material universe is
their choice. they have chosen to say that I didnt see what I saw. it can be described as I
said but can't be *really* described as I said it though it is a cliché of description
the fact is everyone knows you are a machine. wires. or bag of chemicals

the blond wood floor and this is a dream, scattered with poems analyzed by a sour
minded poet also a critic one poems by me. I wake up with a sore eye. it was useless
i'll invent my own   eye oh I have dont be so repetitive one-eyed snake the spine
the long eyed tear the blind   justice, remember?   You dont really look like a
snake No but I'm like one

floor littered with newspapers   in my mind I see   the second body of a plant
which speaks in a faint   whiney voice, and says
I have no eyes to see   no limbs no need to move
it seems made of light   it is a stem with lateral leaves of light it seems almost to
burn. flaming crystal it makes that wind glass sound

More trivial dreams of male poets We are nearly three quarters of the way there
Very interesting Where Driving driving the point is always to be driving there where
Who I'm always supposed to care who the poet is   and what their po etics are
Dream are you still telling me who

So

now he the dead poet who isnt   dead is collaborating with another on an
assemblage a box but isnt very interested. neither am I. art of the dead eye   of the
hardened first body everyone knows. driving to the point where a known dead art is
perfect just perfect. the second body was asleep all night and mostly not driving and
mostly not caring who. was plainly watching. These new dreams I'm finally having
are useless. It has to do with when she started parodying herself, this actress, was it
halfway through her career the way we were nearly three quarters there? these
numbers are *so* interesting but   I cant remember who   whether it was Audrey

Hepburn or Marilyn Monroe. have you finally realized   and am I speaking to
myself   it just doesnt matter? is that how you have a   second body
you are a who   but who you are   it couldnt remember its accomplishments
though it could be it   it couldnt move though it flew it could speak and hear but
not in the way you had thought.

Look at me I have no edges.

Halfway through the movie   so its another nights dream but still probably
halfway through her career   I enter the projectionists cubicle and tell him I like the
movie a lot better than he does. had worried about wearing blue or black chiffon well
that was trivial though a lot less ridiculous than cloning   a woolly mammoth. I
only remember walking across the room walk walk thats what we do   the second
body doesnt do that   it never shows itself right now the second body because
you need me. I'm the only person nearby with a brain a whole long spiney snakebrain
dream you need my tear eye that never shows. you need to look into it with your own

pleased to remember another trivial   dream no it wasnt trivial so my pleasure was
misplaced and I'm ashamed. I dreamed that everything I am using handling every
element I am in, air or water the river, is polluted. everything I eat. I am swimming
in water full of small flagellalike creatures which are pollution not   wisdom. A
onepiece bathing suit from my childhood? violet. down the hill, on the way out of
town. the law of the first world pollution

walk down the spinal staircase it isnt there the fire i see is me lit face facet it is the
second that is primary not pollution how long did it take you to pollute. but nothing
sweeps away either the crystal or the pollution I dont dream because images asleep and
awake fill me with sorrow the law is only the law of this fiery facet self the cold full of hot
that have no qualities and in it are others in me are the others though each is each some
are more to me in a moment there is no moment. The world down there is an echo. all of
it. you are all echoing. down there. the pollution in which I swim is an echo of what was.
the four year old child is polluted now in this dream. the dream is that there is no
cessation of person and there is no escape from pollution.

we stole it we stole the wisdom we threw it
away we dont know the law we are all polluted

I dream of the dead but cant remember it
maybe theres nothing to remember except for presence
my father and kate. except for presence
when you die you die with everyone who is inside you in the canyon
I mean the crystal (you use too many images)
then when are you ever alone   any time both at once like a mind
she wore her messenger clothes again blue
and messenger hair shoulder length thats all I remember

its all here no one seeing it how edgeless it is because everything manufactured must
be so edged it can razorcut   how else does it work. we will do some more
things to your first body today. the law is weeping reason the tear. reason is nothing
but a tear. you know nothing at this moment unless youre crying or unless youre
dead. you have nothing (I have nothing) to defend there is no defense. but as for the
law down there avoid it escape it ignore it not just the legal law but the laws of
relations behavior and every form of asskissing as of the I couldnt leave the métro
through my wonted entrance yesterday   because of an exceptional

state visit he will be assassinated or he will bring good to his country he is a man. he
is trying to be good. he is a leader. he is a man. he is nothing but another scum
leader. it is necessary that he be a man. in order to be a leader and bring change.
your boss man will never know anything until hes dead and then it will take him
aeons of swirling time to even become as conscious as amoeba he was only trying he
was only trying to tell everyone what to but he was a good version of trying to tell

what do to do he was aeons of swirling ignorance arent you? what would you like to know? ask the dead. the psychiatrist has promised to guide us through this important passage of life as if he or she had died the doctors seem to believe they have died too. thats how they know everything.

something egyptian they knew nothing either stop kissing their dead ass.

it is possible to call the real self the second
body. when they say angels they mean
some people not all of whom are dead
you have already been an
angel of the crystal I mean you have
been that unwittingly. the murderer was an angel there too
he had a look of stupefaction on his
facet/face We dont care if hes here or not. yes its a system
I refuse to leave anyone out. my own
hatred is of no significance nor my suffering
except that I'm conscious because of it
I think I am fully conscious right now. I
wish I could dream instead I know things are edgeless

POISON

at night near the
auto supply
I hang on a wall
my poster   which is framed
next to another
poster its larger than and
the glass in its frame is
composed of pieces
of shattered
glass glued together into the rectangle
maybe its a circus poster with a tiger or man or
something else dangerous
no I dont know
something I still cant   see except for its unity.
except for the fact that I've finished the crystal
rectangle which I dont think of, in the dream, as crystal

I now think both posters are by me. one is what the poem would have been. this will
be a larger work, must be.
all the shattered pieces have been put back together but something is under them what
do I see? why can I
only see the image after the shattered glass has been
superimposed upon it

          its all coming from you a live voice might say to me. I mean a not from the
crystal   voice   Answer *Theres nowhere else*   *for it* to come from I
cant trust anyone   for this information and, actually, I can trust hardly
anyone   intellectually because   I was brought up in an auto supply.

I was running in a long gray cavelike tunnel there was a turn ahead then there were
people running away from that direction towards me thus away from where
obviously I must go and those people,   they shouted the word, Cloak!
then, figures appeared cloaked in white covers   over their entire substances or they

were simply white cloaks   and had no facial features and no limbs they
were images as was the word the word Cloak. I awoke and someone had said it's
seven o'clock. Clock is cloak. time is a cloak for   your second body perhaps. there
is a prevalent fear of the cloak Im going to rip off am removing

the second body is what youre looking at because youre not looking, hardly ever, and
also thats how you talk. without edges

                              I remember first the rose petal on each's forehead, cant
stop seeing it. these were people in a field. there was a rose petal red on eachs
forehead but it was later a ruby towards the end of the vision. first we'd entered and
stood in a cave with a cobwebby entrance and in the cave was a large and bright red
rose without leaves, we stepped through and outside the cave then   diverged
from its centrality into the field. the cave was the cave of wisdom, we'd agreed to
have a vision together of wisdom and I'd said a snake or snakes are in that cave but
you said they couldnt be there or theyd kill us. So we saw the rose instead and then
outside we saw a green field a field of folk, *as it says* you said, and each had the petal
on each's forehead   and they werent all people in the green field. these were
perhaps all second bodies I said, but our visions werent exactly the same   and
shouldnt be even though we have them together

so in yours it was a question of who had been helpful and good and   who hadnt
and I asked you to enter   the rose petal or ruby in your own forehead there
where we were among the people in the field who also included animals and plants
others not even organic   so you said you saw origin and origin was also
the future,   but you saw it as a whirlwind   I cant remember with clarity I mean it
was yours to see   and I, I said, can only always see now
                              the crystal city and
know how everyones   ruby is how each has experienced   eachs own story
because by now the petal was a ruby   but each has no choice but to give up the
story and come here, gives it up gives up memory of all that individual action in
order to be conscious, that is, wise. gives up whats thought of as the conscious in
order to be conscious. the rubys what youve done and how youve given it up so that
you are finally an individual the only you the one without your story. you are the
only you to have lost your own story no one else will have either. you are thus equal

to a plant. I still havent described the second body beneath the shattered crystal glued back together and its not that its nothing. its not at all that the second body is nothing. nor is it that the future which   is also origin black whirlwind is nothing. but we still cant remember the language

I think the snakes were in the cave   and I dont think the snakes kill you   I think that their poison as Ive said before is   one version of the wisdom. another is the thickness of the petal red with its veins   flower texture is wisdom.

          my own problem with helpful and good   I would say to the figure of love   is that we've invented all the circumstances that make them necessary   so we've invented them ourselves and a hierarchy judging what they are, how theyre fulfilled. its often what you might call a humble hierarchy a decent family a town full of sexists and also racists (this is *my* town one says) entitled to their things because they are in their lives helpful and good to the lovely others, in the humble town of sexists and racists, where everyone has enough money. the town thinks itself responsible for this modest prosperity this goodness. The crystal is calling but the poison is calling also sometimes theyre the same I was bitten like Robert so you wouldnt know the next note I hope I hope you listeners never know the next note whats coming except suddenly telepathically that is you understand its significance as its sounded out of nowhere. thats the real city the blues is a form but it is also an abstraction like the second body that is, its real. not knowing the next note except telepathically is like the second world the crystal and down here most of everything is predictable. thats why fates nearly sacred   and the only good

several hospital stretchers
are at the foot of the bed
I'm supposed to select the correct
one for the figure of love but
I cant wake up because
I'm rarely
allowed to sleep and
right now
I'm sleeping

I respect my poison my poisonous speeches. there are fangs in the crystal crystalline fangs which poison the story youve brought to the city and kill it. it must die finally. there is no the good though whats badly done be despicable you arent allowed one you arent allowed one deed nor is any other person. this world down here will only change if you are not allowed deeds as you arent up there. though you are allowed to have suffered since that makes you conscious there is no dee because rememb that I never I never did one it was for a man or if you that is one but then it all presumed that you one were vulnerable over something besides food and shelter and being hit so everyone we know doesnt know. I will nevr h a dream again he the the poison had entered my system to help me about not dreaming so I could despise daily acitv activity enough hate it enough to get me through these days. I thought of writing the most poisonno poisonous poem I could when I die I dont want respect and love I want to enter the red rose petal poison veins through the forehead door and whats there for me is the second snaky body the only awakened. the poison. I dont believe I live in this go out there and live in this no i live in the poison as i said at the beginning of my childhood. spit it out at all family gatherings   if you can. spit it out at all the panels do you honestly believe that a philosophical   tex text know more about the real than a slave song? or was it w a white one theres no sickness trial or danger, in that bright land to which I go

       when we got bit by the poison we became conscious of the language everyone speaks but doesnt know just a little more. robt never know he a sexist and so who I am hard and there are no vitu virtues bite him back bit him back with the poison is one thing I do here. as I also bite you here   the bright   river of love is
                              the poison of truth

                                            the poison of truth

these are poison tears too reason is more poisonous than ever and love most poison refusing you your illusion. this poison tear is so strong that it fills the crystal city with sensation a definition of beauty it makes you hateful it makes you hate down here.
                                            the poison of truth
                                            the poison of truth

you have three gold cells inside you I see, I said, they are the love the wise the good and they arent yours you are permitted to be their conduit   their temporary bearer or conductor. maybe not even temporary, though not the only one, and they arent what I believe   but here no one has to be right.

I myself believe in reason, love as for everyone but with further intense goldred sparks where individuals love each other, and the red of the individuality that one lives then must throw away. and the poison. I now believe in the poison. There are

thirteen gates to the city and one is specifically the gate of poison. I'm so g bl badly in dr need of a dream loss here o sequence no pois too tired. I jus cant remember there were massive bodies were they the seconds but theyve nothing to tell me know i have to be in the language in some way I can demonstrate. we have to go there but it isnt a have to like this world which came from nowhere reut returning in w whirlwind to nothing black as bad dust I remember remem you the beautiful dirt that was also the cyrs crystal a city made of the clean dirt in shapes of creation for no reason Reason is different it is how we sing in reason and cry of the theft of love I so bn so need a dream a piece of bright story undoctored, as all this world is doctored so the poison works because its counter its snakes. the poison is wisdom and also intelligence. they don recognize it unless they can use it to make something bad. I stumbled over the stone in a certain world. in a certain world I lost everything but I was going to anyway pass wat passway through pass way through the thirteenth gate my second body oa painted with glow in the dark white paint for existence. its there so something can be since none of this down here is my second with the white on it so I can be some paint some kind of ai paint you don need. its poison paint denoting my second body. you will try to use it for purposes but it will poison you. I hope I can poison you with it, my
radiation

I sit in a meaningless doctoring office conscious and unconscious dead and alive
am I conscious now or unconscious   I am very conscious   though in such a
stupid place   I know I'm conscious because colors   approach me massed in
gray and gold. I am very very conscious can I poison you   they are going to
examine routinely my own body without even seeing my body of consciousness the
second body though they use echography mammography   and other first body
graphy.

I sang of an evil thing
but I only sang
I spoke and sang I'm hurting you but
in fact I didnt act and dont
so I didnt and dont hurt
the waves are burning
the blue lights are burning all over

I knew I was conscious because the colors approached me gold and gray   in my mind in a mass The colors approached me telling me without words and without shape I am consciousness. the poison of change. I'm conscious I'm so glad glad glad

tell me if you can/wont some body tell me/what is the soul of a man, sings another johns son. that is the poison of being real philosophy and I heard it all night in my sleep of trivial dreams I had two trivials another large   patriarchal steel medical   apparatus at the foot of the bed   which I must "wake up for" but really I must sleep and really all medicine and philosophy which   counts has its depth in sleep. Then am with some others perhaps out in the open at night We are being fed toast   We are being told that they our hosts whoever are allowing us more toast than anyone else in that country more toast than anyone else ever gets. I now have seven pieces of toast

the figure of love will feel guilty about having so much of it. I am just looking at it I dont want it

now I'm inside the tear the tear of poison again the tear of everything. philosophy contains no tears and so is stupid I am trying to see beneath the shattered put back together if its a beast but maybe its maybe its the figure of the second showing itself as because it could change   being an image though it isnt really. when youre conscious you dont really go about much in this lower world, you just look at everyone and hope their edges go away. when the pieces get put back together and you see under them another kind of it was just a shape so you wouldn't feel lost. seven toasts are ridiculous, it would have been better not to dream. the clock is cloaked but the second body isnt but is poison poison poison its radium its uranium

LOVE

tall woman shortish pony tail high on head in smalltown theater not as movie
house which it primarily is but   theater. because has a stage. she is or isnt me. it
or she (do I still have to call my self a she) sweater and pants angora breasted pullover
and plaid slacks of the fifties. Yet at same time sense of leviathans whales cavorting
and sweeping about like in water So you are made trivial you vast thing. Beneath the
shattered glass was a trained girl but other now No I still dont know what   is and
I am as always in the space between the audience and the stage, in the walls, or in the
coincident fluid element of the leviathans, all night. you didnt know it was wonder

because you feared sinking drowning, the leviathans   might seem dismal to you
since they didnt wear the clothes of sex and eras but they are edgeless rather than
whalelike and everything is you. or I. you are everything, *the soul of a one/ not of "a*
man"/ is a leviathan/ untrained to shatter/ to matter wouldnt matter. And so I dont have to
have a face in any jubilee. Your strikingly soulful presence with its
edgelessness and soulful fluids body fluids went to the stairs now I remember that that
was tomorrow in some sort of spiral or whirlwind in the telepathy if I could only
remember more of being leviathan as big as all the sea I feel in my skin and heavy and
light with my many metaphysical fluids. Dont you remember?

The same texture as wrath   is a stone   tear
to be like a stone is to weep stones
thats to be like oneself not a striking imbecile   I'm awake
no one is here–no one is ever here
the affect is very no the
affect permeates me deeply. thats why Im a rock   Never use the word 'is'
the therapys to move the rock, render the affect flexible Why bother Nothing
wrong with rock, sings a rock You are not stone not stone soul, sings another thing
Yes I am Dont cry youre not allowed to. I will cry stone
I'd rather be stone than their imbecile.

tears are the slave planets
called moons of Jupiter. that big at least
as big as slave   planets   titans

I will cry and will cry for more than   us two or three or few
I dont have to be alive in this instant in the way of the
imbecile. No nothing happens. too nothing happens. too, no one is here
we are enslaved to a disease to a situation in which the first body. becomes any
         trained fools object
not just us but everyone
And all night leviathans of light and fluid reason and bulging ruby foreheads speak
and speak invisibly in this room now. All that makes things tolerable
those other bodies dont exist. I am the biggest leviathan just like you and no other
kind   will ever be here. weep speak sing and maybe its like a
singer you
cant understand but can   understand entirely
the whole to live is not quite to get it but to be exactly here No in fact   we are getting
it. I am in the process of getting it. the blindest willy or johns son big as leviathan
heavy with   metaphysical fluids don them the flowers for the watch train blue light
red light gone down and we bawl brown green and brow. all that water in the train I
mean the river   didnt   divide us. all that mud all that mud We are here in
the corrupt real worl because they named it, all you named it   but we're there in
the crystal element because its there. we are here because they named it but we're
there because its there. I cant dream because I dont exist here. And because I am stone

more women in slacks, I do remember that
first there was a vat
of white rice or ricelike stuff
thats the antarctic as food
thats the ice of no images as food
the vat was as large as a. I dont know what it was as large as
comparisons are stupid the queen soul and I
were walking later at night of course in our slacks as if we were being
slack, no thats   stupid.   into a theater space again
She is a silkyhaired brunette and
is dressed in a bright red sweater and pants tight sweater and slacks
we will die gendered or sexed   in your unknowing eyes
though it is only in your eyes or is it lexicon we will die (have you ever seen)
white Im wearing white because Im nothing now at all

white for nothing or white for ignorance the
ignorance of the meeting of leviathans all leviathans of light at night and not
remembering. never never remember
what we said in our core of light
cant remember what   we sing or say
we sing that light water light in   syllables we cant understand though
we understand each other
perfectly

Later there was the phrase "life support system" it would make you want to vomit.

there is nothing to tell me.
          tell me something to
nothing to tell me
no life, nothing to tell
soul has nothing to
because reason and the color blue are gone   *not for long not really*
reason gone. my red is along
just being scarlet red
reason is quiet because she doesnt have to speak now

Everyone and their excellent body parts their good looks their life support systems
how stupid can you get. they think they're their brains

you remem doctrine not doctor of ignorance it isnt a doctrine it is itself the
simultaneous nothing we are in where everything happens that doesnt happen but is
the only thing that counts. it counts up to one. ive gotten to this place. im in another
tubulous hospital room and a gaunt featured stranger a thin man runs happily
towards me thats the only image there are none usually in this doc but im not anyone
else and so i say and see what i please the gaunt featured stranger rushes towards me
wearing a gray suit

                    because we will escape you you world ones into ignorance together
this is our heresy we can have the mystical experience together or we can have the
vision of the cave and the folk together we can unite with real together and if two can

cant all and isnt that really the doctrine of the crystal city.

I can't remember the rest of the night except that I
talked to him. that stranger I knew to be you.
I did nothing but talk to you

There are hardly any there are hardly any more images its like drug withdrawal
tell me the story of. there is no. I said to him, But I have never seen you I couldnt I
see something we've invented that stands in for you an image but I could never
see you or anyone. *You* are not visible the only visible things are the ones we
manufacture that we agree to the appearance of so that we can endlessly make them.
We did not originate ourselves only the way we look at each other
in the great ignorant deep where I have a red in my forehead,
a ruby of depth of experience, we dont look at each other. the stone I am, the stone self
is changing but its still there often or maybe its ice it was usually ice in the images of
the past I mean my past though I dont have one I mean things I wrote before.

this life has been carefully constructed
to make most people suffer. they did it
themselves. we did it

I was supposed to stay interested in the testimony of the great mystics as of the great
poets but I only care about my own now. It seems to me that I am in that deep state at
the same time as when I am angry or sad for example it doesnt preclude affect it contains
it. Thus I was able to conceive of the Crystal City, which has nothing to do with religion
or sainthood, but a little something to do with philosophy since it rescues sophia from its
male rules from games. I am in that City now and I am not in a trance. not tingling. I
may be dead I haven't accepted your sense of what is or isnt I am conscious and many of
you seem to be here. There are not images at this point but I still crave them. I would
describe the crystal as it doesn't exist in such a way that you would never want to be
elsewhere. But I can't find images. I wear and am in white.

buried images
all night forgotten again, hospitals   clusters of hospitals we   were driving
towards as into the movie screen at that same theater   at that theater that we
women/girls in slacks keep entering. Earlier   someone had said a leviathans a

206

monster and I felt pleased, I had thought it only whalelike but mythological or then too it is a ship a monstrously vast construction faintly outlined in gold light on the horizon distant at night. we drove toward hospitals all night   they had nothing to do with truth only a contrived necessity   They are images my only dreams, plus the women in slacks.

the codl that is cod code or cold   all codes hurt there is no real code. we're just like its dirt or snow to is it speak its communality all the dirt or snow we'll ever be all the blood in the river run. its just. it isnt a code. i hated being explained to and meditated at as well performed to formed at and made the object of anothers desire to seem to exist as a difference when any one is and there are no fools and we are all equal. and yet i did it too i cant avoid it its like the hospital all the hospitals, all there are are roads hospitals and also, i know, airports. but the world is really composed of hospitals smelling of profound brown-dark fluids collected and disposed of as cheap stuff the cheap.

> I will include the old dream I've already included twice
> Dec 24, 1998 I dreamed variously and in this dreams final
> transformation in which I lived under a theater marquee
> with another woman with whom I
> was always trying to find food: I am no longer on the sidewalk
> I am no longer in the dream as I. Audrey Hepburn
> perhaps in India, outdoors in a natural setting, a womans cloth over her
> head but a physician, is testing a member of her own family for
> cancer. The cancer is there. In the traditional manner of grief
> she paints her eyes red–red circles. She is riding on a cart,
> horsedrawn and heaped with things. A voice says to her
> that it is good to paint the whole body red. There is a reference to
> the figure of love, my love, and the color brown, which in my symbolism
> of color relates to reds spectrum and the soul, and in his to kindness
> I have the right to include this.

this is where love becomes the target of this poem its pure eye

stone or ice or nothing love nothing. at the bottom of the hole of images   is the
nothing of love   the ultimate image is the hospital   or the woman as
woman as if that were   at the bottom   of the hole of images is   love.
images of evolution transparent in their lie fly past my tired when it was only ever the
word love will do. it is white   and thats why my outfit of sweater and slacks is as
pale as love a hospitals   is a urinous paleness different from that its a bleaching
out of any image but its own. Love is white   because it has no shadings it
doesnt think, its selflessness is unimaginable   it has as a reality no image
whatsoever It is nothing and I have been reduced to it I am still praying for dreams
praying for images as others say they pray for the sick but who can understand that?
the soul I say is the second body or is it the first, first or second no difference Ive said
second so lets stay with second. Ive been left with nothing and thats where it is. the
second is here. red is here for the life, white is here for all that counts nothing, blue is
in abeyance here but not really is a surrounding skirt of element for the monstrous
whales who sing white they sing white im in what they sing. if i paint my body red
youll know whats happening but   I dont care if you do. not all the voices are
true. how is your own horse-driven cart of junk doing, speaking to anyone? The sun
rises over the red eyes of the mountain gods who have wept blood and stone for their
eons of lives so everyone says but when has anyone ever said what counted. they
were just more males. and in the deep and in the deep the whalish presences are
growing whiter and whiter and the deep itself is white icy white but fluid

          there is still the matter of the image beneath the shattered glass because
it is matter.

          It was like a circus but maybe that was the smaller one since I wont settle
for this circus down here. there was an image once born of love what was it? was it
simply a baby was it that same old baby. probably not or probably

THE FRENCH WORD FOR FOR

towards where   and in a dirty wind
the rue Bleue crosses the   rue du Faubourg Poissonnière
becoming the rue de Paradis
                                        I'm a man and I fly,
I lift just off the ground in low flight
am movie hero trash in this dream but I
did fly and   whoever I was I was certainly myself inside,   flying
first there was a rumbling in my ears
signalling I might leave my body? the image I flew as
seems chosen by   the sense of humor of the soul? (who is also   I)

later I am a woman but really only a witnessing   consciousness i.e.   an older
woman   the scruffy young men   have a bag of white powder
this is so   oldfashioned
last night and at breakfast theyre dying to take it. drink the drug in water
I stare at them and their short dark beards. I had a better beard   when I was flying
I had a beard and long, vain hair

So, some dreams are back.

                                the heavy lapis beads unstrung, an ornately
framed photo of a dead one
                        and the sexism in the side chamber, a famous dead poet is
coming over hes already in the side chamber   making telephone calls, as any
important person does, though he hasnt come over yet   and the floor is still
to be swept   because this is a dream
                                If I sweep up the dust   and am
the only woman here,   though a poet of equal talent   isnt that sexist?
In another room a jewel sale. because I'm smarter than you and can write better.
Because I'm smarter   does that mean its okay to sweep the floor anyway
or to listen to the blather   of the rich woman buying jewels enough to cover her
head her ears her whole neck? because I can put up with it better   because
I'm so smart
                        So I must be happy
at the return of images of how things are

209

and   that to want to fly   as a second body to paradise   is   only a wish for
a tacky heroism.

                              Wasnt this all supposed to turn to love?
turn to love for all and love larger even than two and than sexedness?   and the
heavy blue beads are back,   the heavy deep blue of reason is back.   they are
my beads and I have them still   as well as loves white shirt.   *dont sweep*
the floor you need to know what the dust thinks what the dust thinks   *doing all the*
thinking   *its the only one thinking.*

the dust is the only one thinking. sometimes its beautiful dirt in the desert
but in an apartment its dust, thinking You dont need to fly to know   What do I
know? I cant find you   at a large family party   youve left with others and my
loved dead messenger stares at me sternly she is the goddess   of reason here the
figure in blue or purple tall forbids me to search for you though I will, I will continue
to theres no hierarchy   to tell me what to do, especially in love, there is no
goddess there is no flying no hierarchy and no drug

the party is in memory
                        of my brother and it is a party, so no one is thinking, the dust
is the only one thinking   I am the dust, sorry,   Im dreaming, that is,
thinking. I see everyone except for you and those youve chosen to leave with in the
dream as I am choosing in this poem to be the dust now or is it snow. love is full of
rejection and loss it swallows them useless images of others illusory choices bits of
mercury silly cling together to be bright when theres only light is light an image I see it
and refuse to sweep sweep up myself or be swept up as the dust   because it is
great light   So in the city I am conscious today am the white hole ever,
I am consciousness obliterated image,
                                    that is what the dust is thinking. the dust: I am
conscious. I am conscious

He will give us face lifts, he will give both love and myself cosmetic surgery. he and
his wife have come for one day to give us cosmetic surgery. just what any one or

thing needs, just what any dust. his name is john of course. so we can feel better.
I dont want to feel better I'm

waiting for the poet for the party for the great for the need to group and leave others
and for others desire to help others   to   go   away.

i know what i am inside here, as soul
i am not speaking, the dust is speaking:

swirling dust motes o ligh some one or thing is bothering me   stirring me up to
what, what was it ever about? to be more than crystal, is about what? i still dont
know why theres anything to doi am just here   and the lapis beads,
round and tough are within reach if one wants a thought but i am just here. even
when you left with the others was just dust   are you you or i   are you
really another?   i have always been this   dust or light or snow, it   The
partys for drunks, the world, good people there like drunks. and the lapis beads roll
nearer i am the i light dust the beads are bringing more messages do i want them?
rolled up images in thought. no one can ever sweep me out of the universe whats the
point, you rolled up images in thought? *we are the beads of thought thats all, thats all.*

there are two of him there should only be one. there are two of me should only be

the one you on dont see. I found you awake and later   we said we were this was
the story, walking down the dark mountain path being followed in a parallel manner
in the woods, hear the sticks breaking   by a small furred one called Bear With
Me. it got in the car with us and it changed into a blue skinned angelic figure
clothed in white and we drove, it in the backseat, through the countryside, to   an
isolated house   Then we entered a room–   angelic figure no longer
with us–   on whose floor there were large white gauze footprints   we've
entered through two separate doors   the footprints are under the table, you say
and theres a fireplace to the right I say but the fire isnt fire its a fiery form, for
purgation or maybe ecstasy? is everyone else in this room? I would like I said my
soul as   an elemental form of the body   to enter through that door. That
would imply division of you you said since youre already here. No because Im not
really in this room Im only seeing it I said. I want really to enter through that door.

naked and to talk to the artist in the bathroom where the tub is I must put on my clothes how ridiculous white shirt black pants   talk to him in black and white when I was perfectly naked. how can I take a bath in these clothes   Then, in a later place   everybody talked all night in their pad beds

                                             all the gates to the city all the gares are piled with garbage.
That is a literal
                    am light up a core jewel first theres pain and its burned off by unliteral fire am a cylindrical though uneven crystal inner walking amid the garbage of the gare de l'est. ignorant of the fact, theyd say, that im lit up but im not o mystics im not ignorant of it and im not using it as power. the lie here is that im in the gare that is the image and some of the words   that i use but i am lit up and that is an all. i seem in this state to want to be amid the garbage of the gare de l'est   being the origin of light myself there is no outside or other light. there is no other there is no use there is no god or great light, i am not a crystal i am light its not light and it isnt coming from anywhere else. the garbage is like snow   or is it dirt and has its own beauty thats why i want to be here   walking up a staircase littered turn to take a métro as I do most days. the light has come from nowhere the mystics are wrong   fills up fingers eyes mouth so that they arent they that is, there.

there are frames like small rectangular paintings—such as the figure of the soul was once painting in a dream with barely a line or two on a blue or violet background— these new rectangles contain a density of the lines which i had, after that first dream, characterized as dimensions lines: the beginnings of the world as our perception of it. These new frames contain as I say those lines but each holds a thick black line in particular. One of the frames or rectangles was trembling as if it were on my eye trembling. I heard voices but now cant remember what they said

San Francisco, they always say   and that   always means poverty.

I have a new map   is it what that rectangle became?

of a green and beautiful terrain
when I remove the old one and affix the new to the wall (like the shattered-glass
poster?) everything changes from being worn
brightens, hills and grass, greenery
the map is shaped like a cross, in broad strips like the floor
of a cathedral

               What is the French word for for? pour   poor

all night they rearranged the parts of my or your or our bodies. that was a dream since
there is no they but I cant remember it. burn the icons first, that was an old old dream
at least a year and a half ago when I presided over the burning of icons in a football
stadium, you burn your icons you rearrange your parts you give away you give way I
have nothing to say Go somewhere on the map the top of a hill or inside a grotto just
go   there and sit. im in the grotto of course, and i must be burning again
burning off my own image What is the french word for for? burning it away its of no
use the they cant have it any more the icon of me because the blister the blistering of
the cameo is burning the profile the filigree and wings the hat of wisdom and the neck
that holds it all together everythings twisting and burning while i see i mean sit here.
burning in the fire in the grotto or is it the blue room. whats el left your bird love id
said love, so its love. thats just a good name for it there are these names for it love
poverty and reason i must have left out something well its alright to leave it out
because we know what you mean. why is this so long? because it takes more than m
more than one poem to go through it. which parts do you think they rearranged i
think they changed my liver and heart to pieces of crystal that is stone and smoothed
them down with sanding paper. who were they they were my agents they were all me.
and your eyes? right now theyre burning but theyll come back   blue again blue
rocks. and my skin. i dont expect to feel different i just know this is happening it was
happening before and before now its nearly done. whats the point. to make a new
being, not human. not part of it. not part of the definition. and if helplessly left with
love then thats because despite all of our previous centuries of words it has been left
out despite the overuse of it as an or the icon it hasnt ever been there except in
moments when no one even recognizes it but thats all there was and is and so i dont
want your hat. my skin will be covered with grafts of sand and i will know how to fly.
dont bother. dust and all the garbage in the gare de l'est because its the love you and
not the not the icon. it will do if the worlds turned to garbage the true icon and the
one i wasnt burning smooth me out now cool me down finish sanding and grafting.

look what you got and you thought love was a song or your ass or the emotion of loss.
look what it does it transforms you they said well it does.

on luna vista rio vista or flora vista street, we are or I am being treated
for post traumatic stress disorder. but I cant remember the treatment or
why I was being treated   how convenient
well it was a dream and so   I gave myself the treatment. now on the subway of
the american nations capitol Im talking to a young   brownskinned woman with
an aquiline nose   and her friend   Im telling them about my poetry and

how easy it is to understand   tell them about *When I Was Alive* and suddenly
remember the first poem   its about the hair of the dead lover of a dead poet
isnt that easy?   its about time   the poets hair was there too   when I saw
it in real time while I had post something else depression   how poor I was
without new body parts   I have a new body   I have new hair   No you
dont   I have a new   I have a new   body

FLIGHT

the male principle as seen from the back
in white shirt jacketless and dark pants walks
towards the female principle miss monroe
sitting in light jellolike dress breasts upturned
at the seaside in a large tent amid other large tents

she is the star and prize, I am not in this story
though feel how she embodies a power found

she revels in her own overwhelming
reality. in the dream I
begin to believe in her and her strength

I cant tell you how much this disgusts me

I dont believe in that moment or those
opposites

                         then where do i go. here   where the torture of
female and male its delusion is preeminent but where i have now   an inhuman
body, because i have an inhuman mind. soul. and i saw the whole train in its
fickleness the whole train   crisscrossing the city of earth entangling us in its
machinations on the surface of my own eye, so you could go anywhere do nothing any
way do nothing as something on the surface of your eye. but i have white stripes
painted on my under body at this moment. the dead are whispering the love song
Poor Soul in my ear   *poor soul go to the failed crook/ tell him to rise to the*
occasion/ of our failure.   my uncle is there   no longer to say goodbye   to me in
spanish but to refract   the sounds of the crystal city. *go to the used girl/ tell her.*
We are no longer the humans, so we dont need sexes or leaders, *but go to your lover*
and tell him/ you are each others because/ you have new bodies now. I have new body
parts now. that is because I have

an inhuman soul.

i went home and it was an
inset shed room full of
dust a doctor and boys
the home i grew up in
with dust or steel wool

i expected to see everyone
it was bare brown wood
dusty steel wool
everywhere like angel hair.

thanksgov thanksgiving dust full of skies
where were all the other people i'd come home to see?   it is a dream of loss poor
thing, well wont settle for that in the inhuman soul there is no poor thi   We are
calling you now to look and see, the more you lll the more you sss

I am reading a French newspaper   in the south of france, in an area of olive trees a
young girl went missing the girl   grisly discovery ah has been made. she was
murdered and then gangs separate gangs came and ate her   in small pieces
almost all of her,   over a period of time. what's left of her is intaglioed into the
rock ground of the area which is round rock there is the shape of her head and two or
three smaller round shapes inside, small organs of the head   inside what would
be the facial outlines,   a sense of hair and nothing else uneaten except for long
long fingers stretching crossways unending so they disappear. it took the police some

time to find her riding their horses along the green riverbank because their horses
refused to go near her corpse if you can call it that even when they gave the horses the
tranquilizer temesta the horses wouldnt help find her but then someone did find
her   now Im there and I force myself to keep looking at her. I realize I am she
awaken falling back asleep ask if I cant now see a better thing so I climb into a bed with
that rough blue blanket   available hospital-type metal sides,   Will I fly? I
ask. The voices answer You will fly

there wasnt a point they just kept making it up and making it up torturing and
torturing. no one even knows who they hurt, you do it in your clothes   but I
dont wear those clothes for a body any more
tell my mother she had me so I could fly

                                        the inhumans mass together nothing
doing nothing the tall tapes the wide songs the wide wide songs as long as fingers. if
you killed me   if you ate me   you probably did me a favor   and this song
can be for you   though I despise you. despise despise?   in the crystal city
despise? anyone who wont fly   when they can (myself)   Calling to
flight which is not what you know. calling to my own   flight.

more   shit   it has to be shown   to a doctor (Ive negated doctors)   A
woman has it in a jar now, masses of it its, stinking up the whole house before
she gets her strange glutinous shit to the doctor (I have negated the doctor)
she, just someone, with the same name as her husband   has taken her shit to the
doctor and come back   from the hospital with a baby a large baby. girl baby same
name as her father

run run run to the skies if you can   have hastened to the run to Im running.
its just my empty head emptied out eaten by you ghouls thats flying. if its too hot for
your hand   become fire   if its too airy for your head become air air. they made
me   they made me do it anyway   they made me like this and now they
cant catch me *dont know what im not thinking*   *we found your body on the rock*
ground   peaceful in full flight   which body   body soul dont know
you saw it

I keep looking at these things done to me
I keep flying away. by the sea in a large tent, fly away from the repulsive yin yang
symbol, in full flight
away from the repulsive mother goddess   and her manly adept,
away from the notion of oceans of hormones away from sexual frequn frequency
waves sex atomic photons neurons male diagram of spirit   Flying out of this
poor   away from the better word for it away from the brain

and So too leave the house of women.
                                say goodbye to woman alone and her daughters
in the night in their solitary house. she says goodbye in her bathrobe. go home homes

a different house A lot of people A cartoon principle a childlike mechanical thing a
babylike gadget   is happy   to be home, performs cartwheels and I think 'It's
happy, inhuman shape.' I walk about in black bra and panties but soon I'm

graduating.   wearing my graduation robe   among the male graduates
I lower my head into the cloth   make a bill-like shape with my hands
and pretend to be a duck...   I'm the only one who thinks this is funny. on a
stone bench my robe gets mixed up with the mens they take theirs away and say, "we
dont want ours mixed up with yours" mine is a different color of course. Still I've
graduated. so, duck

I wouldnt want to stop. I still dont know how to love the

arrogant botchers.   get tangled up in the crystal branches an instant
preferring the philosophy songs of the literal slaves to that of the hi philsophers will
not make you p p p popular. He is singing about union again blind union is singing about
god by which he means the equalizer   because no one you know ofs the
equalizer or will be. he is singing about the voices he is singing about the friends
who are all dead dead already your graduation gowns gone dust I went up on the top
of and saw tangled line a hair snarl where there was supposed to have been the

future

I thought I saw a book there now Im in the tingling and dont want to stop but here
maybe you dont the air dont the air look deep?
you never let me in but here the doors open air   they cant fly no they never could.
those   graduates

amid the colors of earth no wild place. the carefully preserved trees   in the small
parks with their yellow leaves breathing fumes the color of a but you know it that
brown-blue the color of a clue that you dont. I was walking near the carefully
constructed hill with its humanmade grotto   speaking of people to a person   or
I could have been   working what color   is human work? I know the color of
inhuman work but the color of human work is rust brown its very rusty. the color of
inhuman work is red of course. Then I flew over these things a sort of topological map

from that height and there was a sense of reasonableness what color the gray of densensitization smeared with shit. There was more shit the smeared brown of situation streaked the walls of the decent houses I flew above and further above the colors changed to pure blue and then pure red in the air that I was a mannish being in wearing a horned hat what an interesting view theres a mountain up here somehow leading up to the red mist where I'll find a message and the bird to ride back down. I have to walk now walk up a path. theres no one to get a message from as usual but theres a message it is STICK. its a crystal stick. ride the birds back which is black. the birds wings are slow and wavy I am no longer a man I am a hollow girlfaced outline with the organs inside it of. stick love sticking. black hawk. apple of eye. those automatic words can now come true oh automatism you always knew what you were about I you. we are riding up a little little higher above the grand canyon and then over a white polar cap and down, down into the stuck situation. I have a secret stick. by which I tell I feel it the little futures and I also tell the truth just feel it along the surface here you can feel the skulls but also feel the grape leaves and snakes twining round carved into the truth as the truth bites with loving fangs. this stick is a pole as long as my finger its a pole up through the colors into the crystal and down back down.

a chasm in the dead earth
so narrow a book can lie across it like a bridge
a manuscript with a black binder
in the chasm light someones there I can only see the arm I think its a girl
child in a Chinese brocade jacket red   red.

if we have made both hell and heaven and they exist now and we are god
and we have made the earth and the universe because we've defined them,

I still have to go for a walk with a john   as if he were a little god outside amid the
boulders and pines where on earth is that? somewhere I will never see again
no place remains the same now and I'm trying to get it over and there's this walk,
during the course of which at some point I'll be embraced, I'll say No   it happened
the last time as this dream knows. It's getting too late let's get it over with. I'm
putting in the proper punctuation   because I feel very emphatic about the fact that
I won't be embraced.

        If you use the book as a bridge. without stopping   or maybe
you go down there where the hole of images might be. the book shows you where she
is. because I still dont know why that hole is How did we make it Why do we ignore it?
how did we make it
                    did we come from it? nothing but us all it and our
phantasms
on the walls might be another story, just another story.

here in a life here in a house, back from the truncated   vision of the chasm, its
hard and sweet at the same. the inevitable girl babys kept in a decorated
recessed square in the wall. I wear a red full-skirted tulle dress no those two things are
images dreams and they are also true in some sense that I must wear the foolish dress
of soul of   grace its a very foolish dress I have covered myself with red though
nobody knows.   I'm not a human   am I the arm in the chasm   am I the
book that crosses it am I the chasm all those as well as the flight and owner of the pole
up which one flies to the crystal city using it as a guide

up the pole and spiraling around it
through the blue and the red
or
down the pole   around it into the chasm
same the same

down past the earthen walls
to the crystal mist of supposed   beginnings
the voices are down there too   past images seasides and episodes
theres something very thick and white lovelike   I   suppose

FIDELITY

big sunlight house littered two or three stories a moving process and beloved relation
is talking to everyone upset at them   She turns to me too and upset about my
diaries they're my younger diaries   Whats wrong with them I dont know what
shes found Does she have the right to read them?   do I still know them care for
them   am I faithful to   them and her

　　　　Ah I've included my younger diaries in here,
earlier in this poem embedded buried in a layer. Both to cast off dross of self and keep
it true, or is it be true　　　Now　　my diaries are this these dreams this
thinking/speaking and crystal How do you like my diar   so big

No sun small room
someones coming up the stairs. I'll　　　　shrink

my diaries werent good and I wasn't　　　　that might be what she

　　　　Getting on a plane, a different dream
　　　　　　　　　　　　　　　our cat goes in the back　　so does my
aunts her cat. oh my cats really dead   my aunts beloved relation is was   dont
say her name I have a ticket for the front of the plane, because I'm not a cat Do I have
to take a plane Like a person or a cat   for   flying

　　　　climb up the pole and no   plane no. Watch out for that airplane,
invisible flying shaman Watch out for people, airplane, for people in sky.
that shaman there had younger diaries   and was a girl   who couldnt
even write, it was thought, because   she wrote like a girl   I'm glad. thus
she was faithful   Now I'm faithful   writing like an inhuman an
unshaman too

　　　　fidelity sought when anothers diary is read am I really trying to be faithful.
faithful to Fate   Sun no sun climbing the pole Is it enough, love asks, that they
just be voices? in the crystal city But they arent
　　　　　　　　　　　　　　　f voices a shifting in the spectrum

of reason to love to souls sum of experience, blue to white to red in any   order
fills the leviathan soul identity light dragging words out dragging words that arent
words across the sky. dd dont even looook am I faithful. I go to a party in a big house
another one of those houselike houses   to which Im not faithful   out of the
past   theres a doily on his chair back   when I must ask   the figure of
love, sitting with two other men,   if hes faithful, because hes ignoring me, if

hes faithful to me   Yes he says So   he pursues me across   the old
campus, in the form of another at night. in the form of another man, one who grins a
lot   Because people present themselves to others with a set of fixed
characteristics The most boring part Of being alive a sort of fidelity to ones set of fixed.
which arent really fixed   Across the sky listen to the sky across the

       sky. I am now sometimes marked with a dark X on my breast. was sitting
in the corner of the toilet I mean the train and it was, could be, a toilet   seat,
where I sat, it gradually transformed   into the respectable seat of a train. so I was
next respectable. going somewhere always somewhere. respectable faithful to our
ways   of all outward train seat   Across the sky listen to the sky, all   the
people   youre trying to hear down here   are there too   speaking to you. you
are fixed forever among others where there are no qualities like   boring and
respectable   but faithful? does that resonate have I been   so to the or to thee
or to   to this poem, what good is that? I thought that   fidelity was built in
Built in to what Built into the fact that one doesnt get out of it, this mess
except for those flights up and down Ah Out

We floated down together, love and I

into a chasm
into a deep chasm at night with green pine and it would be blue   stream,
nearly full moon. rabbits. We   walked on the path. There were orange flowers
along the way, you could see they were orange and   that they exuded spiritual
vapors,   on the way to the cabin   theres a cabin for us   with hard cots a
wood-burning stove. deer outside, because we're still outside, on the way to the cabin

discussing what form of chasm this is that contains this landscape a cabin and such
flowers which he hopes are marigolds but   I say have three large petals. This is a
chasm in between times   in between minutes of time   There is time and

there are times We live in times and go to time. This is more like time because its In between minutes of time. floated down   probably spiralled   round the invisible crystal pole. Come in always come in. Lie down in the cots and hear the deer and the flowers hear the pines hear the moon hear the rabbits. hear the air the old air to which be faithful

Keep being sent by whom some self to the basement of the castle I remember this castle there was once a knight here   old like leather,   but this is lower than ever
          maybe its below sea level nothing
          remember nothing happening so I'm
back in a diner with a guy. sitting at a diner counter, coffee, I know who he is am not looking at him, and talking just that view of the hand coffee counter that landscape. he has always   had fixed characteristics   a diner man, so everyone loves him hes faithful. and hes faithful to computers, eats in a diner faithful to computers. faithful to a woman he faithful The worl and pollu All the smoke of others between between the teeth all the fume he has car. faithful faithful the vision of 1950 he has sometimes had prosm promiscuous 60s times too faithful to them and   faithful to radical politics in   countries other than his own. he eats a piece of   faithful pie

          Later,   eating,   another and I, Love? and will have dessert white dessert before the main course
both are of tofu
          Must get on the airplane The people in the this house and in particular one man arent Going to let me get to the airplane on time. this man thinks that hes the king of tofu   of tofu healing and knowledge of mind and he wont let me get to the airplane   on time and on my own, sits in his smug chair like knows everything This is all useless The desserts on the street and in the air the tofus every where like   a lotus the white and has no king king of tofu. like the desert desert of love no king of
          theres no one in the center of the lotus   you dont have to be faithful to someone   to someone or thing in the center of the lotus an ancient   manlike thing   not faithful to the godlike human

223

Keep being sent back down to the basement of the castle. again again
then Leave a house Torn between leaving and staying Oh   leave it

Outside is the countryside in its new pale of pollution People are staring at birds
in pale nearly leafless trees   The birds are perfectly still They
are birds I've rarely seen in my life
There's a red bird there's a bluebird both
are somewhat pale but yet Are Red and blue
I walk towards the bluebird since I've never seen one it remains still
Why are they still?   And something is flying
a form in the sky but it's probably a shaman   or me the inhuman one
hovering faithful and trying trying to
What do   you do about this pollution? this pallor

                                        Must fly more. men are
carrying   a large   marilyn monroe doll, and acting as if its real. later castle
castle all night   and two medical situations   one in which everything's all
right and one in which it isnt Theres a sort of struggle   The first one gradually
wins   Both situations are larger

than a person Though not the size of a room they are the size perhaps of a table a
rectangular dinner table. ones medical situation is larger than ones body and is a
shape   the shape's size isnt important because the shapes   edges dissolve
There is no size There is no size of a person   The medical situation of
the figure of love   the   positive mode gradually wins.

        We will make love and will fly too   will be shamans and lovers so you (not
you) cant make the definitions. we're making our own definitions   and may or
may not be faithful to them. there is no faith but there may be fidelity It is a univer
principl how the cosmos sticks together I suppose   so   dont think about it   I
do know fidelity of rock. always rock in the   scrubby forests in the pallid air

                                        I walked
down the stairs to the basement again, not of the castle but of a cave   there was a
snake there it rose up to greet me, from its coil it stood first curved then straight. It

became my stick the pole up to crystal city the carved crystal stick. I ascended curving round and round it up through the hills out and up still spiraling then left it   to fly over the world. air was brown both cloudy and brown but I felt full surprise to be flying flat and caught by the wind but safe, the pole disappeared. I was over the fields of france. I looked for a message to bring back and only saw patch of blue sky it seemed to be the message. I descended soon around spiralling there it was the pole again, into the cave. I'm hopeful I dont know how or why. I dont feel like telling anyone except for here no one is watching. I dont what what its hope of it doesnt say anything a rag a ragged piece of the sky the old sky. that is the message *A piece of the old sky piece of the oldest sky/older than the human/because I am older than the human.*

Soul is back and wants me to go   out to dinner with her the dark the figure of soul the mature woman. someone else wants to too all go together perhaps I dont have a lot of time. walk down the street   Nothing nothing sky nothing landscape. Old enemy reads irrelevant prose theres no enemy this part must be long time ago a fragment of stale time flickering here. all the relevant pieces are both in and out of time. irrelevant pieces of stale time hover and go

the figure of love and I, and the woman whos usually with women, in a field. a field on grass and there are several cagelike structures here dovecotes pens open sheds she used to, she says, in the past, write her poems in such structures. theres an odd partial light, brown   clouds. I'll never write in such again   am carrying my fragment of blue reason's sky about with me all out of its time like a tornup handkerchief Shes so nostalgic for cages Are they her youthful diaries Love and I enter a bleak city room hear the gossip and make love Because we always do it is part of past present
          and future And later and later a mere child has scattered
my jewels all over the floor. perhaps its dead cousin pick them up I've found
my topazes and moonstones
Birthstones and unshaman stones. *I think a shaman doesnt fly high enough*
We are the sky itself Heres my blue letter Coming roughedged
out of my pocket again Air And a propensity
And a spherical sense of time   Unfixed propensity. what happens to me is
unimportant so unimportant soul fl bathed in blue which spreads via tinli
tingling from here to you Can you feel it? stop Stop. feel it and stop Poetry has always

been for stopping
Beneath a piece of the old sky nothing older There is no older

crystal all around me down here earth cluttering my things, so get rid of my things
its in between us but can see through it so Can hear it
the glints, I can hear them of the special colors. they go into this soup I'm
cooking so scrupulously, faithful   it's different from   fidelity to my clothes and
to the deathshead   in my suitcase   throw them away   thats in a kind of
disposable   past   mind   I'm supposed to be packing up to go into
another hospital room   pink nightgown red shorty nighty highnecked flannel
for cold old night, nighties all for the hospital   of this world   and the
deathshead face lying on top of them all in the suitcase throw them away. throw them
away   out the high window. throw out the suitcase clothes arent the real
diary   I have this sense of being watched   being watched in this hospital
leave it   They are watching us they   are interested in our pathologies. the
path is wide I   stand at the penned in ocean An ornamental fishpond
watching an edgeless golden fish with scroll-like fins which seem to dissolve
supposed to write it down on clipboard. dont. am watching   watching the only
godlike
beautiful

Shapes metallic or iron blue so would be reasonable
with ragged edges like the old sky's These are love's
pain   I'm caught in a
fight with them all night
They are in charge of me or us in
a negative manner again and I fight them down, they stabilize
they lose their negative power

Are they older than the human the mammalian reptilian bacterial are they
old
Shapes metallic or iron blue   which become reasonable

SUN SUN SUN SUN

a row a strip of tall, crystal cylinders   a model of the crystal city
if it were composed of cylinders perhaps we're each cylinders, like   cylinders
extending up and down with a surface curved round bluish Where is this model?
somewhere else, or not, two lovers sit at a   reception table that's encrusted,

along its edges, with semi-precious   stones which make a changing grooved or is
it ragged   edge, something whose configuration   modulates slowly   the
encrustation's   thickness topology and colors change before your eyes, all along the
table's edge   like   No not like. unexpected   beauty

It is here   perhaps that there is mention of "the most beautiful sight in the world"
somewhere nearby.

earlier in mothers house a curse
written high on her bedroom wall
in crude red letters, a curse against
figure of Love and myself he

shows it to me Ive been
ignoring it tangled like in
shadows from a tree before now
as we've been lying in the bed

        An angry girl from this town
and in a gray dress
                broke in and wrote it,
with her boyfriend,
                just jeans
They   hate us. Who are they?
Shes young tall overweight righteous
but hes taller, limper yet sly
who are they,
                some tacky   Shakti and Shiva?

her name may mean crazy. what does that have to   They wont allow us, but why
not   Crazy, here, means double duplicit, lies   The pleasures of the curse in a
gray dress. unreason   hugs a twisted rag rose baby oh the pleasure of hating,
the pleasure of justice? why us?   is it because we're not double? not enough of the
shallow   enculturated male and female?

        shes with in fact another john a
        manipulative man named john. she

        changes. and changes others
        disruptive with mood. as a goddess
        would be
        The hole of images produced her
            as a choice for
        a demon lover. who's even less
        compelling
                      Wheres City?
        Crystal   Cylinder   City

        the world chose language not life–
        that is, to curse–   but
        neither are it.
                  sun sun sun sun
        vs the game of pain in mind

           life and its language, not The language.

The table of beauty and love
may come directly from the hole of images, or even
be it, operational. a show of edges a world's
surface a demonstration of the real which

also produces the insanity of cursing others called freedom or randomness
Probably has mathematical equivalents who cares
its all tyranny,   pain in mind.   and the lovers at the table
are exhibitionists   adonis and venuslike Dont   trust them

we are denied our original beauty? our light   must be split into characters
into fem and masc   as these couples are.

A woman long blond hair and an important man another couple, he is the poet
but   she seems even more important,   he is the giant but she is the
blond Somebody. And when they "return"   –everything taking place   in a big
day house–   the Laws   are quickly established. that is, there are other
couples   in this sunlit bedroom, and somehow even in the bed, perhaps in a
simultaneity of times but when this couple return, an   intricacy of laws   is
established all over the bed like a written lace. it seems to be written   into the
bed   Same room   contains a large bathtub we could all   bathe in.
I get in it, some others too   Same room: Abby is sad   shes a blond too
Abby   Abby, Abby

       We the other kind of couple, awake, invent another story:
                                                  You say   that
there is a point of light emitted   from one faceted crystal towards another. What is
it doing, saying What is the message Who   well I had a vision then of how
everything we are being   was that crystal communication, underneath the usual
world,   the emission of points of light between crystals,   was   being
conducted   as in the other the City that I posit   All of the colors and facades of
this world covering that. images   somewhere perhaps on the table   of
semiprecious modulating edges   So,

I said I see a fifties man a drawing from a childrens schoolbook   in a suit and
hat with a briefcase or is it suitcase   carries the point of light in his case
A drawing seen against   the non-drawing of the world. But it is so drawn, the
world   He is colorless though, hes a hole in the world. carrying light
                                                  carrying light
       Abby Dalton, the fifties movie actress is sad.   at a table she is sad He will bring
her a point of light she already has it but shes still sad,   another couple

       This is a room of huge white
urnlike vases gleaming marble ivory but

white of all whites. filled with flowers,
a man's here just taller than the vases
arranging the flowers
a lot of them blue.

it feels like the City too   and obviously isnt couples
split into that prized and symbolic disunity woman and man   Then my old love
deadbutdidntdie   is here in eager radiant youth and shirtsleeves. He has a stain
on his face a scar or mar   but hes full of light,   finally,   uncoupled
Couple   comes from   the hole of images but love itself doesnt. around the
edge   of the hole of images   where semi-precious stones change and
glitter   love was only an exhibit. We're still down to this: a *truer* love, the fact of

sorrow, and how to be reasonable Is this hole   the origin of   the sun which burns
it away? the socket for the sun which burns sorrow away. This isnt sex talk its the
process   of union/disunion we've invented as a universe   but I know
gender's irrelevant   I know more than our universe   The couple
curses   the figure of Love and myself because we arent double, we're something
more than a couple. we are the point of light between us   we are the points of
light between us   we are the point/points of light between us and others

          And I saw this from the top of my STICK   because we two love
like inhumans   like crystal cylinders light pouring vertically through and also
radiating from   its round one surface. And we are *all* practically STICKS.

this is the old dinosaur   this is the old boxing ring.   not as old as old as
the hold Go.   I'm the allosaurus No.   I'm the cit itself and a part a cylinder a
facet a point of light and the one you return me. is there a reason but shiva and shakti
arent it. it's origin, that point of light, whatever its being or saying between   it's its
the point light no message it isnt a message but it's   the universe the universes,
the one enormous faceted crystal that is both totality and the point of light between us
(thats why she hates us) I smell the hospital   smelled it all night the human

odors of urine and sweat and bile but I also smelled crystal   you have senses so

use them find them all use them. This is the old dinosaur, This is the old boxing ring
Gets into the ring with   the human types and loses. Nothing loses Sun sun sun
sun   burns off the vanity of couples burns the world of the dinosaur burns its own
birth Three gorillas stand   in front of the same ring the next night, the same old
boxing ring. Get into the ring No. thats all I remember one was weaker he lacked a
certain layer of power but had sun sun sun sun on his side if he didnt enter it. dont
enter the old boxing ring in the same old void space of same old world. dont go into
battle dont participate in   the Gita an old farce worlds full of them   so
solemnly adhered to

          Sun sun sun sun is burning me as I swirl to the top of my crystal   stick
it is burning away the   I saw the smiling face   of therapist I dont need
I saw the three dismal choices against the black mount of montmartre and one was
cracked   the young man must   take the cracked one because
someone must take the cracked one, this is our why dont you   take the
cracked one instead? so I grabbed it and took it up   all the way up with me to
the top of the stick sun sun sun sun is burning that crack away. that if you choose you

might choose the best of something,   and someone else get the worst Burning
so there is no choice. The crazy woman the goddess the grievanced for no reason
young   woman who wrote a crude curse on my mothers wall   doesnt exist at all
and now she is simply burning words are burning everything that isnt the only
language that which is   the simple point of light   anyone carries between us.
The most beautiful sight in the world   have you ever seen it? it isnt visible of
course it is only imaginable Imaginable.

There were three boxes in front of the mount, the dark mount. Two were large and one
was smaller but in it food was being cooked, it's strangely the small one that
contains the preparation of the food.

In a school a high   school a youngish teacher with long dark hair the soulish
previous figure of reason I was, in another dream   is organizing an early day
The classes will all be held early   so there can be a tribute afterwards, to
Blind Willie McTell. and to Ruby Glaze   the blue light of blues, reason and

the red light to be there, which is which   the red telling, itself, to be there
presumably disappearing   into the music itself The language   but thats
just a figure   And so   a letter is then composed on this subject. Our return
address   in the righthand corner is S.T.Y.X.   I couldn't see the addressee

This all takes place again in front of the dark mountain.
but also in a room full of
brilliant peach light Sun sun sun sun

    The man with the suitcase
    reaches Abby and they
    both become
    points of light.
    sometimes one point of light
    Visible Abby's still sad

There's a blond woman in a basement room a sort of a prison still waiting. it's a well-
furnished room. she's sitting on a blue couch. You can see her there waiting, through
the small barred window. I'm looking in, looking down

did we invent the sun We are all this as image   Always were as point of light. and
The language   We invented the hole the edge the   sun sun sun sun
Abby's still sad. there's a woman in a basement   room, a sort of prison still

waiting   Waiting and not waiting

POISON II

find myself in a large warehouselike establishment where live white chickens are sold
by old men behind long counter. They are special chickens which become when
cooked–I am shown the literal result here, the final outcome of   my chicken's
being cooked–a single round cutlet with   a bone and white fat rim. I hold my
cutlet it's very small so compact. possibly disappointing? Other woman next seen
working on her cutlet as a scientist testing it examining it because it's suspicious
However, an outside force is using it to poison her in this world's way   and I am
told she has been poisoned simultaneously to my observing her from nowhere in
particular at her work in a dark office   with file cabinets a desk a chair she works
against the wall, it is almost a part of a corridor this room

                                        Then she is dying, sliding
down the wall   In celebration of her poisoning a troop of small schoolchildren in
blue costumes with skeletons outlined on torso stupid frilled hats are sent out by the
poisoning force to run through her room in clamorous triumph they've been
unleashed on her they run out of the room disorderly in whatever direction they
please   But shes still alive and I talk to her through a glass wall with an opening
she hands me a small round disk of evidence embossed with silver information
it will be poison, wont it? I am holding it.

                                        Latterly there is a woman in a dark cloche
hat so that you cant see her hair, her hair color at all. I think the poisoned woman's
hair was blonde and she may have been Abby. am I Abby all clocked up? keep dying
keep losing my life Do I need what they call my life

Always the mountain behind us.
waiting for a medical examination the two of us Love and I
and we've already had the same one before   Our mushrooms and snakes are
examined, a relatively thin   layer of mushrooms, as was previously seen, and

healthy snakes rise up in a row   inside us.

        The life part as shape and significance   is meaningless
because you can't imagine certain lives
there's no one to imagine   the lives all the lives No one entity doing that–

I can say mine's meaningless, as a shape, if I want to

Do you really want to see everyone you know at the end of time?
No, not *see.*

       the cave is full of snakes. and today the snake doesn't turn to crystal so I will know I am using poison to get up above us, using my venom. round and round the tall tall brownish smiling snake. smiles like me. Up here I'm above the peak of dark mountain and there are other peaks dark and smooth, some lightning, small lights also of human stations last stations left on going up. I fly up in coat and cloche hat my face darkened with grease camouflage in the dark. Seeing in the dark...transitory teeth smiles light up irrelevant. Is there such a thing as the dark if it's all that and in the mind there's never, so die and see, die of the poison a moment and see. No one comes for me because I only believe in myself–I attend the snake all the way to. into–crystal frozen venom or is it just dripping with it like spit like spit on glass in the dark One of these facets may be me Like a cemetery made of glass there's nobody here nothing but rest. Then the snake sinks fangs into my heart and the crystal lights up Sun shot Why and the glass is presences one-eyed and disappearing coming back like one's attention. Welcome to you. Am I seeing you? Not *see.* And what what do you want? To know it more. The sun goes angular and ripping into my side with heat burning and cleaning the sun is putting something inside me it's a piece of it the sun which isn't the real sun it's Sun sun sun sun. So you can burn your rest of the way through down *and I mean* the way through down. Aren't a person as you've found so now you're burning, burning it. Burning through. The tingling has changed to burning burning poison The sun is a snake The sun hurts the sun hurts to bless me Sun sun sun sun is a very poison snake.

             later in the real, lets make up a story he says
             of going down the road where the sides are fenced off
             with those white fences for the rich We are thus
             confined to going on. We are always made to keep moving
             There are mountains ahead I say
             There is a black house then, he says, With the sign of
             healing on it, the staff of Aesculapius on the door
             the serpent twined round the staff. What's inside he asks
             Snakes I say. Obviously one must be healed by snakes

All the dreams are unpleasant or dangerous.
in womany satiny bourgeois room discussing great danger their husband and father
is about to face and   it's just that in an arena he'll twirl a rope a lasso for
chrissakes I stand directly in front of him he's speaking spanish but swears–Shit!–in
english when he's handed a second frayed rope yet where's the danger It must be
symbolic Children come and speak to him   just a   dirt arena   may be
my uncle the cowboy who has died. he got handed a bad rope or deal? go into the cafe
of no that's just personal Whereas the arena of action oh yeah and the manly and the
worrying satin bourgeois older daughters of who's in a novel and if the   rope is
frayed is it a frayed snake Need a healthy healthy snakes a lot of snakes to get out of here
this performance world. Well I went into the

                                        healthy food cafe Unclear and
scary sequence   another murder later because   the healthy food cafe and its
ambiance of us two women, one who doesnt want me there becomes a

large room full of people an orgy of enforced life pattern, a stupid party of irrelevance
everyone pretending relevance So a blond woman places   a black hood over
another   blond woman's head and strangles her with   a rope. another
rope. Later on a night bridge then later still I'm in the larger version   of that
violent room it's a zoo City of cages of monkeys and apes its built on both banks of a
river   so it's Paris I'm becoming lost from my companion love   it's all
cages I will go search for my father here. I can't understand your accent: she is a dark
dark woman whose rapid french is hard to understand. Soul? I'll go off on my own I
can be my own soul

to find first the one then the other through the streets of cages of monkeys and apes,
an exact inversion of the crystal city

we need to find the right poison. only the opposite of here and now can work

My poison is benediction How I'm not sure yet. it's the strongest poison on
earth that's for sure it turns away everyone everyone fears it in any form except as
given by an ugly old pope or male potentate. you need the poison blessing of the right
snake and I I have a very smiling snake mouth as I have said. I will bless you.

Here is the dream of staying with a queen on her blue carpet of reason because
she is married to a scientist so she owns half of all our house. There is an
all our house though she is a woman and not much attention still is paid to
her part of the work of owning and ruining the world. She's letting us rest
awhile isn't she nice?

Here's the dream of baby. I'm going to give her a bath in a random house on a
random street of houses like where everyone lives who has a little My lover
the baby's father is running running down the street, because   the richer ones
make us run for money or out of the guilt they give us   he enters for a
moment   to say hello but I will bathe the baby girl well arent I the female?
the baby shits a strange smooth   fruit pit onto the floor.   And also
a smooth blue nugget. She is soul. I still take care of her. Someone has to,
you say, but I have to run, you say. Now   I will bathe her

We are making love in public we are having sex in public. Cops are watching
us at a distance. We have to be watched we are older we are sick we are
snakes The medical profession   has thrown away the snake   and the
pole it would curve around   on its way to the crystal city.

the benediction of the poison. it seals you from making the mistake, as I said in the very
beginning–'im poison youre poison robert johnson is poison'–of living in the collective
imagination both venal and decent, horrible. the poison is benedictive, and I am. I bless
but only if you want that anyone can bless anyone I bless anyone. if you die you can die
in your own imagination not that of the medical establishment or the world
establishment, if you live you can live as well in your own imagination. there you will
find that living and dying are the same I've already said that as have others this is a large
night full of strange gray days something inside me is burning up all my food as soon as I
eat it I am tingling but not really burning but burning's a figure isn't it. I know more and
more every day and become more irritable for it my coils a figure aren't they are always
rustling my constant smile is pasted on. I can still bless you it is possible both to dislike
and to bless   What good will it do you Why must it do you some good? it could do
you an else you've never conceived of

I'm the burning sun up above the zoo rising morning   in order to look for
someone Love not my father. He's sitting there staring at cage of monkeys he's
stretched out on an ancient parisian slab of municipal monumental edifice we should
be so proud of staring at the small gestured monkey forces of now which add up to the
destruction of the, and you know it all and that word, monkey money being always
returned in massive proportion to corporate zookeeper. How can he the observer, let
the monkeys out of the doors to all the cages when they are unlocked of course, so

how can you let them out? a life's work, his life's work to figure out how to let the
monkeys out of the cages which are and have always been unlocked. This entire city
was built to intimidate you that is why it is so quote beautiful unquote (beauty is in the
hole near the hole and in and in the true city of crystal not here, it is in oneself) we
should be proud of and staring Now my face is covered by the clouds of the new
weather You know the new weather, there's always the new the new science the new
philosophy the new novel and there's also and now, for long ever, the new weather

                    little person dream I had
                    in a marble manse
                    woman in tulle-skirted
                              dress
                    sidestepping small
                    pieces of shit
sidestep it sidestep it in the tornadoes all over france   uprooted trees
and the oil waves nipping at your knees I am the sun snake I bless all of you
idiots. anything I please the shaman of the gare de l'est the woman who stands near
the hole of images trying to make them stop coming out like dead meat bad weather
money   I still don't know where they come from. the sun is a one-eyed bitch
who can't see everything she's too much in the middle of the burning light. stop all
images for one sec but I'll dream again tonight about a baby and turds about violence
between two women about how I keep dying about houses and roads.

sidestepping all the debris on the artist's floor, so he can show me   a loving
artwork a portrait from a former   time it's like a book the pages each framed in
scrolled bronze. all very former   another portrait of a man one whom he found
beautiful. a rat on the floor   I'm suddenly part of a burgeoning   group poetry

reading so first I'm   trying on clothes like mad   like in a former time
There's my purse, check it my wallet's been stolen. Something's been stolen What's
there to steal but your soul? I knew that, in the former time, but not *really*

      The branches of that tree of home are so swollen I know it's a huge a long fat
snake up there. they're everywhere (like the sun) I do more meaningless things with
dresses, I meet more significant men. One whose name is like insane is a guard in a
combination museum and courtroom, he herds me with others into an enclosure so
we can go upstairs to. it must be madness   Burn out all of it more and that is
benediction a burning towards you and all your possessions, they may catch on fire or
not but I can't help it this is what I do now   I   burn   that is tell the or

embody the truth the   Then we crossed the border into Mexico finally just across
the border Love and I Look   all the graves of the one-day-old babies who have just
died all in a row there We are going to live near here awhile the graves are beautiful with
careful slabs and things written on them by hand not inscribed in stone as if this were the
city of paris Red flowers affixed here and low dirt hills are all about It's a
beautiful small crystal city a home of mine as a one day old baby   If you conceive of
this broken universe as one day old one day one day one sun one sun sun sun sun

JUICE OF A RUBY

round white beans are soaking in blood No they
aren't beans they're pearls No
it isn't blood because it's thin and ruby-
red the juice of rubies

No it's the blood of souls
in which food is soaked
it contains the blood of my soul

     I knew my people were all in one room, on a floor of a multi-storied building. with difficulty I climbed, for there were no stairs but some footholds in the corners of the one-room storeys, from floor to floor searching for them, for their floor. I gave up ascending and, descending, found their room finally, though they aren't here now, in this clean and airy daylit firstfloor room, which would be in america a secondfloor room. They don't have to be here to be mine, or for me to communicate with them. Benediction is the masterpiece of anyone being inside it not that it's a work of art, it's this moment, the same moment it's always been. So, everyone's in this empty room all at the same time from all times, all of them are here and all of their food and everything else the mossy shapes of ferns and cypresses traced in the air appearing and hiding near rocks the boulders of peace and the darkest crocuses that ever Aren't you claustrophobic No There's no one and nothing here, not at all. No, they're all here

     Anyone can bless you and no one can curse you
     there are no curses in this universe,
     there is no such thing as a working curse.

Elsewhere some broth is being cooked. Everyone's worried they think it's empty it's just transparent, there's nothing in it, they say, but agar-agar. Perhaps the bloody beans a few of the bloody beans will be added   it could become saturated with red, my blood or yours at any moment

     there is still some temperament   knocking about inside me
needlessly. people think temperament is necessary to cope with or be one with fate, but nothing nothing inside, a nothing which is a kind of emotion but different an

ethereal thickening of the spirit through an angelic medium like agar-agar, might be
better. thus this soup? another good thing about this soup is that no other being will
be eaten except for the algae in the agar-agar, from whom I must cadge a blessing: We are
all in the same soup it says in its inaudible voice in my head. Was there a primal
soup? There wasn't a primal. everything is now,   no primal anything

        American underwear the sign says. actually, something like
alfredo's american underwear, a sort of factory outlet whose
goods change entirely several times a day. I get off the métro and
enter it changes while I'm there, no underwear exactly
there is a shawl nearby   which I like, flat black with flat
red roses no leaves but I never get close enough to examine it–no

under or over wear what is

distracting me? the fact that I have to go, I'm leaving I'm in one
of the houses I often dream about and a woman dressed for business
in a light blue suit and short-heeled shoes has said she's leaving right
away so I rush off to get my things, I'm going with her. Where?
I don't think it's to the screening of old movies I might be in
old movies made by a dead man (died but didn't die) I might be in

I'll go into the benediction, perhaps in a more   finally conscious way.
                                                          I don't have a
form here that you know head limbs stuff the persistence of a memory of looking
like something but why when there isn't necessarily to look or be looked at, see or
seem. some people will find this repugnant being in love with their particularities
and their analyses of how those work but I've always found such analyses so concrete
as to be suspect and there is nothing more suspect than my own eyes, or was, but now
not seeing, I might recognize you you see I always used to think you were in some
sense manipulable, not psychologically but with my own senses and certainly in my
thoughts I was making of you what I wished of all of you but now I can't. bump bump
but without the darkness and without the demon shapes of our supposed specificity.
it is all light in here and we are a blessing to each other, that is a serene and endless
containment there is no one outside of us to say we are a thing, for we are the all of it

knowing each other   No one outside us will ever say anything about us again
in definition.

the soup it's always a soup. a single bowl on a bare table. watery with a few greens
today. a blond young woman with a broad round forehead   is there. the eating of
the soup   will be out of sequence with the rest of the meal, so what, everything is
out of sequence. But I *know* when things happened, you say. But when I'm floating,
floating and tingling, or even burning,   nothing ever happened it only

happened   if I return to the story.   otherwise the stories float gloss of light
disappearing down river. have you lost the desire   to be

human in any way? but you must also lose the desire   to be famous among the
cruel.

          I'm bleeding again from the vagina but it isn't my period, the blood might be

a serious symptom of cervical cancer I'm alarmed in a house Which house Light-dark
room I must have a smear a scraping of cells from the cervix, Shamanic? surely not
that dream with the shame of the woman body and the longer hair on the head, long
and brunette without gray in the light-dark room   a white oval rug and perhaps a
blue-covered bed? Yet   in this system one has ripped off a mask, remember? a
long time ago in this poem. one does not wear the mask of the shaman to be one or
hide one's own blood   to heal in this system is to rip off the face itself, is to
acknowledge   that there is no face at all.

                              I had fear in the dream, fear and anger
I will show you the no-face of their flow from the hole where the approximate head wears
a hollow I'm trying to master my emptiness I have worked so long to achieve
but   the citizens of this area refuse all except the demonic presentation of being and
face and so the tempers can still bang around in my darkness that is the same
darkness or hole from which the benediction itself flows it becomes the definition of a
being when   the old emotions are done   I am showing you I am showing what
a being is,   though you only see the old mask that old face dreamed up so long ago
officially to be seen   and not the flow

of benediction. *which heals in that it makes disease irrelevant*
the soup is the manifestation of benediction's healing
in that we make it   it may be the only thing to do, down here
really do

the children are given   two long-bladed serrated knives as if this were normal
I am worried. the children the children, everyone hates them as they grow older
the knives are wrapped lightly in paper towels in such a pleasant house
                                                                                        Take back the
knives and cut up an onion and a carrot.   I've cut my hands with the knives
and   my blood will be in the soup. you can't heal unless you've first been
seriously wounded, but perhaps we can put an end to that and the children won't
have to cut *their* hands with serrated knives   it's my blood not theirs, heal
means to use your blood not theirs or the duck's or the rock's or the Danube's or the
lichen's   All my wounds have created my   knowledge of benediction

                    There must be a moment when the wounds stop
                    But this is all the same moment
                    There must be a point inside the great moment when the wounds
                    stop I intend to be that point within point within the moment
                    It's not that I have the right, it's that no one else will do it
                    It's that you're the ones who haven't done it the
                    history of the world   is   the ones
                    who haven't ever done it (anyone can be I here

these dark tents or any dreamed edifice which body of mine are they in the old one not
now, they are behind my non-face phantasmically   these dark tents in which we
will read the poems of he who died but didn't die once more and where she who died
but didn't die is a child with happy piercing voice   these dark tents are inside
this time I won't tell the story transpiring   except to say there will be a reading
and she's in the audience apart from the reading because there is   not only no
sequence, but every part of something is whole. and so   we will be reading later
but she is now in the audience   listening to the reading   in the dark tents in my

soul   tents and tents   or a narrow cobbled street an esophageal passage   on which I meet two giggling young men. I won't tell you the story, about old-me the story about nothing. about some drugs, about nothing. the next night it's an art

opening in white-boarded warehouse-type space but   I am both in this space and not in this space. we are led away from it and back while we're still inside it we never leave it actually though the story says we do a young   artist the brother of one who died but didn't die is taking us outside, singing songs to us though we're really still inside   So neither time nor space   is a fact Only the story is But we know the story is nothing as well   that's what we know from this poem *I've ripped off my face and lost blood*   *in order to tell you this*   I've ripped off my face and lost irreplaceable   blood   Up the pole in a black starry hood and back down in order to   empty   so I can be, that may be traditional, so I can be   So I can stay honest, honest   *Your face isnt really ripped off, is it*   I have no face, except in your story, which I don't   honor.

> it isn't anything but words no
> it is a peculiarly fated life no it isn't
> and it isn't blood but it's   ruby-red a spillage
> of soul in that sense I have lost
> so much of my
> "blood" That much of me   gone to the
> Crystal City I visit it there
> I visit my blood there, I visit my red
>
> I feel as if I've finally explained red.

In that Crystal City, nothing I valued or feared. There is no disease there, nothing of fate remains but its red tincture Nothing is worthy any more there is only benediction the speaking of *that language* of our mind. If you are consciously caught in this one moment can stay in this instant you are charming fate away you are charming away all the conditions *you aren't them and they aren't yours*   you don't have to accept them   as long as you   remain in this   moment *If you are consciously caught in this one moment without disease or fate they are banished*   What I now know.

I am an ill male religious master thirty years ago in a dark hall with a stage, I am being conveyed about on a stretcher and I will be healed soon this is known because of the letter H nearby, what will I be healed of? all the remaining bruising superficialities of my temperament, then only my self will be left. A woman who is I informs me there is a surprise awaiting me. I don't think there are any surprises really. I am in the same hall the next night oh yes it's a "stage"   A voice says that this is a castle in

the deepest possible place. We are knee-deep in water there is some fear that the entire castle will be flooded   an ordinary man says that he will overturn its values, the values of the castle, I wonder what they are but then lose interest. A great poet shows up in the company of a political figure a demon, they are both   ones who died but didn't die and I   want to block out the demon as if he were words on a computer screen and erase him with a keystroke, because he is only an

image, but I can't. He is in me I am the castle and he is hurting me by being there by being me   We must be each other in the better way we can only do this in the Crystal City. let go of the demonic now and finally   and have no hidden depths

HEALING

the bean which   the figure of love puts in the cooking pot   outside a house
and near an old car   the slender bean he puts in   changes without changing
form or appearance,   *clicks* in the eye, to become   a healing element,
this   white or green legume,   though he doesn't quite believe   the food can

heal.   Oh then I have to pee and it's night   and I go into a dark   enclave a
car   but people are in there, and one's   a dead beloved young woman,
in the backseat   staring ahead   without affect as I
try to relieve   myself in the car of the dead   In the car of the dead

where I'm allowed. but where the messenger of death sits, waiting for him

          Benediction today
          will come from the medicine,
          which is food, of the
          past, and also from
          the car of the dead.
          I refuse the present
          I'd fall down in red in
          the present, fall
          looking demonic
          in a red fullskirted
          dress with a
          scribbled black design.

have I further defined, or have I implicated   benediction as healing?

when things used to happen twice in dreams it was probably   once for it
happening and once for understanding it. Now   nothing has to happen twice
because there's no understanding, in that way   In the Benediction nothing is
reprocessed   in the story way, the story is   refused. we don't go over it so
we don't have to experience it, the first time   so we don't have to have time

Back at the healing, with which the benediction coincides Who is being
healed Anyone The figure of love but also anyone What does heal mean Heal means
the soul Heal means bring to intersection   with the benediction (we were lying
there in it...and in no dream, remember? I never
remember)
                    In a dark truly unlit and moonlit house, down by the old hospital
which is no longer there, near   the old civic center   in the old desert town,
shelves and chairs a clutter. there are four tiny beings there which are helping spirits
whirlwindlike have no faces or bodies   Who are they I don't know I   never
asked. Something successful is being achieved a healing four is for symmetry   four is
for the four times three gates to the City   four alive is for the fluid corners of
love. The dream takes place in different episodes several times during the night but   I
don't remember the stories they must not matter. Except one, except that in one a

crack-head and I are given credit   for the actual achievement of the healing. Why not
It was he and not his critics   It was he and not anyone else It was
he. In the dream I thought he was dead though he's alive   because he's treated
like a dead man, he's treated as dead in life   so therefore he can heal   in the
world of dark and white dream   where benediction intersects with this world.
                                                  So benediction is represented by
a crackhead, an anti-social   not true he's social with other   crackheads,
person   who heals others within his sub-crystal   city perhaps and I
perhaps reach out to him in the night for help from his force. As the Mohaves know
it's all done in dreams But it's done with food But also it's done by   lying together
beneath the dark of it.

            I'm running downhill again in
            that same old desert town, now in the area
            of the old post office, mortuary, library, and also
            water department. But nothing's there I've ever seen
            and I don't know who I'm with. I ask he/she if they're

            really going to go into that church to
            sing in the choir Yes he/she says but I, I keep running
            downhill. benediction isn't with the choir

singing in the manner of a herd, its song or voice
goes back and forth around up and down, all anarchically and

your voice doesn't have one range, can't be catagorized
your voice doesn't even have a sound.
How do you sing? aren't you always?

the benediction pulls me in it *clicks* me in but I don't look different. what do you think a body is it a voice a made it's what and so you're taught a view of it but you've not *seen* your thought rushing across to the dead though ha how many times youve all spoken to them and they seem to have sent back an intersection like sheet lightning or some zigzag lightning in a dream no that was the zigzag crackhead thought like a plot. its the pace he says the pace of death thats the pace of the benediction that I bump into in my frenzy and change for a moment, because its cells are everywhere. they aren't cells. who said this? Yes. I'm right there again and there is no fuckin choir in the crystal fuckin city as I say there is no mass there is no all together all of us together being made to do the same thing, because no one made us. so, no one makes us sing the same song. so, a healer is a crackhead. No one made us so you can't make me do anything! except be in the Crystal City because that's where is is.

no memory again except of the addition of the soft white cubes that you must eat, that happened over and over last night. Then the next night voices came and said their pieces, There ain't nothin to ya but I I I I love you still. Then 'j'ai augmenté,' love laughs while a woman gets in a car   stopped at an intersection in front of Société Générale. gets in a gets in a car The car of the dead. leaving   Société Générale   *What you mad at that I said/ that lion bound for glory sho ain't got no head*   Then, finally the snake appears, slender, black, blind with black velvet capped eyes. It's always what you don't have, it's what you don't seem to have that gets you into the Crystal City consciously.
          after you add the white cubes you put in something darker I believe Keep drinking this soup keep changing it a little and drinking it it is like an ocean, which is not our mother, we don't have that mother we reject the yin and yang every mental tyranny that has contributed to our unconsciousness over millennia despite Crystal. I clean the room clean round the bed where a couple is making love in their modern newly built room I'm cleaning for them because they're too self-involved to

know anything, and that was never lovely   or natural   it was simply self-involved. the room's too nice, they're unconscious

so your legs hurt all night but they were mine   I didn't know whose love's or mine   they ached and ached through dreams and we put   shiitake mushrooms on each leg. I'm different this morning so I know it wasn't me my legs. That was the real part I undertook love's legs so I could help them.
                                                                    Then deeper at the turnstiles of the métro or was it entrance to a freeway though underground,   sat, blocking the entrances, three buddhist monks in red robes. I am told they will have to be killed   because they are blocking my way or our way?   a man tells me reasonably that this must be, but instead I   fly off   into the sky in a white box   There is always a way around them, and around violence.

                    went everywhere, and I've forgotten, don't need no legs, don't need no trains, or cars Don't need no lion's head to be a lion no eyes to be a snake No gambling healing is not   a gamble It isn't the body it isn't really to the body it is to you.

          I am lying on my back with my chest exposed
          with my clothes pinned back like skin flaps and
          my inner chest exposed, not exactly my heart but
          it must be my heart
                              perhaps it still isn't large enough but the pilgrim woman I take to be myself is on fire, I saw her just behind the man his dark back to me She her clothes white cap and bib and dark dress all in flames   how can I get, get there this is agony get through take you Bene   is this hardship because consciousness has been repressed for so long, consciousness being also the body its true shape and location its   nature has   been repressed for so long that to come to know it is through pain and something very like torture   but of course only the dispossessed will have this knowledge, dispossessed of this world's materials and knowledge, dispossessed of this world's body as diagrammed.

a man took off my shoes and said that they might have l e a d pronounced leed in them. he was a cyclist himself. because my feet are so tired from taking on the burden   of others' legs. give it all to me one says but you have to know what it is   is the burden your pain or a weight of the mind is the burden unconscious so you feel uncomfortable and thus must strive for a new thing material or power-giving? in the world of the cruel, power and possessions in the world of the cruel, the knowledge that you're right in the world of the cruel. I don't want to lead I want to fly any time, you will accuse me of many things but will never not know I have flown on fire the flames on my pilgrim's dress are wings and if I could stay there long enough one says and bypass all suffering if I could stay there and not suffer for you here but would the flames my wings go out and there is no consciousness without this torture consciousness is no longer natural it is affected as if by the thrust of long needles through the heart the brain the parts so wrongly named that I have lost them through my training my dreams my vocation I have had them removed in the sense of being my sole insides, the long needles are thrust through my soul exposed in this dissection and as everyone knows that is the pain of it. and if I flew away with the flames and I flew transpierced higher and higher without returning, up to the high crystal once again I would find that you are there too as on earth so why aren't you there in your consciousness? because you won't drink the soup of reason you will only eat the fat of the cruel the thickness of the self's food the west's matter more matter for a tick blood of herds of animals and humans. gorging yourselves on the soul colors of others

when the frayed rot comes/when your old chance fails/those are the words we can't use. do you understand? we can no longer use the words for the body or for luck. The sapphire is turning in her hand fast as fast as it can A man says "You were the one who launched it weren't you?" What is it? the bullet of reason.

                                        Yes, am, shaman
            though bird first think a crow, then a sea
            eagle fly up up 'If I can just face the sea' float ecstatically then
            it glitters below, a calm sea. Some voice says "where god
            sold his arms" which simply refers to a nothing, a story of
            some custom there will be, in the past. Tell me a question

            no Shaman is back on the ground

she has a crater in her heart, is
lying collapsed in the original littered space

place your balm in the night against the ringed fist sphinx paw,
the crater is speaking.

Love later says, 'It begins with the minder and then is passed
along the three categories,'   in a renaissance stone room, curtains and flame
torches   'But that is to perpetuate the ancient categories' I say.   'I know,' he says.
I am a minder   I will not pass them along the three categories though I don't
know what those are now

I covered him with wings but first must remember
taking down the building   and not to lose the children   Snake is freeing
herself from a tortoise shell.

'The sun and the moon have found me. Pain is a capturer from the enemy.' 'What
enemy?' 'The sun and the moon and the forest.' 'Then it is not an enemy.' Then, this
is the body: as red is your accomplishment, that is, your blood used, so your body
apparent body, the other body   sings and speaks with others

MINDER

while they weren't watching it was the whole movie   it isn't that they never
got to see it again it's that they never saw it All or rather Whole. voices are telling me
things now *the geological name for this is sub*   that's because the figure of love
and I are leaving the destroyed castle via   an underwater passage a grotto beneath,
whose waters pour out towards open waters

the edifice of past is crumbling   all of history, built as it was on a
misconception of time, a misperception of others, and an urge to power which was not
biological at all   Yes, I am a minder I   mind that our world has become this
I mind, that is, tend to the unconscious others the best that I can and I live in mind.
consciously consciously

> civilization or one might call it the
> man-made cover of the globe
> is the empty coffin I've been handed
> I will send it on its way now
>
> "Send it away on the next train" says a
> voice.
>
> "Send it away on the next train
> in the place in the train
> where the most stress is."
>
> This feels illegal. The voice says,
> "Write down on it the name
> of any coffin company
> and send it away."

Some people are making cute little dolls in my grandmother's passé house,
some poets put dolls in a special container one is a dog with a bronze leaf attached to
its tail. the poets have to be somewhere at seven, everyone has to hurry together not me.
they're all off to the next event I am going to stay home and mind. that is, I'm going
to be leaving with you through the grotto

Went into the dark and opened all
the colors   a black tee-shirt in a basin became all the colors, all the colors we
needed to leave and now   *while we're building the ship the problem is...*   but the
voice has stopped before telling
                              me what it is. It may be stress   enough
tolerance of stress for the train and the ship to do their respective   jobs or that I
am stress myself as any one is in the Crystal City   a stress point from this lower
red plane. Endurance and insight, having enough are the problems. Is there a ship?
          Now the bird comes to her shoulder because her face is all and only light
but that is me, that face. Remember what one looks like and reclaim it from politics and
from the sense that we're a short   history of imperfection. *If all the land*
can take the moon so we can take the sea   I don't understand you, voice, escape by
sea escape by sea of air   past the moon and the sun?

          I have to go up again because I
          cried all night. with the bird
          can rise to yellow air
          this time in mind

staying powers second or other body I, remember I am hard and dead emptied and so I
can do this, rise in bliss and look down with some indifference since they aren't only
there they are also here.
                         and you have come with me, perhaps this   is the ship,
this flight of us spiritually soldered together gone into the golden place in the air
nearing the sun, which burns but strengthens   and changes. now we can walk
into the city I say walk but no walking's needed, past the flames and into the crystal
with no qualities. it is all presence as you fill but I meant to say feel. we both became
grotesque to achieve this you ill and I mentally deformed and estranged in a way that I
have figured as physical—sometimes it seems as if I've said just anything in order to
make it happen. but we are really here we have always been here and you are soothed
past all notion of healing,

the name of that is love, bigger than its use as word, the name of love is 'here'
transpiring   the name of crystal is 'here' transpiring   we have been here so
often that all the oftens are the same and seem unremembered down there so that you
might not get what the crystal is, because it's so familiar. why there's so little to say of
it since it holds everything together including us. what else is there but this

transparence of connection, so how can it cease at death   he who died but didn't die has only ever tried to tell me that, appearing to me in dreams garbed in the awkward clothes or nudity of my own imagination   leave gender and shallow coupling but recognize that one is connected to anyone and all natural entities. the connection endures held together by our stress points

> down here
> earth quake
> no one can be trusted
> Bear
> can be trusted (bear with me)

> flat things against a
> wall are all that's left

> two flat colorful
> leggings
> among them
> yellow and red like decals

I've saved a huge shopping cart full of rice. of course I haven't left except as always. can I change everything that was once green to blue, no it is brown. there is little water and   there is no reason. everything that was once three-dimensional, full and green is dried and shrunken, without nutrients, cannot even be made into tea.

I'm at the Gare de l'Est its gray making soup again miso soup. Later on the rim of a deep and layered archaeological   excavation I am dressed with others in colored scarves, red perhaps, playing at   a physical game but lose and what I lose is some sort of poetry award. The depression in the earth is a great canyon   No I am back at the Gare de l'Est here are some paper bags   people wonder what they are,

garbage? whose are they? They are mine and I take from them handfuls of snakes,

they must be my poems. Earlier I was carrying bags these same bags full of eggs along
the rue des Recollets where small boys bumped me and taunted me, pushed
themselves against the eggs   I shoved them away they chased me, mad, small
French boys Now the eggs have hatched   snakes, snakes   then voices:

They tied up the rose last night, because another one was time
they tied up the rose because they wanted their notion of time
they tied it up and now the dead earth displays time and invented roses

A body's being blown from one hospital building to another. it is large it is female and
statue-like. Another woman says to the figure of love *I'm going to give you
some poems for leader*   that must be lieder   She has a harsh silly voice
Love has his own songs and music. She turns into my ancient girlhood friend who
wants to run me   wants me to share an apartment with her   and save money
in some tandem plan for what? the earth is destroyed I say, I don't want my money
subject to your   rules

The earth is sinking   We are playing at poets along its dead rim.

                                                                    I always love

you
          Open this book   which tells how we should bomb   the southern part of
this Asian country   rather than the northern part   because the agricultural
fields are all there   There are also some chapters about the author's   early
religious training

the geological name for this is sub. this world down here   I dreamed of nothing
worried last night the air is full of false springtime, full of false breath.

we are *there* in our supposed fragility as crystal is also supposed a fragile thing, down
here   we are frangible carrying each other carried by the crystal holding it together
in our part of it. we will never break   a song of peace or humming from the crystal
frangible grass and colors themselves are loose and tend to billow. if there was never
any point in being here except to be a point which spreads everywhere we can stop
everything. I wear a cloak and have no face an entity of transparent bones and you are

wearing blue the gown of reason over your illness, *it is a reasonable illness because*
the voice doesn't finish again   Perhaps no statements from this place can contain a
clause after the word *because.* They are singing our lied

> *all our leaders*
> *are mute here.*

but so much can matter all along the waterfront, imagining comfort, keep it to our
touch, comfort's not imagined, only enough   water for the future is. that's just an
issue, some say, our destruction   All our leaders are mute on this issue of the
water the air the animals the trees and so the song in the Crystal City *all our leaders/*
are mute here;/ all our leaders' souls/ are unconscious/ they are not our leaders.   It is a
reasonable illness   because it is in your body and you are reasonable Which
body Not the one you have continued to improve all your life but the   supposedly
perceptible body   Your ill body's full of stress   Your stress point is in both bodies
It is serene

A painter must make a figurative picture of he who died but didn't die, I am the bearer
of this news to her in a strange city She goes out and stands in the street Is it the
Crystal City? and sings a single word so he will come to his window. She beckons him over.
She tells him He wants to know why I'm there I must be waiting for the portrait
in which He has no face his hands are rays he's wearing smooth skin, no clothes just
something like skin.

down here: "I'll...put over" various people say this   over and over, swaying
against a steel wall

down here: some dark woman waiting, me, with a man's poster plastered over her
face.

On a hill a clump of different white lilylike flowers and plants have been
transplanted. large, some resemble yucca in bloom   these might work in a
drought, danger of a child tearing them out of the earth. Then my mind changed to
black with strips of messages appearing in the darkness white messages

is there any difference between
trying to heal a loved one, trying to save a
doomed planet, and trying to find a key
for anyone to their conscious crystal city?

night-time around the house   up on the hill in the old desert town. the air is
mild at night. bleachers have been built outside for performances of sung poetry. the young
have organized this event and we are each supposed to sing a poem that is a
short footnote suggested by what we've been doing so far   that is more of the fact
that you never get to sing it all: *while they weren't watching, it was the whole
movie*   I perform a poem but   it is the work not the footnote and I
intend to do so again, after the break on front lawn   where everything's being
discussed at around midnight

Alice Notley was born in 1945 in Bisbee, Arizona and grew up in Needles, California. She was educated at the Needles Public Schools, Barnard College, and The Writers' Workshop at the University of Iowa. She lived in the Southwest for eighteen years and in New York City for about twenty-two years altogether, and she has now lived in Paris, France since 1992. Her poetry displays in its scope, complexity, and formal contrasts those different geographies and mental tendencies, desert and urban, American and European. She is the author of around forty published books and is especially known for her epic and narrative poetry.

LETTER MACHINE EDITIONS